CHANGING INDIA

An Economist's Autobiography

CHANGING INDIA

An Economist's Autobiography

An Inspiring journey through time;
Though started on a rough beginning;
It ended on a high note of success.

V.S. MAHAJAN
Director
Centre of Indian Development Studies,
Chandigarh

DEEP & DEEP PUBLICATIONS PVT. LTD.
F-159, Rajouri Garden, New Delhi - 110027

CHANGING INDIA: AN ECONOMIST'S AUTOBIOGRAPHY

ISBN 978-81-8450-038-7

Typeset by SHRI GANESH COMPOSERS, R-3/120, Balaji Chowk, Mohan Garden, New Delhi.

Printed in India at NEW ELEGANT PRINTERS, A-49/1, Phase I, Mayapuri, New Delhi-110064.

Published by DEEP & DEEP PUBLICATIONS PVT. LTD., F-159, Rajouri Garden, New Delhi-110027. Phones: 25435369, 25440916. E-mail: ddpubs@gmail.com • ddpbooks@Yahoo.co.in
Sales Showroom: 2/13, Ansari Road, Daryaganj, New Delhi-110002
Phone/Fax: 23245122

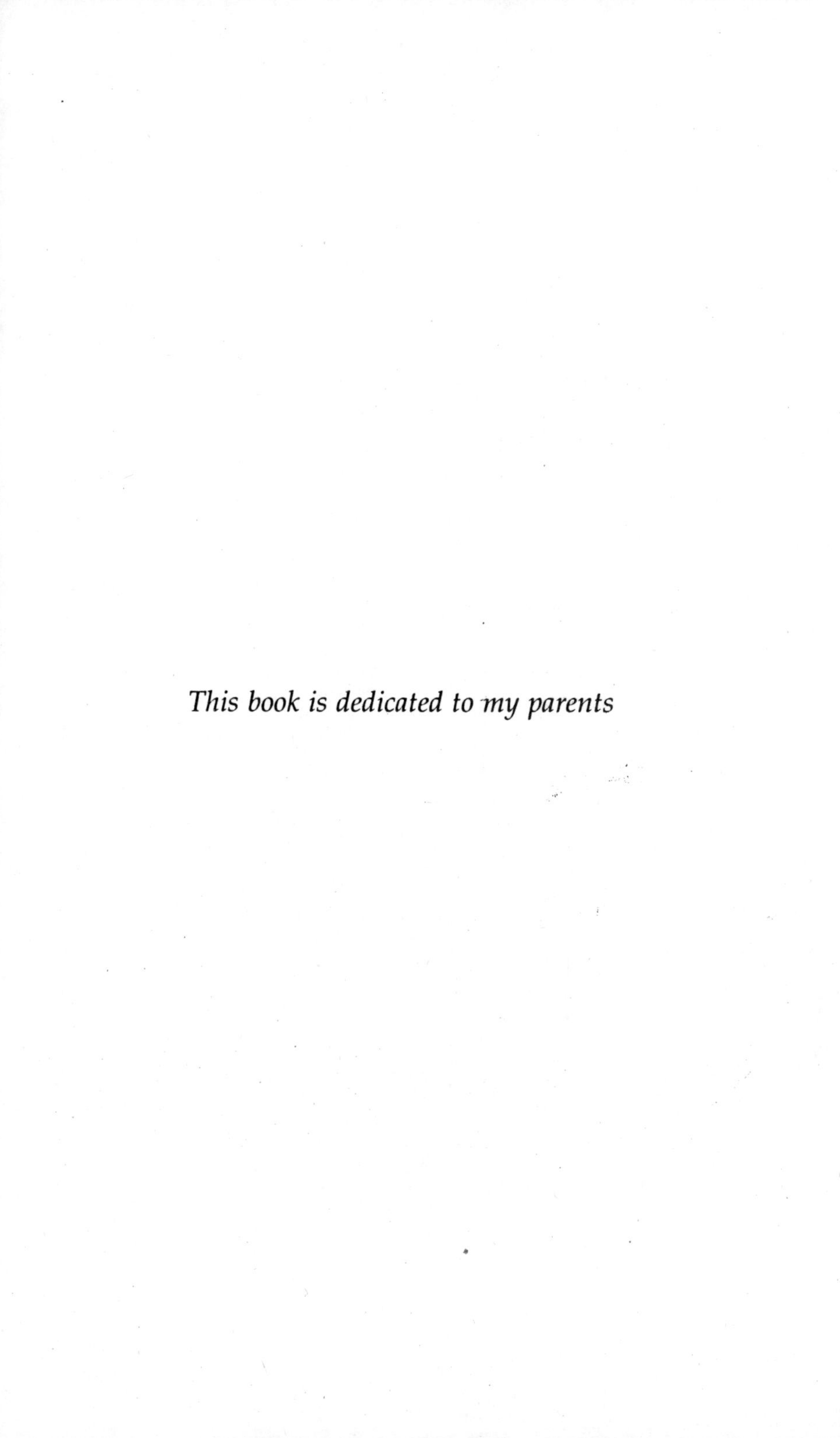

This book is dedicated to my parents

Contents

Introduction

August 1947 will go down in the annals of India's history as a time when the country faced the biggest dilemma of partition that created a new land of Pakistan. It satisfied the long-cherished aspirations of Muslims for a separate homeland as they felt oppressed under the Hindu-dominated India and thought that if they did not have an exclusive territory of their own, they would continue to suffer and hardly progress the way they wanted to.

This Partition, however, led to a large-scale communal fire. Both Hindus and Muslims started slitting each other's throats in the holocaust. Hindus felt unsafe in Muslim-dominated areas and Muslims in Hindu-majority ones. However, the worst affected were the border areas of the East (mostly Bengal) and North-West (mostly Punjab, Sindh, Baluchistan and NWFP), which ultimately constituted the majority territory of Pakistan.

Among all these states, Punjab bore the maximum ire of Partition. The communal fire was at its highest level here and lasted a long time. It got extinguished only after the total exodus of the Hindu and Muslim populations. The state suffered the biggest loss of human lives.

It was under these circumstances that we left Lahore, just a few days before Independence. In Lahore, we stayed in a predominantly Muslim locality in a house owned by a Muslim, Captain Nur Ahmad. He was retired from the army and had built property on Mozang Road. We shared almost half the portion of his house with his family.

He was a God-fearing and pious Muslim and was greatly attached to my father, whom he would consult in his affairs. He was so fond of us that he even refused to raise the rent of our accommodation, while he did so in several other flats owned by him.

We had never imagined that this would be our last stay in Lahore or that henceforth, we would not be able to visit it. That was unthinkable for we had spent our whole life in Lahore, and it had become our homeland. How could we remain away from this place for long? In fact, we very much hoped that soon after things settled down, we would be back in our home.

With this in view, we didn't transfer our luggage, except for a few boxes and beddings that we would need during our "temporary stay" elsewhere. On the advice of our landlord, a couple of boxes containing precious goods and warm clothes were sent to the house of his army officer son in the cantonment area where he was posted.

Our landlord as well as his wife were greatly disturbed by our move to another city, but they also quite realized the delicate situation that had arisen and didn't stand in our way. They very much hoped that we would meet soon, but alas, it was never to be.

From Lahore, we shifted to Ferozepur city, which was just a couple of hours' train journey away. Here, initially we stayed with a close friend of my father who was also a lawyer. The long journey of seeking a settled life had begun. The wandering continued for almost eight years, when at long last the new capital of East Punjab (now Indian Punjab), started emerging from a cluster of villages.

After losing Lahore to Pakistan, a protracted struggle ensued to build a new capital for the Indian Punjab. Ultimately, it was decided that instead of developing an existing city into a capital, a totally new city should be built, which would represent the new spirit and aspirations of Independent India and also act as a model for the new cities to be built in other parts of the country. The Prime Minister, Pt. Jawaharlal Nehru, was greatly interested in gifting Punjab an absolutely new and modern capital, which was comparable to any other developed city in the world.

To attain this goal, he invited the world's best-known architect — le Corbusier — to plan the new city. Leaving no stone unturned, the maximum possible amount was sanctioned for the project. There was, thus, no dearth of funds for building this dream city.

In 1954 my father and other family members shifted to Chandigarh where they had been allotted an MLA flat in Sector

3. I first came to Chandigarh in 1955, when I was posted in Calcutta and from where there was a direct train to Chandigarh railway station.

Chandigarh was then no better than a cluster of scattered villages, with small link roads comparable to rural streets. Most of the places were covered with thick growths of wild grass and bushes. The only mode of conveyance was the cycle rickshaw. The rickshaws are thus the oldest mode of conveyance in the city. Had these not been there, it would have been extremely difficult to move from one sector to another.

We have hardly recognized their services. For years, they have served the needs of commuters and reduced their hardship till alternative modes of transport developed. In fact, they are still prevalent, though in much smaller numbers.

While the buildings of the High Court and the Legislative Assembly had been constructed, the multi-storied structure of the Secretariat was yet to emerge. Several offices of the government functioned from temporary premises in Sector 12 and other places.

The offices of Panjab University operated from a single storey-building located in the corner of the university marketplace. The largest building with a couple of storeys, which now constitutes the Department of Chemical Engineering and offices of the Vice-Chancellor, was the first major piece of construction and occupied the central place in the university. Several departments were housed in this building at that time, beside the offices of the Vice-Chancellor.

Arts Block One and possibly Block Two had also emerged and some departments functioned from there. The other blocks were yet to come up, though Gandhi Bhawan had been built with a waterbed around it. This used to be a major attraction for visitors touring the campus.

Houses for quite a few teachers and staff members had been built. The university was spread over such a big area that it could only be covered on a bicycle, which then was the principal mode of travel on the campus. Except for a couple of other vehicles, it was the cycle that almost every one possessed.

Thus, most of the university buildings were yet to emerge. Around ninety per cent of the campus was vacant, giving it a look of no better than a modern village.

Sectors 22 and 23, which mainly housed residential quarters of government employees, had registered a fast growth. Sector 22 had also sprung up as the main market centre of the city, where one would find crowds of people exchanging greetings and looking to their daily shopping needs. Aroma Hotel was the city's first modern hotel building and proved a boon for visitors to this city. It still occupies a central place among the city hotels.

It took hardly a couple of decades for the vast tracts of empty space in the city to get filled, with a brisk construction of major buildings and houses. Even so, the city presented a desolate look. It was looked down upon as a city of mainly government *babus* who could not match the growth of a modern commercial city, as not many businessmen were prepared to open shop here.

The land prices were quite cheap, often less than what they had been purchased for. The rents of houses and shops were low as there were hardly any takers.

The situation, however, changed substantially after Chandigarh was declared a Union Territory on November 1, 1966 and more so after the 1971 Indo-Pakistan war.

There was brisk business activity during the 1970s, accompanied by a large-scale construction programme. Practically every vacant area was booked and land prices soared. However, it was nothing like what followed the globalisation fever in the 1990s. Economic reforms brought about an unmitigated upsurge in commercial activity. Almost all major Indian and foreign firms were anxious to have a foothold in this city, which had become the prime business gateway to the entire North-West India. Thus, the nineties was the most successful decade, when the boom in business, trade, education, health, consumer durables, automobiles and several other products was unprecedented. And the city continues to grow, also emerging as a favoured information technology destination.

Thus, within a few decades, this once sleepy cluster of villages has transformed into a very powerful metropolis.

STRONG LINKS

I have been a permanent resident of this city since 1964 and that is what justifies the title to this autobiography. I transplanted my roots here, after having been deprived of a revisit since July

1947 to Lahore, which was my original hometown for several years. Memories of that place continue to be green even today, though physically I have not been a part of it for a long time.

Chandigarh, my second homeland, has to a large extent compensated for this loss and I am sure the same is true for a large number of other *Lahorians* who, like me, have been uprooted from their homeland.

I would be failing in my duty if I didn't pay homage to our noble landlord in Lahore — Captain Nur Ahmad — who was to us more than a close family member. He stood solidly by us at the time of dire trouble and wrote regularly to my father; years after we had left Lahore and were yet not settled. He helped my father in getting back his library of law books, without which he could not have restarted his practice in India.

Reproduced here is of one of his letters:

4 [illegible] Road
Lahore
22.7.48

My dear Mahajan Sahib,

After having passed some anxious days about you I received your affectionate most welcome letter of the 16th inst. and hasten to reply to it immediately. I know Court Road very well. The quarters are very comfortable & in a good locality. They are not big ones though. I wonder whether you are sharing the block or you have been allotted the whole of it. At any rate something is better than nothing. I sincerely hope that you will prosper in your profession soon. We pray for your success. I do not know anything about the cotton oil mill Multan & Montgomery, whether it has been allotted to one person or to a syndicate or to the co-operative society. There are no buyers at present for anything, such as houses, land for house construction or business except shops & cultivation land. Land for crops has gone down by 50%. Your [illegible] my bungalow in Davis Road pleader [illegible] has been offered Rs 50000/- + [illegible]

Rs 100,000/. I would make enquiries about the Mills shares and let you know. If you let me know further particulars I will advertise for its sale in Pakistan Times. The other day as a result of my application to have Mr. [illegible]'s furniture removed from my premises, his furniture fetched a ridiculously small price in the auction. Furniture and utensils left in Lahore by the non-Muslim evacuees, have flooded the market of Lahore and very few people care to buy. I will ask some auctioneers to show them the furniture. I would suggest you to wait for a short time more. We hope things will get settled gradually and your furniture or shares will fetch better prices. Don't worry about my fees; just consider it written off. And let me know if you would wish me to send you some money. We miss you all. Not a single day passes when we do not talk of you & yours. Oh how can we forget those happy times. I do not know my neighbours & have never met them. We pass as strangers. There is no social life for me. I feel lonely. Kaikaus's portion is now with an Afghan subject trading in Lahore. He seems to be a bird of passage. It remained vacant for 2½ months and may become vacant in my time. R.B. Tirath Ram old advocate is occupying Bakhshi's portion now. S. Gurbakhsh Singh was killed but his furniture & library were sealed by Govt. I lost my rent for 11 months. In fact rent recovery became a problem. Let me assure you that we will not forget you at all, with sweet memories of the past & affection.

Yrs sincerely,
N. [illegible]

4, Mozang Road, Lahore
22-7-48

My dear Mahajan Sahib,

After having passed some anxious days about you I received your affectionate and most welcome letter of the 16th inst and I hasten to reply to it immediately. I know Cart Road (where we stayed in one of the MLA flats in Simla) very well. The quarters are very comfortable and in a good locality. They are not big ones though. I wonder whether you are sharing the block or you have been allotted the whole of it. At any rate something is better than nothing. I sincerely hope that you will prosper in your profession soon. We pray for your success. I do not know anything about the cotton Oil Mill Multan and Multan Ginnery (where my father had made a large investment). Whether it has been allotted to one person or to a Syndicate or to the Co-operative Society. There are no buyers at present for anything. Such as houses, land for houses construction or business except shops, and cultivation land. Land for crops has gone down by 50%. You remember my bungalow in (which) Daulat Ram pleader lived has been offered Rs. 50000 and I bought it for Rs. 100,000. I would make enquiries about the mills shares and let you know. If you let me know further particulars I will advertise for its sale in Pakistan Times. The other day, as a result of my application to have Mr. Nanda's furniture removed from my premises, his furniture fetched a ridiculously small price in the auction. Furniture and utensils left in Lahore by the non-Muslim evacuees have flooded the whole of Lahore and very few people care to buy. I will ask some auctioneers and show them the furniture (left by you). I would suggest you to wait for a short time more. We hope things will get settled gradually and your furniture and shares will fetch better prices. Don't worry about my dues—just consider them written off and let me know if you would (wish) me to send some money. We miss you all. Not a single day passes when we do not talk of you and yours and how can we forget those happy times. I do not know my neighbours and have never met them. We pass as strangers. There is no social life for me. I feel lonely. . . . (Much of the rest is about the old tenants). . . . Let me assure you that we will not forget you at all. With sweet memories of the past and affection.

Yours sincerely,
(Nur Ahmed)

(Bracketed writing is mine.)

How strong the bond between the two families was becomes further obvious from the fact that once a strong mob of looters, after we had left, gathered in front of our house, having learnt that it belonged to a Hindu family, and was poised to loot it when the wife of our landlord came to know of their intention. She immediately rushed to the place, and risking her life, threatened the looters that if they dared to enter this house they would be shot at. She told them in an emphatic tone that the house belonged to her brother. Sensing trouble, the looters ran helter-skelter. Later, some security arrangements were also made through the intervention of her son in the army.

We have yet to come across such an affectionate and friendly family.

* * * * *

While the names of the metropolitan cities of Bombay, Madras and Calcutta have been changed to Mumbai, Chennai and Kolkata, I have in this narration stuck to their earlier names, which are more acceptable and popular the world over. Also, a hill station like Simla has been renamed Shimla, and several other cities have changed or are in the process of changing their names like Poona (changed to Pune) and Baroda (changed to Badodara). Incidentally, Poona and Baroda are still more popular than their new names.

Acknowledgements

Thanks are due to Ms. Harvinder Khetal and Mrs. Asha Mahajan for editing this volume. Thanks are also due to Mrs. Santosh Mahajan and Mr. Rajeev Mahajan for helping me in several ways to complete this volume as early as possible. Equally, I am thankful to Mr. G.S. Bhatia for rendering possible assistance in publishing this book. Last but not least, I am thankful to Mr. Badri Prasad for typing out several drafts of this book before it could take final shape.

Note: Precise order in which certain events mentioned in this book have occurred could be tentative because of memory lapses.

1

Tough Land, Tough People

Lalian, my native village, was a typical village rooted in the tough land of *kikar* (acacia) tree valley in North-West India—now a part of Pakistan—which would not easily open up even to a blade of grass. However, once grass surfaced, it would survive the harshest weather. Similarly, the people of Lalian—stern, adventurous, innovative and hardworking—were equally brutal in the use of the language and would coin up the most abrasive invectives to express their anger. This was the way of life in Lalian, where tough people believed in using a tough language.

It was in these environs that I was born in 1923 on 22nd September—according to middle and high school certificates, the only authentic record that existed in those days. It was left to the sweet memory of the family elders to vouchsafe such date and year and that would finally settle the issue. The modern day compulsory birth registration practice was not prevalent those days.

Soon after my birth in this village, I was shifted to Lahore where my father practised law in the High Court. Thus Lahore became my permanent home till 1947, when we had to migrate from this place as a consequence of the partition of the country.

However, my love for Lalian remained so strong that I would often crave for an opportunity to visit it and spend a carefree time amidst its surroundings.

A train journey from Lahore to Shakargarh in the old British Raj used to be very exciting and I would always look forward to such travel. Shakargarh railway station was housed in an old shed without any protection or platform. From the station, one had to walk or ride a horse to travel 15 miles to reach the village.

In those days there were no roads and en route one had to negotiate a big patch of a *barsati cho* (seasonal rivulet), which would assume a dangerous posture during the rainy season. It was quite risky to negotiate this unpredictable *cho* when the water level suddenly rose to endanger one's life. Often when it was flooded, we would be forced to stay overnight at Shakargarh town than risk crossing this *cho*.

Despite these hardships, a journey to the village was a fascinating experience, particularly because we got the opportunity to enjoy a horse ride. We took great pleasure in making the horses run at a reckless speed, unmindful of the warning of the elders. After zigzagging through a rough and often bushy area and encountering quite a few more small *chos*, we would eagerly look forward to reaching our village; and the moment we spotted its outskirts, where the majestic marble top of the village temple was the first to greet us, our joy knew no bounds and we goaded the already tired horses to run still faster, till we neared the village boundary.

WELCOME TEMPLE BELLS

From a distance, we could hear the temple bells ringing with their melodious sound of welcome and the temple priest rendering *arti* (prayer). This pious atmosphere was a great solace to our tired and aching limbs and we would breathe deeply in the surroundings.

Later, till our stay in the village, we would regularly visit the temple not only to attend its various ceremonies but also to attend to our hefty homework. We would linger for a long time in the cool recesses of the temple *verandah* and often fall asleep or indulge in gossip when we felt dull.

On the temple premises was also located the village post office in a small rickety room in one corner, where the middle-aged postmaster presided like a lord in the evenings. A group of anxious villagers would surround him to know about the welfare of their dear ones, mostly working in the army, or to receive anxiously awaited remittances, which the dutiful children would rarely fail to send home, howsoever small the amount.

In those days, even a remittance of a couple of rupees was highly welcome by dependent elders, which helped several of them to clear their debts raised on a high interest rate. It was remarkable that the lone postmaster performed every conceivable duty, like going on foot to the *tehsil* headquarters to pick up the village mail and return before sunset. Often, when the big *cho* en route was flooded, he would be detained at the headquarters, much to the displeasure of the anxious elders. Quite a few of them would have trudged a long distance to hear news about their wards or receive the much-awaited remittance.

POST OFFICE

In those days, very few villages had the postal facility and one post office catered to the needs of a large number of neighbouring villages. The postmaster, thus, had a tough job of covering several miles daily, often under harsh weather conditions. The government had provided him with a white umbrella and a leather bag for carrying the mail, money orders and other documents. Thus, it is not surprising that the postmaster often missed quite a few days from work when he was not well.

Even so, he appeared to enjoy his job, which earned him much dignity and respect from a large number of rural people, who did everything possible to make his life comfortable.

He regaled us children by narrating exciting anecdotes. We would eagerly wait for his arrival in the afternoons and the moment we spotted his white umbrella from a distance, would often rush to catch him and lighten his burden of the mailbag, and carry it for the rest of the distance. He also felt equally happy to see us and allowed us to open his office, where a heavy lock was put and sealed carefully as a safeguard against theft.

In this chamber were stacked items of postal stationery—postcards, envelopes, stamps, money order forms and other postal documents, as well as postal seal, wax and an earthen *deewa* (a substitute for candle). He also kept some cash of undisbursed money orders. All these were placed in a wooden box, which was again securely sealed.

It was a very elaborate system and much time had to be spent before embarking on fresh operation of distribution of mail and money orders. We would help break the seal and feel important while reading out addresses from the mail. The moment a particular name was read out, a sense of hope and joy would light up the face of the person concerned, who had been anxiously waiting for it and possibly had made quite a few rounds of the post office for this letter.

The postmaster, when in a relaxed mood, would interact with people and read out their letters. Of course, some carried happy news while others were harbingers of sad news. He would console those confronted with sad tidings and sympathize with them. He would also share happiness with those who had received money orders. It was indeed an occasion of mixed feelings, though mostly happy ones and youngsters would touch the feet of the postmaster before parting.

The temple premises also housed a promising school for girls, to put them on the literacy map, which was nothing short of a miracle those days. The operation of the school was the result of the efforts of some enlightened village elders. In the highly conservative society of those times, girls were expected to stay at home and concentrate on household tasks. A middle-aged lady had been appointed to run this school. In order to provide her further inducement, her husband too had been appointed as a teacher in the primary school for boys, which was located on the premises opposite the temple. Here, in a big thatched hall a couple of jute rolls had been spread out to seat the students.

As this was the only school in a number of surrounding villages, boys from adjoining villages would also seek admission here. The school was government aided and provided education free of cost and also paid the salary of its only teacher, which was rupees ten a month, indeed a princely amount in the 1920s. The teacher would also get all his daily necessities free of cost. These included a house, foodgrains, milk and buttermilk, which came from the rich houses of the village.

In the village society, both the teacher as well as the postmaster were highly respected members and received much regard and affection from the local people.

ADVENTUROUS SOCIETY

During the summer afternoons, siesta was a routine feature when villagers would take respite from the scalding day temperature under thick shady *banyan* trees. The village was fortunate to have many such trees around its water tanks, which attracted droves of siesta-seekers. They carried their stringed *charpoys* and spread them in the shade of the banyan trees.

It was an exciting experience for us and right from morning, we would look forward to it with élan. Just after lunch, when the sun shed its maximum wrath, we would walk down to the nearest tree around the cattle pond, which had the thickest foliage and spread out our cots at vantage points and would soon be snoring in the cool shade. Here, we would also have an opportunity to share interesting experiences with the village elders, who would narrate the history of the village, its past spread over several years, the multiple troubles it had to face, as well as happy events.

It was the British, who we were told, had ultimately brought about peace and law and order. Invaders, who before them had often made the life of local people quite difficult, no longer harassed the people. Those who had actually fought in the war, narrated the special role played by the village in the recruitment to the army, particularly during the First World War. We listened with rapt attention about the exploits of the brave soldiers who had fought the enemy in pitched battles, often endangering their lives. It showed the bravery and total commitment of our forces and we felt proud of them.

Their tales were so absorbing that we anxiously looked forward to the next day to hear more of their adventures. Also, there were quite a few families of adventure-seekers who, even in the face of heavy odds, had ventured into far-off lands in other countries and settled there, earning high income, reputation and fame. Many returned and built spacious houses in the village, purchased lands and opened lucrative businesses.

Thus, the village was a conglomerate of families who were not quite content with their present position and were keen to explore the best of the opportunities available. They wanted to move into the wide world and bring back wealth to invest in the village and other places.

POVERTY IN ABUNDANCE

Even as all this happened, a large number of families failed to emerge out of poverty. Their houses were located in low areas and they were almost huddled together in single-room mud tenements with a small courtyard barely enough to stretch themselves during the summer months. They led a miserable life, with large families where children moved around semi-and even full-naked. The mortality rate was high in these families and they were often victims of malnutrition and did not have sufficient food and other necessities of life to satisfy their basic needs.

I was often touched by their lot and they were in quite a large number, almost double that of the better-off families. Early morning, their children would gather, in good numbers, outside the houses of the rich with their dirty pots that often leaked, to collect *lassi* (buttermilk) for their families. Most of the children were deprived of milk and a drink of *lassi* served as a substitute.

They were mostly landless families or belonged to such categories which performed menial jobs in the village for which they were paid in kind. This helped them meet their household needs. Several of these families comprised Muslims, who had a large burial land close to their houses, which was a good indicator of the high mortality rate among them.

SOCIAL LIFE

The village had a rigid social hierarchical system. On the top were rich members of society—*sahukars* (money lenders)—as they were called. They were also big landlords, owning most of the land in the village as well as in the neighbouring areas. Then, there were *Brahmins* who stayed in houses close to those of *sahukars, and* though their houses were comparatively modest, these were spacious and well maintained, compared to the houses of the poor.

Brahmins rendered various services to the affluent class and had easy access to their families. Their ladies worked in rich houses and male members rendered other services, including fetching water for their domestic needs, etc. The Brahmins would draw water from a nearby well exclusively meant for these families and carry it in brass pitchers in remarkably balanced *behangis,* a system of carrying a large number of water vessels balanced on the both sides of a shoulder, thus exerting minimum pressure on the carrier slung across their shoulders.

These wells were out of bounds for the low class families who had to be content with drinking water from tanks and other unhygienic sources.

While all this was a part of the village social life, yet the depressed sections led a satisfied life. The village provided them with opportunities to participate in its social ceremonies, where they were served lavish feasts, earned gifts, extra ration and other facilities.

Marriages were celebrated with much pomp and show. The preparation for a marriage, particularly of a female member, would begin months in advance. The whole programme was chalked out with much care, not leaving anything to chance. All elders were closely associated with it. Elaborate arrangements were made about dowry, ornaments and gifts to be offered to various relatives whose list ran quite long. All these details would start circulating even before the betrothal ceremony was performed. In fact, someone from the joint family itself was closely involved in providing details about the families of the groom or bride, as marriages were solemnised within known families. There was no question of going beyond the caste. The rules were strict and closely observed.

Because of lack of communication in those days, the visiting party was comfortably housed and elaborately treated to various functions, including breakfasts, lunches and dinners for days. Much, of course, depended on the convenience of both sides. There was no hurry. Ceremonies went on at a leisurely pace.

The village temple would gain special prominence on the occasion as quite a few ceremonies were performed there. This brought the temple priest into special importance.

Interestingly, after the marriage, when the groom arrived at the village with his bride, he could not straightaway enter his house. He had to visit the temple first, where some ceremonies were performed by the priest, and for the first night the couple was expected to stay on the temple premises itself. It was only the next day that he was permitted to return to his house along with his spouse.

MARRIAGES IN THE FAMILY

In 1942, as a student of a local college in Lahore, I had to seek permission from the Principal, who was an Englishman, for attending the marriages of two of my cousins. When he read the application requesting for the grant of a fortnight's leave of absence from the college, he was greatly amused and said, "Surely, you don't propose to go on a long winter holiday! For how long does the marriage ceremony take place? My dear boy, you can't afford to be absent from your studies for such a long duration."

In fact, he narrated to me an incident from his life. "When my mother died, I had my exam the following day. After the church prayer and burial, I was right back to my studies."

I had to argue with him about the functioning of our social system and tell him that more time was needed for visiting a village, which lacked even elementary communication network, and then I had to attend not one but two marriages. Ultimately, he allowed me 10 days of leave but asked me to return earlier, in my own interest.

In the village, while the first marriage ceremony was performed smoothly, during the second marriage it started raining heavily which delayed the departure of the groom's party. And when they left, their vehicle bus got jammed only a short distance from the village. A side wheel got trapped badly in the slush and even after a lot of effort it was not possible to extricate the vehicle.

Arrangements, therefore, had to be made for petromaxes, tents, food and other needs of the groom's party, a tough demand on the bride's family. Thanks to the solidarity of the village community, where every member was available for help, soon the arrangements were made for their comfortable stay.

This shows how even the most vexed situation was tackled under the prevailing social system and the entire village community cooperated to save the honour of the family. I am sure it must have been an almost impossible job for the family to face this unexpected problem alone, more so when they had yet to get over the accumulated fatigue and hustle and bustle of the weddings of two girls.

JOINT FAMILY

The corporate family life, where the joint family system ruled supreme and elders enjoyed high respect and played a crucial role in the family matters, was a unique experience, and I loved it. I felt quite comfortable and elated in the company of elders. I also enjoyed the company of the youngsters of my age. We played all sorts of games in the village and, of course, kabaddi was our favourite.

There was a large family divankhana/haveli exclusively for the male members. It was an imposing structure. Close to it were spread a large number of structures, some bricked, some semi-bricked where the joint family's food and allied requirements were stored. Also stored were items of cattle feed. A large quadrangle-shaped open space separated the haveli and other buildings. Here we usually played the game of kabaddi, often perspiring profusely during the summer.

Thus, a refreshing bath in the nearby *bagh* (garden) was looked forward to eagerly. Spread over 100 acres of land, the bagh was partly used for growing fruit trees and partly for agriculture. Tobacco was the main crop of cultivation as there was a huge demand for it among the large number of *hookah*-addicts (smokers) in the family.

In fact, from morning till late evening, the *hookahs* made brisk rounds among the elders as well as guests. It was believed that a puff at the *hookah* cools down angry moods and thus helps build better human relations. Sharing a *hookah* with other members, whether from the same village or other places, provided a good opportunity for the people to discuss things of mutual interest in a leisurely and cool manner.

Often we children, out of sheer curiosity, when the elders were not around, would have a long puff at the *hookah* which mostly ended in a major bout of cough. Hookah water had its own medicinal qualities. The nicotine in it served as a medicine to cure swollen eyes suffered during the hot weather. Washing these affected eyes the first thing in the morning with *hookah* water helped overcome the swelling.

The cultivation of tobacco was thus given top priority and the crop raised would generally meet the demand for tobacco for the season.

This *bagh* also provided a good opportunity for studies and we would often spread cots in the thick shade of trees and get engrossed in doing homework or reading. Often, we would be tempted to sleep in that cool environment.

However, our honeymoon in that soothing place came to an abrupt end with the arrival of one of our young uncles. He would shrewdly lure one of us with his art of narrating interesting anecdotes and gradually prepare ground for sexually assaulting his victim. He was a sex maniac who needed someone to satisfy his lust. It was a very sad experience and no matter how carefully we tried to avoid him, he was too clever for us and managed to get at one of us for his gratification.

My cousin and I were his victims in particular. He would seize the opportunity of roping in either of us and take the victim on horse back not far from the village to a hidden lonely spot in a *cho,* invisible to an outsider. Then without a preamble, he would unbutton the dress and start his assault, unmindful of the severe pain caused by his continuous stroking of the sensitive spot. I would restrain myself crying out aloud for fear of being heard. It was only when he had satisfied his carnal desire that I would be released from his clutches.

It was a bitter experience and had an adverse impact on my mind. During those days, it appears that sex abuse of males was far more common than assaults on females, for the latter stayed indoors most of the time, with little contact with males. On the other hand, boys were more easily accessible as nobody bothered to keep any check on them even if they were sexually assaulted, which happened to be a common feature in large families, and not much attention was paid.

Strangely, he was married to one of prettiest ladies in the family and I had high regard for her. I often wondered at the fate of this lady who had tied the nuptial knot with this boor who had no control over his sexual urge. She raised two sons and, as expected, did not have a happy time for she found it difficult to adjust to the strange behaviour of her husband, who made foolish demands at odd times.

It was not long before a situation arose when he committed suicide. His younger sister was found in a compromising state with an employee of the family handloom business. In a flush of anger and without considering the consequences, he swallowed the cartridge of a gun, which soon poisoned his body.

That was the end of this sex maniac, leaving behind his young widow and two small children to struggle in this world. Her misery was further multiplied when the whole family had to flee after this border village went to Pakistan. The family had to face several hardships to rehabilitate themselves. She had to perform odd jobs to support her children.

Incidentally, in the big *ghar* (residential accommodation) that we had in the village, there resided three families of my great-grandfather. The family of his third son, who was a lawyer practising in the district courts of Gurdaspur, stayed in Gurdaspur. His eldest son too had graduated in law and his other son was a sales tax practitioner. Similarly, his three daughters were well qualified and settled.

One of them was Principal of the local Government High School. (Incidentally, Gurdaspur was a district headquarters but did not have any college in the pre-Independence days, though its tehsil Batala had one—Baring Christian College. Batala had a large population of Christians as well as Muslims. In fact, Qadian which is a part of Batala, is the homeland of the Ahmedia sect of the Muslims.

Among the remaining three families, two were of granduncles and one of my grandfather, who was dead. In fact, I have never seen either my grandfather or grandmother—both were dead before I was born and *my taya* (elder brother of my father) stayed here. He had read up to matriculation, though formally did not qualify for this.

My father lived in Lahore. He was also a law graduate and practised in the Lahore High Court. My third uncle, who stayed in Nainakot, a well-developed town close to our village, ran a cloth merchant shop. He had hardly read up to primary class. My youngest uncle, who was also a graduate, was a bank manager and lived in Lucknow.

The story of the other two families was the same where hardly any member read beyond matriculation —mostly they were primary read. My eldest granduncle, who was also the head of the family, had five sons. While three of them stayed in the village, the other two had also settled in Nainakot.

Despite the scattering of family members, the joint house in the village had a large number of children, as during those days there was no concept of family planning even among the educated. Further, the mortality rate being low among the well-off families, a large number of children would survive.

I remember how happy I felt when during the summer holidays, we five brothers along with my cousin who stayed with us in Lahore would troop into the house and renew contact with a large number of other children. The house was full of noise and gaeity and we all loved it.

CULTURAL LIFE AND VACATIONS

The village did not lack in cultural moorings. *Baisakhi*, a highly colourful and exhilarating festival dominated by *bhangra* (Punjabi dance), was the most popular. It unfolded the joyful spirit of a good harvest though there was no Green Revolution those days and we hardly heard of any bumper crop of paddy, as we do now.

Malaria took a big toll those days with mosquitoes flourishing in unhygienic surroundings, filth and squalor. It would claim several lives. While families were large, so was the mortality rate, thus ultimately a natural balance in population was ensured.

My cousin, who was two years senior to me and attended the same school, and I would save some money from our daily pocket money and invest it in buying stationery and other similar items to be given to village schoolchildren. We would also bring a large quantity of quinine tablets for distribution among the suffering villagers. How far this actually helped them, we hardly bothered to find out. We thought this that this was minimum we could do to help them fight the scourge of malaria.

Interestingly, the summer vacation those days, unlike now, followed the British pattern with schools and colleges closing in of July and reopening in September. Thus, it provided us with an opportunity to stage Ramlila, the drama based on the celebrations of *Dashera* (an important Hindu festival).

This was a befitting end to our summer vacation. The last days of our long holiday were spent preparing for staging this mega event. Each one of us virtually memorized by heart the dialogues for the specific role allotted to all members of the dramatic party.

The dialogues were carefully drafted by senior members to avoid possible ambiguities so that the final version was easy to remember. All of us were filled with so much enthusiasm for this performance that we would punctually gather in the village school compound opposite the temple and sit for hours memorizing our role in the play and would not part unless every word was on the tip of our tongue. Simultaneously, we would also learn the art of delivering the dialogue in an appealing and impressive manner. Initially, of course, we had to get over the sense of stage fright and fear of facing the village audience. It was only through consistent practice in front of other members that this fear was overcome.

On the D-Day, when the stage for the final performance of this play had been raised in the centre of village around a large cleared area, we would have the last-minute rehearsal to rid any shortcomings that may have persisted. To ensure that the dialogue —the most coveted part of the play—was correctly delivered, it would be simultaneously spoken in a low voice by an expert from behind the stage which helped infuse confidence in us and thus, reduce the chance of anyone cutting a sorry figure before the audience or becoming an object of ridicule, which was still worse.

During the play, the time between one scene and another was profitably utilized by the village *Bhands* (akin to circus clowns) who would send the audience into peels of laughter with their superb clowning.

Their performance very appropriately covered up for any lapse committed during the enactment of the play and also kept the spirits of the audience high. This shows that high talent did exist even among the simple village folk, who were totally illiterate and had no professional training.

For a few days after the play, we were the proud recipients of special words of praise, particularly from the elders and ladies, who witnessed the performance from the roofs of nearby houses facing the stage, as they had to maintain a distance from the elders.

The play was thus witnessed by a large number of villagers and it was a superb event for us that raised our spirits and we felt greatly honoured.

SEEKING ADVENTURES

The village also provided a good opportunity for seeking adventure in its not too far-off surroundings where we would often venture into during the early hours of the morning. We would try to explore fresh areas with great zeal.

Our favorite haunt was a *dera* (retreat) developed by some *sadhus (sacred* persons) which was hidden behind a thick growth of trees and bushes. A group of *sadhus* lived there in seclusion. The place abounded in adventure. Located at the centre of a vast forest area, it consisted of a group of thatched huts where *sadhus* lived, prayed and practised *yoga*. It was an all-male place comprising around half a dozen young and old members.

Curious about the life of these *sadhus*, I would not only watch their daily chores but also often engage myself in conversation with them. I would inquire about where they came from, how they spent the day and maintained themselves and whether they faced any fear in the highly secluded and lonely surroundings of thick and impenetrable growth. The leader of the group, who had settled here for the past several years and was one of the earliest founders of this place, was well known as he often visited our *haveli* to meet elders and sort out their problems.

The group was well supported by the village community, which took good care of their daily needs and often quite a few social ceremonies were performed here in the *Bani*, as it was often referred to, particularly when a large feast was to be organized on a special occasion.

Thus, these *sadhus* had become an integral part of the village community and helped the ailing villagers with their age-tested herbal medicines, the preparation of which occupied a good part of their daily routine. They also distributed sacred threads and metallic contraptions which were worn by men to ward off evils. Some of them were quite learned, knew the ancient scriptures and helped perform several rituals in the family. Both men and women from the village often called on them to seek their guidance in solving intricate domestic problems that they might be facing.

How far the faith of the villagers in these *sadhus* was justified, one does not know. But considering the number of families that invited them to perform various ceremonies, it appears that the *sadhus* were quite popular.

This was another part of the village life which made it more adventurous and colourful. Personally, I felt thrilled by undertaking long walks through the narrow paths of the thick jungle land filled with a rich variety of trees, some of which had very thick growth and were tall and majestic. The place was endowed with several medicinal plants and the *sadhus* would use them abundantly to make medicines for treating various ailments.

MALE-FEMALE DIVIDE

In the joint family system, there prevailed a very strict male-female divide. While the *haveli* or *divankhana* was an exclusive male habitation, located in an open space right on the village boundary, it was in the *ghar* (house for dwelling)—situated at a good distance from the *haveli* in the interior of the village—with only one large entry of a formidable gate built of strong wood and metal that women and children stayed. Within the high surrounding walls, after entering the main door, there followed a long *deori,* an uninhabited covered place which represented the limit for the outsiders, as beyond this they were not allowed. This *deori* also kept away dogs and other stray animals from entering the inner quarters.

Beyond the *deori* was a big courtyard around which a two-storey structure of small bricks existed. Half a dozen families stayed in this spacious place and they had their independent quarters and kitchens. Certain facilities were, of course, shared.

The house had a newly installed hand water pump, which was raised after much difficulty as the contractor had to sink deep underground to tap water. This was a great achievement, for it helped supplement the growing water needs of the families.

So this was the *ghar,* a protected bastion for ladies and children to which only male members of the family and those who rendered services had access. Marriages were consummated here and children were born.

The *haveli,* as mentioned earlier, was an exclusive male bastion where the elders met visitors. It also housed cowsheds, stables for horses, places for the storage of fodder, grams, oilcakes, feed etc. for the animals. The elders functioned from here and attended to their daily chores in a manner that suited them. Meetings would occasionally take place with visitors to sort out family and village problems. Thus, there was a clear distinction between the *ghar* and *divankhana* which were the integral parts of a large joint family.

I found it quite interesting, though at times puzzling too, for we had to pay obeisance to a large number of elders and it was often difficult to remember their exact relationship. The whole affair could turn into a big confusion. But we had got used to it and felt elated on touching the feet of a large number of elders and seeking their blessings.

In the joint family, there was normally no distinction among various members. All were treated alike. I remember one of my granduncles (elder brother of my grandfather), who was the senior most member in the family and thus enjoyed the distinct status of head of the family, had called the village tailor and told him to stitch half-pants for all male children from a big piece of cloth. The tailor was not quite conversant with the concept of measurement and stitched uniform half-pants, without ensuring whether these fitted the wearers; so it was a mass tailoring syndrome. The tailor master enjoyed a special status, being the only one who attended to the sartorial needs of all, elders and youngsters.

FAVOURITE FOOD

I remember my village-based favourite drinks and eateries with nostalgia. In the early morning I relished a big tumbler of freshly churned *lassi* (buttermilk) laced with a rich layer of thick butter called *kirar* and it was my most favourite drink. Later, it became a dream only, for rarely did I have the opportunity to savour *chatti*-churned buttermilk that involves a good deal of labour.

Another specialty that I delighted in was the well-known *sarson-da-sag*. It was cooked in a strong *handi*, a round earthen pot with a deep hollow, on the soft simmering fire of dung cakes in a *tandoor*. For the whole night the *sag* would be allowed to cook and by morning it would turn out to be mellow and soft like fresh *malai (cream)*. Topped with a big dollop of freshly churned butter, it made an ideal breakfast with *makki di roti* (maize bread).

Both these favourite delicacies and a few others became a rarity subsequently.

At the end of every stay in the village, whether it was during the long summer vacation or after attending some function in the family, I would bid adieu to the carefree, exciting and wandering life with a heavy heart and return to the urban moorings. For a return to Lahore meant again getting lost in its disciplined, dull and drab life, where getting ready for school in time was a miserable exercise. It entailed carrying a heavy load of books, stationery items, and a slate. All stuffed in a bag which had to be carried on foot for a couple of miles every morning and again brought back home in the afternoon. It was an ordeal that I hated.

And once back home there was no respite. A lot of homework aggravated the ordeal. There was hardly time for relaxation or play and I fervently missed a game of kabaddi that we daily enjoyed in the village.

Thus deep love for the village life has stayed constantly with me even though I had lived in the countryside only for brief periods.

2

Early Days in Lahore

My honeymoon with the city of Lahore had begun when I was a mere toddler and it continued till I was a grown-up youth right in my mid-twenties. This attachment was, however, permanently snapped towards the end of July 1947 when the situation in the wake of the partition of this country and communal disturbances that followed turned out to be very grave. It became impossible to go back to Lahore ever since it became an integral part of the newly created Pakistan. In fact, at that time it was the only major city in the whole of North India and enjoyed an international status.

TRAIN JOURNEY

The train journey from Lahore to Shakargarh was eight hours long. It was the only train during the day, and would move leisurely. It used to be 60 to 70 per cent empty. I am quite sure the railway authorities those days must have been losing quite heavily on this section. But it was the only link for the people from villages in Shakargarh *tehsil* to travel to Lahore, Sialkot and other places in the country. Had it not been there, these people would have had to face considerable hardships.

One of the largest numbers of recruits to the army came from this *tehsil* and it had become a major occupation of the people here. This had become possible only because of the rail link, which increased the mobility of the people who served in several national and international destinations. Our village was a good example of such an exposure.

Narowal was an important junction where people had to change trains for going to Sialkot, Jammu and other areas in this region. While comparing the railway station of Shakargarh, without any platform and with barely a dozen people waiting to board the train starting from *Chak Amru,* with the gigantic, multi-platform and highly crowded railway station of Lahore with its imposing facade, one was indeed filled with awe, particularly when often intercepted by an Anglo-Indian ticket checker, who exuded a false sense of superiority. But then simple people took him as their *Mai-Baap*. He would often question unnecessarily to impose his authority, especially about the age of children or the weight of luggage carried and would let you move only after you had shelled out some amount of penalty.

Outside the railway station, awaited the services of rows of *tongas* (horse-driven carts) for the passengers. Some bargaining, of course, was prevalent. But, on the whole, it was a reasonable demand considering the high quality of *tonga* maintained, as well as the sturdy horses which would dash at high speeds and reach the destination in no time.

Though it was simply unbelievable, it spoke high of the standard ensured by the administration of the time in issuing licenses to the *tonga* drivers, after they had qualified strict tests.

TONGA AND BICYCLE DAYS

After the *tonga,* the bicycle was the most convenient and common mode of transportation. I have covered countless number of miles on this machine, during my stay in Lahore. Of course, during my early school days I used to walk to school, covering about five mitles of distance both ways. This journey during the hot summer days used to be quite an ordeal. In those times, a cooler was unknown, and even a ceiling fan in homes was a rarity. For most families, the table fan was the convenient air blower, for it could be transferred from one place to another with ease.

Thus, one can imagine how intolerable the intensity of daytime heat was, with the temperature hovering between 115 and 120 degrees Fahrenheit. And Lahore was well known for its extreme heat.

The nights too, with little movement of tree leaves, were equally uncomfortable. And with mosquitoes humming through the night, it was an almost choking environment. We would sprinkle plenty of water on our bed sheets to get some comfort. Just one table fan at one end of a row of *charpoys* (stringed beds) was not enough to provide comfort.

Despite the horrendous difficulties faced because of lack of basic facilities, life moved on peacefully and was enjoyable and one hardly felt the absence of basic amenities, as we had become accustomed to that style of living.

To beat the heat every evening, we were treated to a cool *badam sherbet* (almond drink) prepared at home, with a liberal sprinkling of bazaar ice.

POOR HYGIENE

Mosquitoes, heat, insanitation (in the backyard of our house there was a big cow shed which was a fertile ground for mosquitoes), open latrine system (flush system was practically unknown) and several other unhealthy features of the urban life were the main factors responsible for the scourge of several diseases. Malaria was widely prevalent and took a heavy toll. One or the other member in a family would be invariably suffering from it during the summer. I too suffered frequent bouts of malaria, which often left me in a miserable state.

Typhoid was another dreaded disease. Those days, there was no remedy available for this disease and most of the victims had little chance of survival. In our family, we had quite a few cases, including myself, which had rendered me bed-ridden for almost three months during my middle school days.

Though the rains in July brought some relief, it was only a temporary respite. The monsoons aggravated the breeding of mosquitoes as several fresh pools of dirty water would sprout.

LAWRENCE GARDENS

We spent the evenings visiting parks and the unforgettable Lawrence Gardens was our favourite spot. It was a large garden, modelled on the lines of London's Regent Park, spread over several acres of land with carefully tended grass, shrubs, trees and flowers. In fact, there was no other park like this in the whole of this province or, even North India. It had several tennis courts and a large cricket ground where the top world players considered it a privilege to play cricket.

A couple of artificial hillocks had been created to give one the feeling of a hill station. Several paths ran through their zigzag routes from the bottom right up to the top and the area around these paths abounded in rich greenery as in the hills. On the top, where the scenery totally resembled a hill, it was cool even during summer. Here, one could relax comfortably and even walk down the other side of the hill, enjoying the same grandeur while descending.

During the spring season, the whole area was brightly lit with all kinds of flowers that presented a very charming view and one was tempted to linger on indefinitely.

As around the spring season we would also be preparing for exams, we would occupy a lonely corner in the garden and concentrate on studies. However, with our mind occupied with several other things especially the irresistible beauty of the surroundings and of some visitors, we were hardly studious and often gossiped and cut jokes and frequently gazed at beautiful damsels.

An open air theatre was another novelty of this garden. It was located on the top of another hill where a spacious amphitheatre had been built for the entertainment of people and various cultural programmes were staged here. Its spacious stage as well as artistically designed greenrooms for the artistes had been created with much thought and planning. The theatre had a capacity to accommodate a large number of visitors. It was especially active during the winter season when several programmes were performed. In fact, Lahore was the only city in the North that had this unique facility, which spoke highly of its cultural moorings and artistic tastes.

SCHOOL DAYS

In my earlier school days, I was a very dull student and scored the worst possible marks and was a frequent victim of punishment by the teacher. I was, in fact, very afraid of going to school, which I considered as a concentration camp akin to a place of punishment. Even if I learnt something, it would slip out of my mind at the thought of the teacher's stern attitude towards me.

My father, whom we called *Baujee*, had no time to listen to my woes. Rather, I dared not discuss my school life with him. I was afraid that opening this topic with him would invite his anger and harsh language. However, it was so different with my mother whom we addressed as *Bebe*. Though I never understood why we called her *Bebe*, but everybody addressed her so and no one ever wondered beyond that. This word appears to be close to the Persian language, but is not found in the Hindi text.

Bebe would listen patiently to our problems and try to do something to help us. In my case, she told my uncle who was studying in a college, about the bad time I was having in school. The very next day uncle called on my teacher and warned him of dire consequences if he punished me. The poor teacher was intimidated by this and from that day onwards I had a peaceful time and the fear of teachers vanished. My attendance improved and I began doing well in my studies.

In fact, as I moved to higher classes, I showed an unexpectedly good performance. I was rated among the top students. There was a remarkable improvement, further helped through regular coaching by a teacher at home in the evening.

Now I understood what havoc fear could play with the psyche of a child, make him dull, slow and poor in performance. The moment the child is helped by someone in the family, he could do well, rather, wonderfully well. I scored a high position in the class six examinations. In fact, I secured the record number of marks, topping among the total of 250-odd students in a class split into five or six sections. I was also my section monitor and had the privilege of punishing those students who did not fare well in the class. I remember once I was asked by the teacher to slap nearly 40 students who were not able to answer his query. I found it a hard task and by the time I reached the last student, my hand was tired and paining.

Other boys felt jealous of me and I feared that they must be waiting for an opportunity to repay me appropriately. Fortunately, despite all this, no student held any grudge against me. In fact, while once standing with a student who was also my close friend, another student who bore enmity towards my friend, dared not teach him a lesson in my presence. He later admitted that had he not been my close friend, he would not have been spared.

Even in those days, I believed that one should not hate any fellow student, but have a soft corner towards all and help them in case of need.

Not only did I stand first in the class, I also secured the first or second position in individual subjects and thus became the proud recipient of a number of awards in the annual prize distribution function, which was appreciated both by my teachers and family members. This event was celebrated by *Baujee* who distributed a big load of *laddoos* (sweetmeats) among friends and relatives.

GLORY WAS SHORTLIVED

They say fame and glory are shortlived. This was true in my case. Soon after my promotion to the next class, I was attacked by typhoid. It was early in May when while returning home from school, I ran a high temperature and my whole body was writhing with pain. But ignoring the symptoms, I thought it was my primary duty to do my homework first.

I undertook the work, despite my body failing to cooperate. When I could bear it no further, I told *Bebe* about it. My high fever was confirmed and I was totally confined to the bed. By the evening, my condition worsened. The doctor was called in and he prescribed medicine to cool down the temperature.

A couple of days later I was diagnosed to be suffering from typhoid, for which there was no remedy those days. The victim was generally left at the mercy of Nature and the chances of survival were fifty per cent. In my instance, the situation was worse as my case had been spoiled through wrong medication in the beginning.

I was thus left completely at the mercy of Nature. In fact, for almost three weeks I was virtually in a state of delirium, hardly knowing what I talked and where I was lying. I was in a sort of long dream with no knowledge of what was happening around.

Bebe sat by my side tending to me day and night, often missing her food and sleep. Another person who kept a close watch was my *Tayaji* (father's elder brother) who, after hearing of this news, had come to us from the village to relieve *Bebe*. Other members ran errands as ordered by the doctor.

It was indeed a crucial period, a big struggle with me hovering between life and death. It was after a long journey of an endless dream that I came to my senses and picked up the thread of my life and started recognizing people around. When told about what I had been talking during my illness I could not believe it.

The period of suffering had reduced me to a mere skeleton. I was nourished back to my normal health slowly and with utmost care, which took nearly two months. I had, meanwhile, lost complete confidence over my ability to sit or walk. I needed support even for sitting. Initially, sitting for even a short time would make my bones ache. Slowly and steadily, I regained confidence and I could eat my meals without support.

The worst casualty of this disease was *Bebe*. Already a patient of diabetes, her health further deteriorated. Both her hands were in a bad shape, almost nonfunctioning. She took a good long time even for their partial recovery.

Tayaji would sponge and clean my body everyday with care. This helped me recover to my old shape. After staying with us for most of the time of sickness and recuperation, he left for the village to prepare for our comfortable arrival and stay during the summer vacation.

BACK TO THE VILLAGE

Soon after alighting at Shakargarh railway station, I was helped to a waiting family palanquin, normally used for marriages, that had been renovated. This was the only mode of transport that could to be used in my case. I enjoyed the trip, even as the four helpers who carried the palanquin on their shoulders often broke the journey for rest and refreshment.

We reached the village by late evening. The weather was hot.

There was a virtual stream of relatives, beginning early next morning, headed by my great-grandmother, despite her difficulty in walking due to old age. She was one of the first people to visit me and thanked the Almighty Father for leasing me a new life.

Though *Bebe* stayed in the family house, she would be by my side for most of the day to ensure my body massage, as well as to see that special food was prepared for me. All this care and the open atmosphere of the village helped in my quick recovery and by the time we returned to Lahore, I was almost my old self again, though yet fragile and in need of care.

I fell behind in my studies because of this illness. However, with determination, I was soon able to make good the loss and again began doing well, which was revealed in the house test results. I remember the Headmaster of the school called the students of my section and specially pointed out at me as an example of hard work and commitment, who despite having missed studies for long had shown that success could be had with hard work.

MY LAST PRAISE

I must have felt happy at this praise, but then that appeared to be the last one. Soon, I was heading towards a downward move in my studies. All the earlier zeal and commitment appeared to be gradually disappearing for reasons I could hardly make out. In fact, I was doing so badly that I was pushed out from Section A, which was meant for toppers and intelligent students, to a lower section meant for the mediocre ones.

That was a great insult. But I deserved it for having fared badly in the final exam.

Thus, I turned out to be a mediocre student and no teacher, much less the Headmaster, ever praised me. Wanting me to attain a high grade in the matriculation examination, *Baujee* put me under the charge of an experienced teacher to hone my skills, especially in mathematics, which had been my weakest subject, and was a high marks scorer. I was equally poor in the sciences.

How poor I was in the use of library facilities became evident when I went to deposit my totally blank library card with the librarian who was simply wonderstruck at my not having drawn even a single book from the library. He gave me a long discourse on the benefits of the library and how it helped in studies.

How I wish that such a sermon is given at the time when students join the school. We were never exposed to such talk, even though we had a fairly good library.

SOCIALLY SLOW-GOING

I was socially slow-going and during my long stay in the school could strike close friendships with just a couple of students. Roshan Lal Bhatia became my intimate friend and continues to be so to this day and we share each other's joys and concerns. He was more or less at the same level as me in studies and that perhaps was the major reason for our bonding. He belonged to Bhagowal village in Sialkot district (now in Pakistan). Along with another classmate Ravi, I visited this village during his marriage. The preliminary ceremonies connected with his marriage were celebrated in the village, while the actual marriage took place in Lahore. His father-in-law was a major soft drinks and sherbet manufacturer and had a big shop in Anarkali Bazaar. Roshan rose to the top position in finance and accounts before he retired.

Another schoolmate was Rajinder Sachar, who retired as the Chief Justice of the Delhi High Court. We were also together at Government College for two years. Though there were a couple of more friends, there has been hardly any contact with them since. Mostly I kept to myself.

In the final exam, I did well in mathematics, but my performance in the science paper was dismal. The final verdict was a good first class, but it did not make me proud, as even several mediocre students had scored higher marks.

ADMISSION TO TOP COLLEGE

Though I had been a student of DAV School run by the Arya Samaj, for college education *Baujee* wanted me to join the best college and at that time Government College enjoyed the highest status, not only in Lahore but also in the whole of North India. Quite a number of scholars from Oxford and Cambridge universities served on its faculty. The college maintained a high standard of education, sports and cultural activities.

With such a formidable reputation, it was natural that there was a big rush for admission from different parts of the country, while the number of seats was limited. This college accounted for almost 50 per cent of candidates for recruitment to the country's top civil service—the ICS. Even in the arena of sports, the country's top sportsmen hailed from this college. Similarly, in professions like law, teaching and others, including politics, this college had the honour of producing several big names.

Indeed it was a unique institution, nourished by the dedicated and hardworking faculty who assured all-around progress of the students.

G.D. Sondhi, the first Indian Principal, took over after the last Englishman had retired. Sondhi was an able administrator and sportsman and was interested in cultural activities. He was also the main instrument behind the Lawrence Gardens Open Air Theatre, as well as mini open air theatre on the Government College premises itself. He ensured that these were not merely glorified monuments but actually functioned. He himself guided several programmes and helped build a creative urge among the artistes who staged dramas, skits and other programmes. Besides being a keen sportsman, he also brought laurels in the area of performing arts.

As mentioned earlier, admission to this college was very tough and with my score I stood a fifty per cent chance. And since I was not even a sportsman, who were preferred for admission, *Baujee* did not want to take any chance. He deputed one of my maternal uncles, who was on the faculty of the local Law College, to introduce me to couple of his colleagues who were in the admission committee.

Accordingly, he took me around and spoke to them. Likewise, my *Massar* (the husband of my mother's first cousin), a senior High Court Judge, spoke to Principal G.D. Sondhi, who enjoyed a major voice in the selection process. Thus my admission was assured.

MY DREAM GIRL

Hardly a day after my admission to the Government College I found myself face to face with a rare beauty and felt my heart miss a few beats at the sudden encounter. She was none else but the daughter of *Baujee's* close friend and colleague who practised law in Batala. She had come to seek admission in the local Forman Christian College and had stayed overnight with us along with her father. The next forenoon, they had left. But her face continued to haunt me even afterwards.

Later, she stayed with her *nana* (maternal grandfather), who was retired from medical services and settled in Lahore. I could have gone to his place but hesitated as I was told that her *nana* was of a suspicious nature and likely to be annoyed if a young male person walked into his home to meet his lovely granddaughter. I was afraid of facing such an awkward situation.

One day, however, I gathered sufficient courage and called at her *nana's* house. Immediately, I confronted this stiff gentleman. He was sitting around a table. When I told him that I wanted to meet his granddaughter, he frowned and enquired how I knew her and what business I had with her. I introduced myself and on hearing my father's name, his temperature cooled, though the scowl on his face had not cleared.

The next time when I thought of calling on her was after a considerable gap. This time, to avoid a face-to-face meeting with her suspicious *nana,* I located an alternative route through a side entrance to the house, which in fact was used by the family members. Their family comprised a large number of members. Here I first encountered her *nani* (grandmother) and sought her permission to meet my young friend. I found her to be more understanding and she made me sit comfortably before calling her.

I remember quite a few women of the family were sitting in an adjoining room indulging in *gup-shup* (light talk) and enjoying music. Soon, I was ushered into that room, though I was skeptical of facing around half a dozen young damsels. Somebody was tuning a film song.

After some time, my friend approached me and wanted to be excused for she had to get the belongings of her younger sister arranged as she was leaving Lahore the next morning. After she left, I did not feel like sitting there any longer and quietly made my exit.

I had been a student at Government College for two years from 1939 to 1941, pursuing a course for the Intermediate examination (F.A.). I was a mediocre student and not at all a sportsman. My family wanted me to do engineering, an area which was very much respected and in high demand those days, but by temperament, I was not cut out for this field.

Soon after opting for a course of non-medical sciences (F.Sc.) with physics, chemistry and mathematics, I found it hard to pull on. I especially did not relish the laboratory life amidst obnoxious gases, that was an integral part of the chemistry practicals. After finding myself a complete misfit for this course, I decided on a softer option.

I decided to replace chemistry with a more agreeable subject like Sanskrit. My love for Sanskrit was kindled when I learnt that it was a scoring subject and required little preparation because the Sanskrit teachers were keen to make it popular, since it had been unfortunately pushed to the backburner because of general preference for science subjects.

While initially it was difficult to persuade *Baujee* for this change, but ultimately weighing the overall situation, particularly the fact that when I was least interested in chemistry, he gave in. My application for this change was accepted without a hitch as I had done it within the stipulated time.

Incidentally, I was also quite poor in mathematics and found it a pretty dry and insipid subject and not at all agreeable to my taste. But after changing one subject, I did not have the courage to go in for another change for it would mean a big departure from the prevailing trend where science and math courses were prospering. Also, I would be hurting the sentiments and aspirations of my family. The situation even in the case of physics, which I realized later, was not encouraging. It also involved the use of mathematics and laboratory work, though the latter was far more acceptable than chemistry.

Thus, on the whole, looking into my predilections and tastes, I was not temperamentally as suited for a science course as for the arts course, for which I had a soft corner. How poor I was in mathematics and even in physics was well demonstrated during the term tests when my results in these subjects were disappointing, while I did very well in Sanskrit though I devoted comparatively very little time on it.

Later, however, Sanskrit was never used in my practical life and much of it was soon forgotten. Herein lays the tragedy with the classical languages. Under the prevailing system, Sanskrit, Persian and other classical languages have hardly any practical use and thus cannot enjoy mass base, or even acceptability among the educated.

In the finals examinations of Intermediate, I proved to be just a marginal student, could barely qualify for the second division and that too just at 50 per cent score. This was disappointing, as I had passed the Matriculation examinations with a high first division. Again without much thought, mostly on hearsay basis, I had opted for the B.Com. course instead of B.A., despite the fact that the former took a year extra. Because of compartment in the accountancy paper (my weak area), it took me a year more. In all, it took me four instead of the usual three years to clear B.Com.

In hindsight, when I ponder over the reason of taking such an important decision that would have a bearing on my career, so casually and without much thought, I feel sorry. But it also shows that no proper guidance was available either at the college or at home, which could help me decide the right type of subjects for higher education. In fact, I often suffered later for being deprived of such counselling that could have helped me specialize in the right type of course.

HAILEY COLLEGE OF COMMERCE

So with hastily gathered thoughts, I opted for the B. Com. degree course which was offered exclusively by only one college in the whole of North-West India, Hailey College of Commerce. It was a new, upcoming area, which offered high prospects in business, banks and industry. Thus, it was more prestigious and value-oriented than a mere B.A. degree. Further, the commerce college was within walking distance from my house, which I thought was a great advantage. On the whole, I was convinced that commerce education had more relevance and demand than an arts degree, though my past experience at Government College had clearly demonstrated that I was far more suitable for the arts education than for alternative areas, a factor that became a great stumbling block in my subsequent life.

Thus, with me, there was a clash between pure arts education and alternative professional and social sciences education, where unfortunately, the latter, despite its unsuitability insofar as I was concerned, yet had an upper hold on me. This was further strengthened by the prevailing family and market circumstances. *Baujee* was a lawyer. He would have been quite happy if I had joined him in the profession. But then I was least attracted to it specially when I saw him slogging for long hours at his desk preparing briefs. I developed a positive dislike for this profession. On the contrary, a pure arts degree hardly held any market value.

Thus, faced with this conflict I took this decision on my own, which I thought was the best under the prevailing times.

The Hailey College of Commerce, as mentioned, was the exclusive college of commerce, and located in one of the palatial houses opposite the Panjab University playfields. It was an old colonial structure with extensive front and side lawns which were well maintained and there were lots of open spaces. On its eastern wing facing the college was the hostel for students. There was a small annexe in the north adjoining the boundary wall, touching a residential area, which was used for teaching English by Faiz Ahmad Faiz, a renowned Urdu poet, who was employed by the college for this purpose.

The total strength of students in the college could not be more than 100, where, of course, it was the first year students who dominated, because with each passing year, some students dropped for one reason or the other. Some found it hard to pull on with the tough course. Others got disenchanted by the commerce education itself and opted for their family business, without completing the degree. Quite a few unluckily failed the examinations and did not feel like continuing any further, when they were not sure of the end result.

The elite group dominated the campus. A majority of the students hailed from well-to-do professional and business families. Some of them looked to gaining a foothold in such highly rewarding courses of chartered accountants or cost accountants. Thus, there was a fair mix of various types of aspirants.

Lectures were delivered in a leisurely manner both by regular faculty members as well as part-timers. The Principal was an Englishman who also took classes regularly. I remember, after entering the classroom and before delivering his lecture he would inhale a deep breath accompanied by a big smile. Then he would start his lecture which, of course, most of us found difficult to follow, though we nodded in agreement to what he said.

He was the only foreigner on the faculty. The rest were all Indians, and most of them were well qualified from British universities. Being a small college, unlike Government College, one found it easier to strike acquaintances with many students and become friendly.

The college had a good library with quite a number of books on biographies of top business leaders. I was particularly attracted to these books and whenever I found time, I would sit in the library and read these books, relishing them immensely.

Besides enjoying an encouraging academic and social life under the congenial circumstances, we were often taken on business tours, both in small and large groups. Long visits were scheduled during the winter (Christmas) break when students from each class were supposed to join a trip to gain some practical experience of the business life. Though, often these trips turned out to be more of pleasure trips than business trips.

TRIP TO KARACHI

The trip to Karachi in December 1943 was memorable. It was the height of war time when the British were fighting the battle for their survival and quite a few coastal cities in this country were the target of enemy attack. They had already sent danger signals through small aerial attacks on Calcutta and Madras. This was enough to cause panic among the local people, several of whom had shifted to safer destinations.

The situation in the two western cities of Karachi and Bombay was, however, different. Facing the western coastal belt, they were comparatively safe and there was no panic among the local population. So, our trip to Karachi was considered safe and there was no cause for worry.

The train journey from Lahore to Karachi was long and we had planned stopovers en route in Sukkur and Hyderabad (Sindh). The famous Sukkur Barrage across the Indus river was the main attraction. We eagerly went around seeing how the waters of the mighty and awe-inspiring Indus in which flowed all five rivers of Punjab—Sutlej, Beas, Ravi, Chenab and Jhelum—had been harnessed by top engineers to feed a battery of canals that supplied water to the parched fields of this desert province and turned it into a global granary. It was indeed a superb job executed admirably and filled the long-felt need of this region, crying for water before the five rivers emptied their millions and millions gallons of water into the Arabian Sea.

We spent a good part of time learning the working of this highly complicated barrage as well as comprehending the splendour of this area. This visit also provided us with an opportunity to see the functioning a top biscuit unit, the only one of its kind at that time in Punjab and Sindh and possibly in the whole of North India. It was owned by a seth, Mangha Ram, who was a multi-millionaire. It was a gigantic manufacturing unit where we were liberally treated to sweets and biscuits and when our stomachs refused to accept more, we filled our pockets and bags with as much as we could.

Hyderabad was a robust cultural and academic centre. A visit to this place was quite refreshing. Incidentally, during the pre-Independence days, there was often confusion over the two Hyderabads. If it was not specified whether it was Hyderabad in Sindh or in the Nizam's state, a letter could land at a wrong place and fail to be delivered to the addressee.

The train journey through Sindh was highly dusty. Lots of sand accumulated on our clothes and faces. We would be inhaling sand and dust even after windows and shutters in the coach had been closed.

Thus, the first thing that we did at the next railway station was to douche our faces liberally with water to clear up the sand sticking hard on our faces and also gargled the mouth several times to clear the throat of sand, which often failed to provide sufficient relief. In these circumstances, it was difficult to enjoy any eatables. Even tea had to be sipped with care and eyes had to be specially protected.

We found the port city of Karachi very different. It lived up to its reputation of being the most well-maintained city in the country with broad and solidly executed highways and no sign of refuse. It appeared that there was a heavy penalty for uncleanliness. The houses, multi-storey buildings, flats, institutions, business premises, government offices, even bazaars wore a fresh look. Its population at that time was quite small and well manageable and there appeared to be a great sense of discipline and orderly behavior among them.

It was a multi-cultural city, where people belonging to different faiths and religions stayed together and worked and contributed to its prosperity. It was a thriving business centre where most of its residents, called Sindhis, were in some trade or the other. They were so adventurous that quite a few of them could be found in other parts of the globe. Besides all over Gujarat, several of them had spread their businesses in Arab and African countries, to which access was easier from this port. Later, in the mid-1950s when I had the opportunity to visit the little-known but extremely charming Spanish island resort in West Africa—Las Palmas—I was surprised to come across some Sindhi businessmen settled there, some even married to Spanish ladies.

It shows a high sense of adventure among the Sindhis who brought a lot of wealth back home and invested it in property, real estate, stock market and business. This was the one community that owned beautiful and spacious houses in Karachi.

They were also a forward-looking people, free from religious dogmas. One would often come across lovely Sindhi belles who spoke chaste English. It was a pleasure to engage in conversation with them on any area as their response was usually quite friendly and they were well informed. This was so different from what we were used to in Lahore. Though also a cosmopolitan city, with a major education centre, rich in social and cultural moorings, the ladies in Lahore were far more conservative and lived virtually behind the *purdah* (veil) and thus were difficult to approach.

It was for the first time in my life that I had the opportunity to visit the sea. I virtually feasted my eyes on the vast expanse of blue waters, watching carefully the small and mighty waves chasing one another relentlessly to a good distance. Clifton Beach was a favourite spot where we enjoyed a full-day picnic, had frequent dips in the sea, taking care that we did not move too far into the sea, particularly because the behaviour of the sea waves was difficult to predict. It was a vast natural beach and despite the crowds of visitors, was well maintained, like the city. We took long walks on the beach which were refreshing and invigorating.

The other place we visited was the Manora Island area, which was located a short distance inside the sea. Those days, it was under the control of the army. We had to seek special permission to visit it. What struck us was its empty coastline without any warship anchored or any sort of similar activity. It was hardly protected against any possible attack by the enemy. Fortunately, it appeared there was little possibility of such an eventuality as the enemy, both in the eastern and western fronts, was too engrossed to think of this. However, such a situation in a port city like Karachi could pose a big danger.

Soon our memorable trip to Karachi, where we visited a number of historical, tourist and business sites, came to an end. But, I decided to stay on longer with my brother-in-law who was working with a business house in Karachi. This also helped me see more of its social and cultural life, as well as enjoy visits to more sites that had been missed earlier.

FIRST VISIT TO DELHI

The trip to Delhi in 1942 was also quite interesting. It was part of an educational trip to Delhi-Agra-Mathura-Brindaban. It was my first visit to Delhi. The North and South blocks of the Central Secretariat were taking their final shape and so also, quite a few other government buildings, including the monumental mansion for the Governor-General or Viceroy of India (the present Rashtrapati Bhawan) and several bungalows and houses for government officials.

The building for All India Radio's headquarters was under construction and I suppose except for this structure and buildings of the police station and possibly the YMCA and a church, there was hardly any other building on the present Sansad Marg. Most of it was a deserted place and ill-lit, making it unsafe to move during the night time. Connaught Place was coming up, with a number of buildings under construction. Its surroundings were gradually emerging. On the whole, much of New Delhi bore a deserted look and was hardly safe during the late hours.

In contrast to this, Old Delhi was busy, active and thriving even during the late hours. Much of it centred around Chandni Chowk and narrow lanes and bylanes that surrounded it in an endless number, and bursting with population. It reminded us of Lahore's Anarkali Bazaar and its narrow lanes which spread deep down into its 12 historical gates. The pattern of development of both Lahore and Delhi appeared to be asymmetrical.

Considering these factors, it appeared that though Delhi was the capital of India, much of its grandeur was still to emerge. On the other hand, Lahore scored over Delhi in population, business, trade, education, culture, and other aspects. It gave us a sense of superiority, which was amply reflected when we talked to our counterparts in Delhi or with the local population. We thought the average Lahorian was better dressed, more educated, smart and active than his fellow Delhiwalla.

Little did we realize at that time that within just a few years most of us would also become an integral part of Delhi itself.

While in Agra, we rushed to see the Taj Mahal in its full glory against the backdrop of the full moon. There was complete darkness in the city to protect the monument against enemy attack. The darkness enhanced the beauty of the moonlight and we virtually forced the *tonga* drivers to race so that we could enjoy the full glory of the Taj. The main monument had been painted to camouflage its identity in case of a possible enemy attack.

However, we found its main gate locked and there was no other entry. We had to satisfy ourselves with a look at it from a distance. The next day we went there again and went around the impressive monument leisurely, and even climbed to the top of one minaret and enjoyed the view of the Agra Fort and the Jamuna river that flowed quietly nearby.

IMPRESSIVE LIST OF CLASSMATES

In Hailey College, I forged close friendships with many classmates. As said, the group was mostly from the elite section, either professional or business community. Even those who came from other sections gradually absorbed themselves mostly into professional section.

We had a classmate, Ranjit Rai, maternal grandson of Sir Ganga Ram, well-known engineer and planner who had executed a large number of major government buildings and was also in the forefront of planning and developing infrastructure for transport, irrigation and other allied areas. He owned several prized buildings and houses in Lahore and elsewhere. In fact, the building housing Hailey College once belonged to him. Ranjit's father, Aftab Rai, was the Director-General of the Directorate of Disposals, created by the Government of India for selling a large number of products that had been rendered surplus after the Second World War.

Aftab Rai wanted his son Ranjit to form an agency through which he could take the maximum advantage of this opportunity. Ultimately, Ranjit collaborated with Yudishter Nanda, another classmate. Yudishter hailed from a well-known business family owning a fleet of passenger buses, which plied to various destinations.

In the beginning, this group was called Escorts Agents. It kicked off good business and became quite popular and even expanded to other parts of the country.

After the partition of this country, it shifted its headquarters to Delhi. Subsequently, it appears Ranjit had to quit it, perhaps to start his own independent business. Thus, Escorts fell completely under the control of Yudishter, who was a highly ambitious and hard working entrepreneur. He soon expanded the business to new heights and this firm branched out into different fields.

Unfortunately, Escorts faced a big shock in 1951 when the small plane in which Yudishter was travelling along with a couple of his business partners was hit by lightning close to Delhi airport. Yudishter's elder brother, who had a fairly good experience in business, took over Escorts. It grew further under his management. Today, Escorts is one of the country's leading corporate firms.

We had another classmate, Raj Kapur, who also hailed from a reputed business house. His father was a leading paper distributor who enjoyed a major share in the marketing of paper manufactured by the Thapar Group of Industries. After Partition, they had shifted to Delhi and opened offices in several other cities.

Raj had settled in Bombay. I had attended his marriage in Amritsar. I enjoyed his hospitality more than once. Before boarding my ship for travel to London in 1956, I had stayed with him and he was very happy to take me around the city, which I was visiting for the first time. He had also come to see me off.

On another occasion, when I had taken a small group of my students on a trip to Bombay and Goa, we did not have any suitable place for stay in Bo[illegible]d neither could I take the risk of staying at an unfamiliar [illegible]n two young girls in the group. On reaching Bombay, early morning, I rang up Raj and luckily he was available. I told him of my problem. He promptly offered to accommodate our group in his house. We enjoyed his hospitality for a couple of days.

The stay was highly comfortable and we immensely enjoyed the surroundings of Malabar Hill where my friend and his family occupied one full floor in a posh building. The girls, in particular, were quite happy to meet the women members of the family and enjoyed homely comfort and security. Before parting, they presented them with a gift for the hospitality we had enjoyed.

Rama Nand was another classmate. He too hailed from a prosperous family owning large property, both lands and buildings, in Haryana. They also managed a couple of known colleges. He later joined his family in managing vast business interests. Till before his death a few years back, we were in close touch with each other.

In fact, in the hostel where Rama Nand lived in Lahore, also stayed two more of my classmates, Radhey Shyam and Amrit Lal, both hailing from prosperous business families. After leaving college, they too had joined their family businesses. We have rarely been in touch with each other since, though in Lahore I remember we saw a number of English films, together which we were quite fond of. Possibly, the last film we watched together, during the Second World War was "Gone with the Wind" featuring Bette Davis and Clark Gable, a very popular pair during those days. This was the longest film we had seen, with two intervals.

Subsequently, quite a few of my classmates entered professional careers and most of them rose to the top positions in the corporate sector. Sardari Lal had joined Hindustan Lever and before retiring held the top position in accounts.

Similarly, there were Krishna Nand, Parshottam and Chand Kishen who rose to the top positions in their organisations.

I have continued to remain in touch with particularly Chand Kishen Hazari. He joined Escorts and retired as its top man in finance.

On the whole, it was an extraordinarily active group of students who made to the top positions in their respective areas. Even the former Prime Minister of India, Mr. I.K. Gujral, is an old student of this college. He was a couple of years senior to me.

RAWALPINDI

During the 1939 summer vacation, as a fresher at Government College, Lahore, I visited Rawalpindi to spend the vacation with a family friend for getting coaching in mathematics from him. He was a lecturer of mathematics at a local college. Indeed, I was poor in this subject and needed lessons in advance to face the topic with confidence.

While this was a laudable and appreciable endeavour, my mind was hardly responsive to the instructions. Instead, I looked forward to exploring fresh surroundings and perhaps, visiting a hill station, which I had never seen.

My lack of interest in mathematics was further hit when I noticed the stern behaviour of this professor while he taught students at his residence. Thus, I became more reluctant to submit myself to his discipline and avoided him.

I did a lot of running around to new places and also found an opportunity to visit a hill station, Murree, which was not far from Rawalpindi. I spent a full one week in Murree and never missed trekking down to a place of interest. The visit to this lovely hill station, full of greenery, pine trees, fresh air and cool atmosphere, provided a big contrast to the hot and perspiring plains of Pindi. How I wished I had more time to spend here!

The Pindi visit also provided me with me with an opportunity to visit historical places like Taxila and Punja Sahib. Excavation work of the vast ancient site of Taxila had been completed and a well-managed museum had been set up for the preservation of rare relics and other items of historical significance.

One of the most important sites was the area housing the university, where scholars from far-off lands came to be trained from its highly learned faculty. The whole excavation work was spread over several hundred acres of land and it was difficult to cover it in a day. Since we did not have enough time, we limited ourselves to select sites and rounded it off with a visit to the museum. Taxila was without a doubt a well-constructed town and a thriving kingdom. The memory of this place has lingered in my mind, even long afterwards.

Another unforgettable visit that is still fresh in my mind was to Punja Sahib, which is not far from Taxila. I hung around at this historical site for the maximum possible time and conjured in my mind events linked with Guru Nanak, whose life history as well as teachings I had read during my school days. Indeed, he was a unique character who had travelled far and wide, including Mecca-Medina, at a time (in the late 1400s) when there was no regular means of communication. His teachings had a profound effect on me and thus, at Punja Sahib, I experienced a unique mental peace.

GLAMOUR OF WINTER

Lahore was a national, cultural and social centre. In the winter season, it came to its full glory, when a large number of conferences, exhibitions, *mushairas* and other programmes were organized. Artistes of national and international fame would often visit the city to entertain people. The circus, which lasted for several weeks, was a regular feature and it was enjoyed immensely by children and grown-ups. So were *Urdu mushairas* and *Hindi kavi durbars,* when a large number of poets of repute would descend on the city and their programmes were well attended, both by the locals as well as outsiders.

Celebrated films in Hindi, Punjabi and English would be screened and they attracted record crowds. The city had a large number of well-managed and comfortable cinema houses. It especially excelled in halls showing exclusively English films, for which there was a great demand, for the city had a good population of Anglo-Indians, British and other European nationals, army personnel, Christians, Parsis, besides the big number of local population who were fond of watching English films. There were often 'house full' shows and cinema owners did brisk business.

The cosmopolitan character of the city, which virtually enjoyed the status of the winter capital of north India, also attracted a large number of well-known politicians and cultural and social leaders. As a child, I remember the All-India Congress Session was held in 1929 on the banks of the Ravi where for the first time, I had the opportunity to see and hear Pandit Jawaharlal Nehru, who was the Congress President, as well as other stalwarts. It was indeed a great opportunity to see the top national leaders. A large number of family members and friends had come to attend this session and our house, situated about eight miles from the venue of the session, was virtually agog with life, somewhat akin to a marriage occasion.

It was a special time for the children to enjoy and move together among the crowds that thronged the venue of the conference. As we hardly had any interest in listening to the leaders' speeches, we lazed around the spacious area, indulging in *gup-shup,* munching sweets prepared in *dhesi-ghee* and peeling off *chargozas.* Those days we could buy a pocketful of *chargozas* for a song. Indeed *chargozas, badams, kishmish* and other dry fruits were available aplenty and were our favourite throughout the winter months.

These leaders, after the session, visited the city and addressed mammoth meetings of the citizens.

ENCOUNTER WITH TAGORE AND GANDHI

Gurudev Rabindranath Tagore was another top personality who had much attachment with this city and often visited it. I remember having an encounter with this universally recognized poet during my early school days. He used to stay in the house of Dhani Ram Bhalla, a top businessman of the city. Once my father took me to Bhalla's house to hear the poet recite his works.

I was, of course, too small to understand his poetry but could notice the deep impact it had on the select audience that had gathered around him on the occasion. While he recited his composition in Bengali it was rendered into English by his secretary.

Later, I often recollected the saintly personality of Tagore, with a flowing beard and body wrapped gracefully in a loosely worn gown. His face exuded serenity and he was deeply engrossed in his composition as he recited it to the audience. I am sure those who understood Bengali would have been deeply moved by his rendition. This flavour was missing when he rendered it English.

Still later, I also became an ardent reader of Tagore's works. I read his celebrated story *'Kabuliwallah' a* number of times during my school days and it has stayed deep in my memory. It was also made into a film. As I grew older, I read his more serious works.

Another leader I had the opportunity to meet was Mahatma Gandhi, who too had much love for this city. I remember the evening prayer meeting in the early 1930s that he held on the spacious premises of DAV College hostel close to the Lala Lajpat Rai complex, where he would often stay. Lala Lajpat Rai himself was a great leader who enjoyed nationwide respect and played an important role in shaping the political life of this country. He had met a martyr's death in the late 1920s while leading a procession of peaceful people protesting against the anti-people policies of the British. He was hit on his head by a *lathi,* which proved fatal as he collapsed later. The Lajpat Rai complex was raised in memory of this great son of India and was a favourite place of Gandhiji's stay. As a child of five years, I also had the opportunity of witnessing the unveiling ceremony of Lala Lajpat Rai's statue in the *Gol Bagh* area of Lahore.

I recollect that a mammoth crowd had gathered around the raised platform where Gandhiji was to hold the prayer meeting. So thick was the crowd that one could hardly see the end of it. Gandhiji walked so briskly that it even put several youngsters to shame. While seeing him from a close angle, I was much impressed by his broad chest over a small and frail body. He had full command of himself and when he addressed the audience, there was pin-drop silence. Though he spoke in Hindi, rather Hindustani which was a queer mixture of different Indian languages, his tone was basically of a Gujarati, which sounded so peculiar to my ears. He used an utterly simple language, devoid of any difficult word, and, he could cultivate direct communication even with an illiterate person.

In fact, Gandhiji, realistic and practical that he was, always favoured the use of simple Hindustani dialect in day-to-day affairs. Otherwise, it would have been beyond the comprehension of an ordinary person.

I have often wondered that had we followed Gandhiji's advice of making Hindustani as our national language, and not Sanskritised Hindi, we would have succeeded in achieving our national language goal far more easily. Our Hindi lovers have failed to achieve their goal even after more than half a century of effort. Unfortunately, even in Hindi speaking areas, the national language continues to be confined to the elite section and has not gained access to the common man.

Thus, our major tragedy has been to ignore Gandhiji's advice and allow the Hindi Pandits to have their word, which has made the Hindi language so very difficult to gain the status a of national language, even in the future.

LIBERAL TEACHINGS

Right from my childhood, I have been impressed by the liberal teachings of our Gurus, who were above conventional dogmas and made tremendous sacrifices for freeing the society of irrational customs and bringing it on the path of sanity and rational thinking.

In this respect, the teachings of Buddha, Swami Dayanand, Guru Nanak, Swami Vivekananda and other like-minded leaders filled my mind wholly and had a deep impact on me during my early days.

Swami Dayanand, the founder of the Arya Samaj movement in this country, was a great social reformer and an eminent educationist. As a boy, he was deeply shocked when he found that a deity that was worshipped so reverently by countless number of followers had failed to protect itself against the onslaught of a rat that made a clean sweep of the rich offerings made to it by the worshippers. He argued that if this deity was not able to protect itself against the rat, how it would protect its followers.

Thus, he found that idol worship was irrational and spent many years searching for an alternative, more rational path of enlightenment, when he found the institution of universal religion with rational thinking. Thus, Arya Samaj was founded and its main goal was universal education and wiping out of illiteracy, for illiteracy was the biggest factor for the spread of wrong beliefs and dogmas.

Little surprise that Arya Samaj has been in the forefront of education. The body has created a large number of educational institutions right from the primary level to higher education throughout the country, though its maximum concentration is in North India. Its educational institutions have also been opened in foreign countries and they enjoy a high reputation.

Similarly, Guru Nanak has had a profound impact on me. He was also a great 15th century reformist and rationalist. He was a world-trotter even during days when there were no modes of transport. Once while visiting a holy place, he found that people were making an offering of water to *Surya Bhagwan* while taking a dip in a sacred river. Instead of following them, he started making an offering of water in the opposite direction. People were annoyed and castigated him for what he was doing. He retorted by saying that if their offering could reach *Surya Bhagwan* at such a long distance, surely his offering of water would reach far more quickly his parched fields located in the direction of his offering.

In a nutshell, this episode was to demonstrate the

ludicrousness of the belief that by no stretch of imagination could water reach the sun.

He preached the people to follow rational behaviour instead of wasting time over illogical rituals which did not do any good, rather victimized them.

Thus broad, liberal and rational thinking was the message conveyed by most of these leaders which had earned high appreciation and respect even from their opponents.

LOVE FOR ECONOMICS, FINALLY

From the commerce stream, I shifted to economics in 1945 when I took admission in MA by formally enrolling myself in Forman Christian College, a reputed American missionary college. But all our postgraduate lectures were delivered on the Panjab University campus. Senior teachers hailing from various local colleges taught us.

Thus, we were exposed to over a dozen teachers. Ours was a fairly large class consisting of over sixty pupils, including a dozen girls, a fairly good number during those days. It was an indicator that girls in Lahore were active participants in the educational and social life. Some girls occupied responsible offices in student bodies and excelled in oratory and debating skills. Their command over English was quite remarkable.

There were quite a few coffee houses close to the university and these would be often packed with senior students. They would spend hours at a stretch in these coffee houses, discussing politics, elections to student bodies, girls, or anything.

POST-WORLD WAR II

The atmosphere of Lahore was shaping differently after World War II. The days of blackouts were over and so were the war-time austerity measures and rationing, gradually giving way to plenty. Imported goods had almost disappeared during the war days. In their place, we had to be content with shoddy, second-class swadeshi products. Now they were making their appearance again. The harassed consumer who had suffered the tyranny of local manufacturers for years was now feeling happy with the return of his favourite brands.

Soon a big change occurred in the local economic scenario, when a large number of units engaged in meeting the war-time needs started closing down in succession. The spectre of a large-scale unemployment again faced the country. This was further worsened with a large number of demobilised soldiers returning home after the war. The time of transition from war to post-war period was a difficult period for a large number of families.

The war had shattered not only the British economy, but also much of the European economy both in the East and West. The trudge on the path of a slow and painful recovery began. The worst hit countries were Germany and Japan, whose cities as well as local economies had completely broken down. There was a heavy loss of human lives, particularly of young people, who perished in large numbers while engaged in war operations.

Thus, the post-war period witnessed a severe population imbalance with far fewer younger members compared to elderly ones. Despite the dismal scenario, their economies amazingly recovered earlier than expected. This was attained due to the presence of local talent, technicians, engineers, planners and professionals and liberal assistance available from the world's richest country, the USA, whose economy had remained intact during the war period.

The USA had made a rapid growth during this period. During the post-war period, the USA had made liberal offers of assistance to the war-devastated economies. Germany as well as Japan particularly benefited from the American aid programme, and along with locally available talent soon rebuilt their completely devastated economies and before long they were even performing better than the pre-war days.

In fact, this recovery prepared them for new challenges, which made the newly emerging economies far sounder and better result yielding than their pre-war economies. Both Japan and Germany went on the path of complete modernization within a few years and global markets opened up for their products.

We were not directly affected by the war as India remained beyond the enemy attack, except for sporadic attacks by Japan just on the periphery which did not cause any substantial loss. In fact, compared to us, the Americans suffered far more as a result of the attack on Pearl Harbour by the Japanese, and, yet we had failed to take advantage of this golden opportunity. This can be attributed to the poor pre-war economic base, low technology, lack of skilled manpower as also the absence of minimum infrastructure.

VOICE OF FREEDOM

While we were passing through a difficult post-war transition period, the British announced their intention to free India and hand over power to the local leaders. This was a welcome sign and encouraging result of a long political struggle under the guidance of Mahatma Gandhi and other national leaders, and especially after the Quit India Movement launched in 1942. But, in reality, we were not well prepared for it. We were yet a weak nation and despite a strong leadership, had miles to cover before we could become a strong nation. It has been duly confirmed by the post-Independence experience where, even after several decades, we continue to be a poor nation with the bottom score in the conventional growth indicators.

There is little doubt that had Churchill remained in power in the post-war Britain, the chances of India earning freedom so soon were bleak. He would not have handed over freedom on the plea that India was yet not prepared for it or fit for independence.

However, our main trouble was not whether we were prepared for this freedom as it was with the power sharing between Muslim-majority areas on the one hand and rest of the country on the other. Once the venom of communalism was let loose, it led to bloodshed on a large scale. This poison spread deeper as the time of division of this country came nearer. The rest is, of course history. Five million refugees from either side crossed over the border in the biggest-ever exodus in world history and countless number of people were killed on either side. And then followed the long battle of refugees to be settled again.

A NEW HOUSE

In 1945 we had to shift our house from Edwards Road in Lahore, where we had stayed since the time we had moved to this city in the early 1920s. It had been gifted by the landlord to the Punjab government for opening a craft training centre for girls and the government had in turn sent us urgent notice to vacate it immediately. To find a new suitable house so soon was not an easy job, particularly as at that time the city suffered from an acute accommodation shortage.

Luckily, an alternative place, which had easy access to the High Court, to suit the needs of my Baujee, was found. We shared the house, a two-storeyed building, with our landlord Captain Nur Ahmad, a Muslim gentleman who had retired from the army. In fact, our new locality was predominantly Muslim inhabited.

While our new accommodation was smaller than the earlier one, we were compensated here in several ways. It was a new structure and we were lucky to have a very good neighbour in Nur Ahmad Sahib who was a God-fearing gentleman, and his family soon developed a great liking for us. So it was a very cordial and happy stay, which proved highly beneficial in 1947 when communal riots started. This area was comparatively safe and protected and, above all, we had the full protection of our landlord, who treated my father as his younger brother and that was an additional advantage.

The other redeeming feature of this house was that it was free from the scourge of mosquitoes which had made our lives hell in the previous house, particularly in the summers, when it was difficult to have a comfortable sleep during the night. No longer were we disturbed by the constant humming of mosquitoes. Thus, we were also freed from regular bouts of malaria and other diseases. It also saved us from the scourge of open drains, which were a regular breeding spot for mosquitoes and neither did we have that cowshed which was an integral part of the backyard of the earlier house and we had to inhale, almost all the time, the peculiar smell of cow dung.

We were completely spared of these mind-boggling sufferings in our new residence. However, the plus points of the earlier accommodation were: (a) plenty of covered space and (b) easy access to clients, being on the main road.

MASS COMMUNAL FRENZY

We had barely settled down at our new place for a year and a half and were getting used to the new premises, its neighbourhood and the like, when the phantom of the Partition of the country began to loom large before us and turned out to be the vital starting point for communal riots. Being a prominent political centre in the country, the signals of such communal disturbances began to grip Lahore and soon spread to other parts of the country.

In no time, mass communal frenzy started ruling over several parts of North and East India with a dominant role played by Lahore and other cities of the then Punjab. As mentioned earlier, this had resulted in the mass migration of five million Hindus from west Punjab to East Punjab and five million Muslims from East Punjab and surrounding areas to West Punjab. There is no record of the number of those killed, raped and abducted. The number runs into several lakhs. It was history's worst carnage.

It was at this stage that the protective care of our Muslim landlord came to the fore. When we left Lahore a few days before Independence, all our belongings were practically left in the house. They were taken care of by the landlord and his family members in our absence. At the time we left Lahore, it was unbelievable to us that we would not be able to return at all. But soon we realized that Lahore had become more inaccessible than a foreign land as we were denied entry to our motherland forever.

Thanks to the protection provided by our landlord, we were later able to salvage important items of our belongings, including law books, without which Baujee could not have been comfortable in restarting his law practice. The salvage operation was managed entirely by the landlord at a high personal risk. Subsequently, he also maintained personal contact with Baujee and often enquired about our welfare.

Travail of Unsettled Life

After leaving Lahore, there followed a long travail of unsettled life, moving from one destination to another, and ultimately moving to Simla in mid-1948, where the High Court of East Punjab (as Punjab was called after Partition) had ultimately started functioning. In fact, after the loss of Lahore, East Punjab had yet to build its capital. Simla was made a temporary capital mainly because among all the places in East Punjab this city had the largest accommodation available, being the summer capital of the erstwhile Punjab government.

The unsettled life in Lahore in 1947 had also prevented my appearing in the final examinations of MA. Though they were held on the scheduled dates, it was difficult to prepare for them under the continuous disturbed conditions. Several other students had likewise failed to take the exams. After the establishment of East Punjab University in Solan (another hill station not far from Simla where sufficient space was available for housing the new university temporarily), this exam was finally held in 1948 in Amritsar for the benefit of those who had failed to appear during the 1947 exam held in Lahore.

KURUKSHETRA REFUGEE CAMP

Early in 1948 I had found a small job in the Kurukshetra refugee camp at its Vocational Training Centre run by the Ministry of Relief and Rehabilitation of the Government of India, for the benefit of refugees. This Centre was managed by S.K. Dey who soon started the famous experiment on Community Development and Extension Programme. Before Independence, Dey was a *pucca* bureaucrat who had led a luxurious life and donned a European style of living.

However, after Independence, he had completely changed to serve his mother country and its people and offered his honorary services to Pandit Nehru for the rehabilitation of refugees. This is how this Vocational Training Centre was started, which provided training to the refugees settled in India's biggest refugee camp. It was established close to the railway station of this historical pilgrimage place and covered a spacious stretch of almost desert land, housing over one lakh refugees.

The refugee camp bore the look of a vast tented township, divided sector wise, where each tent had an identity, location number, details of its occupants and other particulars which helped the camp administration to run and manage such a large refugee population in an efficient and convenient manner. It distributed ration, and provided medical help and other facilities. A large number of voluntary organizations had also opened their offices and were providing essential services to the refugees. Ample provision had been made for the supply of water and meeting the sanitary needs of this camp. There were also facilities for the education of children and here, the voluntary organizations in particular played an important role.

The vocational centre was located in the middle of the camp and attracted a large number of trainees, including women, who were, in this way not only kept productively busy but also earned a small stipend. Various consumer products manufactured at this place were sold through its cooperative shop at highly subsidized prices. Thus, refugees could purchase items of daily needs here itself instead of going to the nearest town, which was a couple of miles away.

Though thrown into this sort of life by chance, it provided me with an ample opportunity to become a part of the refugee camp life and understand its working and problems. People had converged here from far-off places in West Punjab and the NWFP where they had enjoyed a long settled life and owned houses, lands and businesses. Now, all this had become a thing of the past and they had to struggle hard for a new life under the changed conditions.

The camp, of course, was not their permanent abode, and it could not be by any stretch of imagination, where a large number of families had to share a tiny space and were often exposed to all sorts of vagaries of Nature. Life would particularly become miserable during the rainy and winter seasons, during the long evening and night hours as they had scanty woollens to protect themselves.

It is remarkable how the refugees faced these hardships with undaunted courage and patience. During the daytime, the male members tried to earn some livelihood in whatever way they could, while their women folk took full care of the children and household duties.

Under these conditions, the death toll was high, particularly among the old and weak members who found it difficult to survive the harsh conditions of the camp life which had with meagre medical facilities.

During the evenings, not far from the camp a large number of burning pyres that had been lit to consign the dead bodies was a common sight. It was awe-striking and reminded one of the ultimate destination of life and made one feel humble.

The camp authorities also helped in the dispersal of refugees to a more settled life, where quite a few began to move out before they faced the next Monsoon. An easy access to Kurukshetra railway station proved a great boon. Some camp residents had voluntarily shifted to other destinations, after spending the initial difficult period in the camp.

Even then, it was a heroic job to disperse the majority of dwellers. Some of them had got used to free ration and other comforts of the camp life and had become too lazy to move out even when offered help. They virtually waited to be thrown out.

And this is what happened soon. At the very first flush of Monsoon, the pains of prolonged camp life became too obvious. It was particularly so among the residents of low-lying areas. Their tents were flooded and they had to be shifted to safer places. This disturbed their daily routine and forced them to move out, before the situation got worse.

With the further advancement of Monsoon, the Vocational Training Centre too had to be closed. Meanwhile, the authorities had been able to acquire alternative land in a small village of Nilokheri on the main road, not far from Kurukshetra. The Vocational Training Centre also acquired its permanent roots here and turned into the first experiment in Community Development Programme, which was soon to take its national level spread.

NILOKHERI, AN EXPERIMENT

Thus, within a short time, this one-time thick jungle land infested with monkeys, snakes, other animals and insects was cleared mostly with voluntary labour of refugees. Roads were constructed, as well as, potable water, power and other facilities laid. A regular township with houses, shops, schools and technical education facilities emerged. Gradually, this very first experiment in community development provided a meaningful rehabilitation to refugees who would have otherwise perished in the camp life.

Soon, the fame of the success of this experiment travelled far and wide. So impressed was Pandit Nehru that he made S.K. Dey, the person behind the Vocational Training Centre as also this experiment of community development, the Central Minister of Community Development and Cooperation. He was at the helm of the ministry for a full ten years.

Thus, community development became a successful experiment for the meaningful rehabilitation of the uprooted refugees. It also proved equally beneficial for starting a new life for the lakhs of refugees in India's backward villages.

SUCCESSFUL STAY

My stay in Nilokheri was very brief, less than two months, while at the Kurukshetra camp I had spent around six months. But these eight months were packed with adventure. I lived in tents with refugees who had their own tales of woe to narrate and did not quite know how they would settle down to a new life after having lost everything in Pakistan. With large families, their problems had further multiplied.

But evidently most of them did not lose courage. Their history was steeped in such emergencies when their forefathers had often fought with invaders from far-off lands, who raided this country. Moving from one place to another on short notice was also not alien to them. While several of them perished, they fought valiantly against the intruders and had learnt to stand on their own, settle themselves amidst new surroundings, and with hard labour and patience turn the new area, usually tough, into a rich and thriving one.

They carried the same tradition after the country's Partition when they had to leave their hearths and homes, without any baggage, to face the new hardships of refugee camps, with dignity and grace.

I think it was the same spirit that came to fore among these people. Overcoming the trauma of Partition and of losing their dear and near ones in the world's greatest bloodbath, they not only resettled themselves in different destinations of this country but also did remarkably well in whatever profession they chose, whether it was agriculture, their favourite, or transport, running of small, medium and even large businesses, or joining the army, even visiting foreign lands if they could find an opportunity and settling there. Wherever they found a foothold, they worked hard and left behind a deep impression.

After leaving Kurukshetra for different places, these refugees did not look back, but got settled, and some of them also reached new heights.

I personally have happy moments of my stay both in Kurukshetra and Nilokheri. Kurukshetra is the land of the legendary battle between the Kauravas and Pandavas. Though in 1947, it was an abandoned and dusty land, it must have been so different in the days of the battle. I often visited its sacred tank and listened with rapt attention to the evening prayers recited in its several temples located nearby. The melody of this music would often touch my inner chords, relieving me of the heat, dust and constant din of the camp life.

It was around this sacred tank that one of my favourite characters, in an unpublished love story, had tied the nuptial knot with his dream girl much against the wishes of her family. The marriage was solemnized by the temple priest in the presence of friends of the couple and a few other people staying nearby. Above all, the marriage was blessed by the full moon, which had spread its full radiance over the newly weds as well as the sacred tank.

I was among those half a dozen or so persons who had first spent the night in the thick jungle of Nilokheri, where we had pitched a few tents in a small clearance. And, despite having put more than six petromaxes in different corners of this clearance, we did not feel safe as we could see a number snakes slithering around. The place was full of mosquitoes, which also made it difficult to get even a wink of sleep, despite the anti-mosquito nets.

When the morning cast its glow, we heaved a sigh of relief. We were welcomed by a large group of monkeys who watched us with great surprise from tree tops, probably wondering who had intruded into their domain.

Things improved soon with more colleagues joining us and the provision of more facilities. The thick growth cleared to have an easy access to the main road.

Hardly I had settled there when I got an offer of a more secure and better-paid job in Simla. I decided to accept it. It would also provide me with an opportunity to join my family, who were settled there in a house provided by the government on Cart Road near Boileuganj. This location had an easy access to the High Court, where my father practised, and saved him from zigzag walks in the hill station that he was not used to.

So, I bid adieu to my colleagues, with whom I had had such a wonderful time. Most of them were also tired of leading such a nomadic life. It did not suit those who had families. Not quite sure of how much time it would take for Nilokheri to develop into a regular township, though the authorities assured handsome rewards, most of them also left as and when they found appropriate opportunities.

Soon, S.K. Dey, the architect of the community development experiment, also left to join his new assignment as Minister of Community Development and Cooperation in Delhi. His move dealt a severe blow to the growth of Nilokheri. But the shift helped the country embark on a nationwide programme of this new experiment of community development.

Simla Hills Beckon

I soon became a part of Simla. This was the realization of a dream that I had nursed while in Lahore. However, at that time it appeared to be just wishful thinking. I little knew that destiny had in store for me a stay in Simla for over three years. Though most of the British population had left after selling their properties, some were still around and felt reluctant to leave this place. They were born here, and had grown up in the city and developed great attachment with its surroundings and climate.

Of course, times had changed. No longer could they bask in the past glory, when they were the rulers. Now, they had to adjust to the changed times and live as equals with the local population, though it was tough for them.

Still the level of cleanliness and sanitation and basic services that Simla had enjoyed under the British, was to a large extent intact; notwithstanding the fact that a large population of government servants and refugees had settled here. Most of them worked in East Punjab Secretariat and other scattered offices, while a few had found jobs in the offices of Central government and quite a number of these offices functioned from here. In fact, after Independence, refugees were given preference in government jobs. This also happened in the case of Central Secretariat in Delhi, where soon a large number of refugees from West Punjab had found berth.

After Simla emerged as the new capital of Punjab, it acquired a new status with busy and crowded bazaars and roads. The Mall, in particular, was a very busy road, buzzing with pedestrian traffic both in summer and winter. Earlier, during winter, several shops would close down for lack of customers but now they remained open throughout the year. In winter particularly, crowds of youngsters thronged The Mall, more so during snowfall. The daring and adventurous among them would carve out snowmen from the piles of snow heaped around and write their favourite slogans on them. Often, they would have fun throwing snowballs at one another.

Most of us had not seen snow earlier, and it provided us with an exhilarating experience. When we returned home late in the evening we often had to face chilly winds and walking over snow-covered roads would make our feet and bodies numb and aching. A warm welcome by the fireplace was keenly looked forward to.

The earlier administration had taken pains to ensure that houses had comfortable fireplaces, where steam coal could be fed with ease to warm the bedrooms of the houses in particular, so that the families could spend their evenings in comfort. Equally good arrangements existed for the supply of steam coal and sufficient quantities were stocked before the onset of the winter season.

I remember that a bag load of this black gold could be purchased for Rs 2.50 in the late 1940s and four bags coal were enough for a month for an average family. You had to just walk into a coal depot and hand over a note of Rs. 10, and before you reached home, the coal would have been deposited at your residence.

With coal wagons moving from the East right up to Kalka and then reloaded into the narrow gauge rail line to Simla, there was no danger of disruption of its supply.

I have yet to see such spotlessly clean and shining roads as in Simla during those days. As far as sanitation is concerned, Simla was simply matchless and it showed how the local municipality functioned in the interest of the local inhabitants. Further, the supply of water and electricity was uninterrupted, notwithstanding the big rise in population in the late 1940s. It revealed how the British planning system had ensured that the existing basic facilities should be sufficient even for a much larger population influx.

After Independence, we have completely failed to draw any lesson from their meticulous planning about the basic services. While we have encouraged growth on our hill stations to cross every conceivable limit, we have conveniently overlooked the system of planning facilities accordingly. The adverse repercussions of such unplanned growth are quite obvious now.

Not only have we failed to maintain these hill stations, at least to the proportion they should have been with population growth, we have also not been able to create new hill stations, which could have taken the load of the additional population and also of the fast rising tourist traffic. It has resulted in a total chaos and miserable failure of the current facilities.

All this is in quite obvious from the experience of Simla. After Punjab got its new capital in Chandigarh, Simla became the full-fledged capital of Himachal Pradesh. And since then there has been unprecedented growth in its population as well as simultaneous decline in its essential services, which have been pressed into maximum use without their proper maintenance.

While it used to be such a pleasure to walk up and down the long stretch of the Simla Mall Road, it has now become an ordeal with diggings at frequent intervals and the road becoming fragile and unsafe.

GORTON CASTLE

My office was in Gorton Castle, a British castle-like structure, raised on the top of a full hill patch and located not far from The Mall. Indeed, it was a highly durable structure executed with great care and accommodating a large number of offices in its three-storey building. During winter, to heat the rooms of this large-sized and high-domed castle, sufficient arrangements existed to feed steam coal into the cast iron heating network provided in each room. As the coal burnt, it radiated heat through the pipes with convenient outlets for the gases to escape.

While this arrangement took a long time to heat the office rooms, but once the warmth had pervaded every nook and corner of the rooms, it stayed on for a long time. Rather, at times, windows had to be thrown open to let in fresh air.

During the period of a perceptible decline in temperature, when high-velocity cold winds blew endlessly, the work output would also decline substantially, when our fingers refused to function and the body temperature would get down to an uncomfortably low point.

To reach office or a business place those days, one had to walk, in the absence of any mode of transport. And walking would often turn risky with treacherous roads gone slippery. One had to carry a spiked stick to ensure safe walking. Hand-pulled rickshaws introduced by the British were there for those who experienced difficulty in walking.

As balancing the rickshaws in the hilly terrain was a major problem, these were pulled by four persons, two in the front and two at the back.

But this system was beyond the means of the majority of residents who could not afford it, except during emergency situations. Thus, normally one would have to walk. This was in a way a welcome feature on a hill station, as it helped to warm up the limbs and was also a pleasant experience amidst green surroundings. It also kept the body in shape. Rarely, did one come across a fat person on the hills.

LOVE AND MARRIAGE

I have earlier mentioned of a chance meeting with a girl of my dreams during the time of my admission to a college and she had immediately stirred up thoughts of love and happiness in me. Years had passed since we met last and I had almost forgotten her.

I again had a chance meeting with her in Simla. I was returning from the usual evening stroll on The Mall in the company of my colleagues and near the Scandal Point I was face to face with her. She was with my younger brother and I was thrilled to learn that she would be staying with us. My old memories of Lahore were immediately revived. She had the same grace and charm though she had slightly aged, which was natural with time.

She stayed with us for around a week. She was looking for a job after having qualified as a doctor and wanted to meet the Chief of Medical Services in Himachal Pradesh. Now we had plenty of time to talk to each other, compensating for all our past silence. She was still unmarried.

It was only on the last day when she was ready to leave that I hesitatingly broached the topic of marriage. She was completely taken aback for she had not anticipated it. However, she candidly admitted that she was in love with someone else and planned to get married soon. So, that settled it.

Though it made me sad, I did not think too much of it. Soon I was, very interestingly, moving into a similar adventure. This time it was a fair lady from the neighbourhood. She was around my age. She was also quite graceful and dignified. Often, I would accompany her and family members and neighbours during the evening stroll. We never went far, just covered a short distance, which did not tire the senior members.

I would often find opportunity to talk to her and likewise she too would reciprocate. We discussed topics like politics, social life and economy. The conversations also brought us closer to each other for we found our opinions were generally matching.

Since we were neighbours, I found opportunities to visit her house and share tea and snacks, especially when her dad was not at home, for soon I realized that he held highly conservative views and did not take well to our frequent meetings. Thus, we could not indulge ourselves when he was around.

Soon, he suspected that something was brewing up and became even more cautious and took special care that his daughter did not take much liberty with me.

That was the starting point of trouble. She also became conscious of it and frankly admitted that she was afraid of her father though not of her mother, despite the fact that she was her stepmother as her own mother had died years back.

So, it was a case of another romantic love destined to end without any positive consequences.

And it so happened that a few months later she was married to a well-placed civil servant. Meanwhile, they had shifted to another place and I had also been transferred from Simla to Calcutta.

HIGHLY ROMANTIC SIMLA

Simla proved to be a highly romantic place with the presence of many graceful beauties. One among them was Rattani, a damsel from Chamba. She was married to a close family friend. Though we stayed near each other in Lahore, we had rarely had an opportunity to meet. The ladies from Chamba were popularly called 'Chambe di kaliyan' (tender and beautiful as buds of Chamba).

It was in Simla, where we had shifted after Partition, that we started meeting frequently. Their bungalow was not far from where we stayed. They would drop in during the evenings for a chat with my parents.

Rattani was a social figure in Simla and often participated in social programmes organized by the wives of high officers. The ladies were quite active, particularly in Red Cross work, when they would be seen collecting funds. They approached their clients with such a disarming smile that could not refuse, rather contributed more liberally.

I can't forget the occasion when, one day on my way home from office early afternoon as Bebe wasn't feeling well, while crossing a bridle path to shorten the distance to our house, I was conveyed the sad news of the death of my Bebe by Rattani, which she thought I must have known.

It was a bolt from the blue. The help rendered by this couple on the occasion is indeed praiseworthy. When we returned from the cremation ground late in the evening in the month of January, we were helped by them to settle down to normal life. They had brought food for us and cajoled all of us to have it and looked after us so that we did not face any problem. It was only after we had eaten and settled down that they left for their place.

Even later, for a number of days they would be by our side and rendered every possible help. When for a fortnight, *havan* was performed every evening, they would be invariably present.

BUG OF FICTION-WRITING BITES

Now with plenty of spare time and no plan for further academic pursuits, I seriously thought of giving a concrete shape to my dream of fiction writing, lying dormant inside me for years. I was spurred to give it a practical shape, with my imaginative and creative mind. So, I decided with all sincerity to utilize this opportunity amidst these ideal surroundings for this purpose. Gradually, this dream started unfolding and my writing skills cooperated for preparing the draft of an attempt that I had titled 'Naima'.

Soon I was making good progress, as my writing skills got sharpened simultaneously. Much of my free time was spent on weaving several threads of my very first attempt at fiction writing.

My office routine left me with a good deal of spare time, which instead of spending on gossip, *gup-shup* and similar frivolous activities, was used to complete this work. An unbounded enthusiasm seemed to have caught hold of me. I hardly experienced any problem in preparing this draft. Page after page, the language flowed with ease and so did the dialogue among different characters. The whole work started shaping itself from one episode to the next, almost in continuum.

My impatience to complete this task in the minimum time ran so high that it did not allow me to write it with hand first. Instead, I often fed my thoughts into the typewriter straightaway. Here, I was also conscious about my poor handwriting, which at times I myself found difficult to read.

I was saved of this tyranny because of my knowledge of using a typewriter though I was a slow typist, being used to the sight system. Even that had its own advantage, for it allowed me to pause frequently to punch in the proper language.

I remember once on an uncomfortably cold day of January when it was a holiday, I had hastened to my office, got hold of my favourite typewriter and set my fingers at its keyboard for almost four hours non-stop and without use of any prepared draft. The outpouring was almost from my memory, from the beginning to end. And, I must add, it worked very well. There was hardly any lapse, any discontinuity in the flow of my thought process. And during this time, I typed around 20 pages, entirely from memory. When I read them later, they made perfect sense and were well related to the theme of this fiction work. I found it to be indeed a remarkable job and wondered how it happened, for I do not recall of any similar achievement later.

Thus, it was on a chilly day of January, when people were sitting around fires in their homes, that I had accomplished this almost unbelievable task.

I think if you have the willpower and are imbibed with the spirit of total involvement with your mission, it is quite possible to achieve things, which under normal circumstances would appear to be quite difficult.

I also feel that in constructing a complicated plot where several characters, episodes and locations were involved, it was mainly the backdrop of Lahore which was so very familiar to me that made it possible to tackle it with a single-minded concentration without any conflict or confusion. Much of it was also due to the prior mental preparation, with every minute detail of this particular episode having been thought of that morning in advance.

I was very pleased that the draft of this monumental work, running into 300-odd typed pages, was completed in just a year's time. As it did not undergo much of a change, it was not difficult to get it finally typed. When it was done, I thought I would become a celebrity overnight and that it would not be difficult to get it published. And soon, I was planning my next venture.

Unfortunately, such a jubilant mood and euphoria was short-lived. I found there were no takers for this attempt, on which I had laboured so hard day and night for over 365 days. In fact, it invited some nasty comments, which left me totally cold and sad. Some called it a "total waste of time", "work of a novice writer which would not sell if published" and so on. The more sympathetic once suggested that it be pruned down drastically and carefully edited if it was to go for publication. Of course, it was clearly added that I would have to foot the bill.

I was shocked and totally crestfallen at such comments and suggestions and was ready to tear the whole attempt to pieces.

But better sense prevailed. I just put all this on the hold and shared my work with some members of the opposite sex, who consoled me with encouraging remarks that helped me overcome the most frustrating situation arisen by outrageous comments of some publishing houses and critics. They imbued me with fresh energy and courage.

I decided to forget about it for the time being and got busy with yet another attempt, whose rough outlines had already emerged. I thought it would also help me overcome the frustration of my unsuccessful first attempt. But the disappointment failed to leave me despite my best efforts.

I completed two more, though equally unsuccessful, attempts. All this aggregated to around 650 typed pages, during my two and a half years of stay in Simla. None of these, of course, saw the light of the day. I was to a large extent responsible for this situation as I did not pursue even a single piece seriously, that the publication of a work of *fiction*, particularly from a novice like me, demanded. I thought it could be postponed to a later date, which was a foolish idea, for it never worked.

That was how my Simla days were spent. It was a sort of balancing act between attending to my boring office routine of handling statistical data of major activities of selected large-scale industries in the country for ultimately shaping into the Report on Census of Manufacturing Industries, published annually by the Central Government, with my more sensitive and mentally satisfying writing of *fiction*.

A HAPPY TRIO

In Simla, I struck close friendship with two office colleagues—Banwari Lal Sud and Prithvi Nath Kaul. We were on the same job and had been recruited together. However, while Sud and I were of the same age and bachelors, Kaul was senior to us by eight or nine years, and he was married and had children.

We shared most of our evenings and at times even holidays together. Soon after leaving the office, we would leisurely walk to The Mall and have a couple of rounds between Scandal Point and the other end of this busy road. We discussed all sorts of things and exchanged greetings with friends and acquaintances we met on the road.

It had been, as I look back, one of the happiest times in my life and it lasted for a full three years before the office shifted to Calcutta. On weekends, we had plenty of time in the afternoon when we had half working day. We would invariably pass it in some coffee house/restaurant, followed by a long walk, preferably to a new place, before returning home. During the very cold winter days we would reduce our visits to The Mall, but we rarely missed it during the snow time.

We had once even ventured to *Tatta Pani* (literally means hot water). The journey to the sulphur springs of boiling hot water was a perilous trek down several miles in the interior of Simla hills and through narrow slopes. A few other colleagues from the office too had joined us on this trip.

It took us the whole day. We started very early in the morning and by the time we reached this place, it had become dark and we were dead tired. The local people, however, extended their warm hospitality and provided us with comfortable beds and hot food. We had a sound sleep. The next morning we trekked some more area around this place and had a refreshing bath in the hot springs, close to which quietly flowed the Sutlej river. It was indeed a memorable visit.

'NAIMA' REVISITED

A word about 'Naima', which had taken me a year to write with full devotion. Its plot was set against the backdrop of Lahore and a few other places, which are now a part of Pakistan, during the tumultuous period of World War II, while I was a young student.

The character of 'Naima' was based on a real-life young, highly attractive, easygoing and talented student in the postgraduate department of sciences at Panjab University. She was the sister of a senior Muslim bureaucrat. She was a couple of years senior to me. Though our friendship was casual, her smiling face and graceful bearing was so irresistible that the plot of this story got naturally woven around her. She was projected as a student leader working with other colleagues, where I happened to be the youngest in the group.

We often spoke against the British in the well-attended student meetings for the liberation of our country. This attracted the attention of the police, who often turned violent and, thus, we had frequently to go into hiding and chalk out strategies for the next course of action.

Naima was the only female member of this small group led by a middle-aged person, Rafiq Ali, and Naima was his favourite. Later, as the plot thickens, I realize that Naima was the daughter of a high society lady and was the favourite of a large number of city's big guys.

But she was an elusive person and kept them all at tenterhooks. She had developed a soft corner for me and I was equally fond of her. We often spent time together in lonely corners of Lawrence Gardens and other destinations. She was attracted to my tender age and innocence, while I tried to understand her complex character, which defied any easy diagnosis.

Ultimately, it came to be known that she was none else but a relative of mine, closely related to me through her mother, who had been separated from the family in her early age under mysterious circumstances. She was untraceable, despite a lengthy struggle to find her. Thus, she had to be written off and the family reconciled to this situation.

It was only when Naima interacted closely with me and I was exposed to her relationship with the top guys in the city that the truth came out that she was none other than the daughter of the missing aunt. But then it was too late, for at that stage she was involved in a fatal accident. This, in a nutshell, was the story of the young 'Naima' around whom this work had been executed in detail.

Unfortunately, subsequently, I did not have sufficient time or patience to go through this attempt again and reconstruct the whole plot in a more acceptable way. I never again found the zeal, I was so richly endowed with in 1949. Strangely, that spirit failed to re-emerge again.

Calcutta, the New Destination

As a schoolboy, I was often moved by the life story of Ishwarchandra Vidyasagar, the great educationist and social reformer of Bengal. In fact, my parents had named me after this great man, possibly thinking that I would live up to this name. Thus, I had an ardent wish to visit Calcutta. Such opportunity luckily did come soon, as I was to spend a good part of time in this city, the land of the Messiah of social reforms—Ishwarchandra Vidyasagar—who had encouraged young men to marry widows and was against several evil customs against women. He lived a very simple and saintly life and did a lot for the spread of education among the less privileged sections of the people.

I had also been fed on stories of other great men like Rabindranath Tagore, Swami Ramakrishna Parmahans and Swami Vivekananda and was keen to have a pilgrimage to their land.

As mentioned earlier, in 1952 my mother passed away, in Simla, in the month of January, at the age of 55. It was a big shock for the family, particularly as none of us five brothers was married. I was the eldest but had refused to tie the nuptial knot, though I was over 28. It was during the fag end of 1952 that my younger brother got married.

In early 1952 we had been served with a notice by the government to vacate our flat for structural alterations in the block, and we were the last to vacate. Our new accommodation was almost like a cold store, where the sun would be visible just for a couple of hours during the day. It bore, thus, a big contrast to our Cart Road accommodation, where the sun never disappeared as the place was open from all sides and there were no tall hills around to block the sun rays. Meanwhile, my office too had been shifted to Calcutta. The process of transfer soon began and crates of office record were sealed and forwarded by train to Calcutta. Within a couple of weeks, the move was completed.

This was my first visit to Calcutta, the city of Tagore, Vidyasagar and other noble people who had occupied a special place in my heart for a long time. Thus, I was excited to be a part of this city. It had also caught my attention, for it was here that K.L. Saigal had achieved fame in his film career and rendered soulful pieces of music, which were superhits during the 1930s and 1940s. He had also received special attention from the cinema goers, who virtually mobbed his films, which often ran for months. I too would rarely miss his films and thoroughly enjoyed his music. I was eager to visit the studios where his films were shot.

FIRST IMPRESSIONS

When we landed in Calcutta on a scorching hot day of May we experienced a sudden change in the temperature. The cool and salubrious climate of Simla gave way to very hot and humid weather. Our miseries rose further when we learnt that the private building that had been requisitioned for our stay was yet without power. Also, it lacked proper toilet and water facilities. Thus, we were sweating most of the time, to which we were not accustomed.

Our new office was temporarily housed in an old 19th century Victorian style building on Strand Road, which at one time housed the government mint. Being a discarded building, it lacked even elementary facilities and we were not sure about the quality of water we were drinking. Also, being a part of Old Calcutta, it was full of noise and disturbance. All this added further to our misery and we felt as if we had been transported to a nasty place from the heavenly environment of Simla.

Gradually, however, as we settled down, things began to change for the better. Soon our office was shifted to a more contemporary, roomy and spacious building in a modern business centre of Dalhousie Square, which was well maintained. The best thing about the new location was that it was within walking distance to the place where we stayed, which itself had meanwhile undergone much change and we no longer faced the power problem. This was indeed the biggest relief, for in this city it was almost impossible to survive without electricity. I remember how, for several days we had to use the kerosene lanterns and it appeared we were living in a village rather than a metropolitan city.

VISIT TO JAGANNATH TEMPLE

The Calcutta stint provided me a good opportunity to visit other places of interest in this state as well as in the nighbouring Bihar and Orissa. My earliest trip was a visit to Jagannath Temple in Puri. While the temple itself was magnificent with praiseworthy architecture, it was poorly maintained and the way the pilgrims were treated by the *pandas* (priests) was disgusting. They exploited the visitors, particularly ladies, and made them perform a large number of *pujas* (ceremonies) just for the sake of collecting more money, ignoring protests from the accompanying male members.

The poor, who could not afford to satisfy the greedy *pandas*, were mercilessly shooed away. If somebody dared to come near them for *prasad* (offering), he would be rebuffed and in case he still persisted he would be dealt with in a callous manner, including striking his head or other part of the body with a stick.

It left a very sad impression on me and my inner self revolted against the selfish and dictatorial attitude of these priests. They behaved as if they were the lords of this place and the visitors were at their mercy. I strongly felt that urgent reforms were needed to streamline these places of pilgrimage and free them from the capricious hold of *pandas*.

A group of *pandas* would enter your compartment as the train neared the railway station and soon completely overpower you and not let you move around freely. You had to virtually do the way they dictated and while you resisted, it would be difficult to escape them, if you were accompanied by ladies.

We spent a good time around the seashore close by and enjoyed a refreshing bath before returning to the *dharamsala* (guest house). Soon we were surrounded by *pandas,* who had been able to trace the ancestry of some of us when their elders had visited this place. We added more details to update the family tree.

Maintaining the record of the family history, I found, was a unique way of preserving the details of our ancestry. One could certainly get these details from the records so meticulously maintained by the *pandas.* I was told of the visit of my grandfather along with my father and other members of the family. Now the *pandas* recorded the latest details of the family. It was the best way to know about your family history and this was possibly the only good service rendered by these otherwise greedy *pandas.*

The place was full of beggars. Long rows of them sat outside the temple on both sides of the road. Several of them were physically deformed like lepers and others suffering from diseases. Their sight filled one with disgust and one had to move around with great care as the place was full of pickpockets.

On the return journey, we spent some time in Cuttack and Bhubaneswar—Cuttack was the old capital of Orissa and Bhubaneswar was the new one selected. Then in the early 1950s, it was gradually taking its shape. Interestingly, while both Chandigarh and Bhubaneswar were selected as new capitals in the country and had started coming up almost around the same time—rather Chandigarh a little later—Chandigarh was able to grow faster into a modern city. Bhubaneswar has lagged far behind.

CHANDIGARH *vs* BHUBANESWAR

I have often wondered why this happened. There have been of course, certain positive factors in favour of Chandigarh, which have been missing or only partially fulfilled in the case of Bhubaneswar.

First, Chandigarh was the darling city of Pandit Nehru who wanted to gift to the Punjabis the best possible capital after losing Lahore to Pakistan. Thus, he made every effort to see that its growth was comparable to the world's best cities. He also wanted it to be a model city in the country, to be followed by other new cities.

Second, the best team of architects in the world was employed for Chandigarh's planning, headed by the globally known French architect, le Corbusier. They did their best to develop it into a unique urban complex with modern buildings, residential areas, government and business complexes. Indeed, it grew in a highly planned way with sufficient greenery, parks, valleys, forest area, lake, and other facilities and infrastructure.

Third, its growth picked up speed after it was made a Union Territory in 1966, when it was generously funded by the Centre for its further development as well as maintenance. Such status also saved it from being a victim of petty state politics and interference, which thwarted the growth of other capitals.

Fourth, under globalization, Chandigarh witnessed an all-time high rate of growth. It became the major business corridor for the neigbouring states of Punjab, Haryana, Himachal Pradesh and Jammu & Kashmir. Several multinational firms opened their offices here. This city has also become the major centre of finance and banking with the presence of almost all Indian (both public and private) banks as well as foreign banks.

Fifth, being the capital of the two states of Punjab and Haryana, apart from itself being a union territory, has made it grow still faster, only to be compared with the top metropolitan cities in the country. The satellite modern towns of Panchkula (in Haryana) and Mohali (in Punjab) have added to its further growth. In fact, Greater Chandigarh, including both Panchkula and Mohali, has become a leader in global business.

Most of these opportunities have been missing in the case of Bhubaneswar. Little surprise, therefore, that it should have failed to reach the heights of Chandigarh. Simultaneously, let us also not overlook the highly enterprising spirit of the people in North-West, which has been no less a factor behind its unique performance in a short period.

SANTINIKETAN

My next long-awaited visit was to Santiniketan, the abode of peace and tranquility, very aptly named. It was indeed a memorable trip to this land of Rabindranath Tagore, housing his brainchild, Vishwa Bharati, which moulds the formative years of children to the best of Indian culture, music, dance, arts, philosophy and other areas in which this country has had a long tradition.

The campus was spread over a vast area, full of greenery with well-maintained lawns, trees and flowers. Most of the teaching was done in the open, for Tagore believed that Nature was the best classroom where the minds of children could be moulded in the best possible way. He was against the closed classroom environment with a rigid course of education as well as discipline.

He wanted the children to grow up in an open atmosphere, watch things around and believed in the informal mode of teaching. As a child, he himself had hated going to school and be closeted in a classroom, and learning from the printed text and qualifying for a formal exam. It was perhaps this hatred which helped him develop his own system of educating the children, in an open environment.

This appeared to be the purpose for selecting this place, far away from the crowded environment of Calcutta.

Of course, this system has since undergone a vast change but the basic concepts continue to be rooted in Gurudev's original thinking.

Moving through the sylvan surroundings of this campus was itself a great experience. We could almost feel Gurudev moving around the place, occasionally stopping to see how a teacher was caring for the young pupils. Next, he would be sitting under a shady tree with a blackboard hanging prominently from its trunk. He would participate in the children's lecture and anxiously watch the reaction of his pupils about this system of learning and in the end after making his own comments, would walk to his office, and record the impression he had gathered by talking to both, the students and teacher, and in this light suggest appropriate amendments needed in this experiment.

This was certainly a unique and challenging experiment in the open-air classroom and often encouraged students to express their views about it, in the light of which suitable amendments were made. Thus, it was not a closed system of education. The open atmosphere was meant to arouse the inner curiosity of young students to question, to go deep into this experiment and make it further interesting and acceptable.

Music flowed in rich abundance, rendered in a soul-stirring and mellifluent voice in Bengali that provided lasting joy. Even though I did not know Bengali beyond its basic rudiments, I derived great pleasure in listening to it. Its sweetness, mellifluence and rare joy of the melody made it all the more sensitive to the ears.

That night happened to be a full moon night, as pure whiteness sparkled through the environs of this campus. We took a long walk, both inside as well as outside the campus, and could hear music from different corners. It was also close to the *puja* period, when the atmosphere reverberates with the best music delivered by great music composers.

Somewhere, a drama was being staged, and we could hear the dialogue clearly against the silence of the full moon night.

Later, I happened to witness a dance drama programme of Tagore's classical play *'Tastier Desh'e* by the famous duo Uday and Amla Shanker and their team in Calcutta. I remember the auditorium was packed to capacity with quite a few foreigners in the audience.

Thus, in Calcutta one could witness classical plays, performed with meticulous care by known performers. It was also a place rich in music and instruments, where even in the dead of night somewhere music would be sung, or sitar and other instruments played. While people would say it disturbed their sleep, my personal experience was different. I found it acted as a great balm on the mind and the more disturbed I was, the sooner it brought about signs of cheer.

During the long *puja* period, the whole city would resound with music. A visit to a *puja pandal* during this period was a stirring experience. One needed to have a lot of spare time to witness the performance of various ceremonies.

Ultimately, the long *puja* would end with elaborate arrangements made for the immersion of *Durga* idols in the Hooghly river where these images were taken in boats amid singing and dancing by devotees.

WINTER TIME

Climatically, the month of November was quite pleasant and after the rains there would be a considerable decline in humidity, with pleasant mornings and evenings. Thus, this month, as well as the next couple of months were quite popular for visits to the surrounding areas.

Dakshineswar Temple and Belur Math were of special attraction to me. They also provided an opportunity to interact with scholars following the noble traditions set by Ramakrishna Parmahans and Swami Vivekananda. Situated close to the Hooghly, almost on its banks, they provided mental solace and transported one to the time, when these two renowned *sanyasis* stayed here and preached their gospel, which had a profound effect on their followers.

It was later, when I had visited Kanya Kumari, in the deep South, I learnt how Vivekananda had also visited this place during his long foot journey in his short earthly existence, for he had died at a young age of a little over 39. Here he was totally hypnotized when he saw the *Sangam* (confluence) of the three great oceans—the Indian Ocean, Arabian Sea and Bay of Bengal. It was in this confluence of the three great water bodies that Vivekananda visualized the glory of this great country. He was so overwhelmed by this sight against the backdrop of the setting sun that he swam through the deep and turbulent waters to reach the nearest rock, where he spent the whole night experiencing and visualizing the great glory of his country and returned to the shore only the next morning.

To pay homage to this great saint's historical visit, a memorial in the shape of a temple has been erected here, which is visited by a large number of tourists every year.

During the *puja* period break a large number of Bengalis move to other destinations in the country to enjoy their holiday and almost an equal number of those settled elsewhere would make it to Calcutta and other places. Thus, there is a tremendous pressure on the rail traffic and several special trains are run during this month. Still to finding a comfortable place is difficult unless the reservation is done much in advance.

Shopkeepers do brisk business in this month. They decorate their shops with attractive and latest wares. Big stores, of course, attract the maximum clientele with their vast variety of goods on display.

People spend almost their entire savings on *puja* shopping, visits to other places and on decorating their houses. They exchange greetings with friends and relatives. Costly sweets and other luxury eatables are on the top of their family menu and a lot of money goes into their purchase. In all, most of the families generally spend much beyond their budget and run into debt. Of course, it is also the bonus month, when they look forward to liberal payments by their employers.

Even then, they are always short of funds. So much money changes hand during this month that when the families finally settle down, they have to work extra to make good for this overspending. Of course, this has been a normal feature and they are hardly worried over this.

It was this custom, in which several crores of rupees are being spent without any social benefit, that prompted Swami Vivekananda to advise that even if a part of this money was spent for social welfare of the poor, on their education and job-oriented programmes, it would benefit a very large number of them. Such a noble advice has hardly been listened to all these years.

GREEN PASTURES OF BIHAR

I had also planned during the next *puja* break to visit the green and highly picturesque areas of Bihar, particularly Ranchi, Hazaribagh, Bokaro and their surroundings. At Ranchi railway station I was intrigued at the sight of female porters. I had never come across a female porter before this. As soon as I landed, a young, newly married lady came to pick up my luggage. I hesitated, thinking that she was doing so by mistake, but soon I realized that several other ladies were doing likewise.

I thought, at a time when she should be enjoying the bliss of a newly married life, she was pushed to be a railway porter to earn livelihood. I soon learnt that tribesmen of this area were a poor lot, though blessed with picturesque countryside, with verdant surroundings all around and blessed with rich minerals.

Such is the unfortunate lot of most of the tribesmen, which called for a determined effort on the part of our leaders so that these people of the soil can also enjoy the fruits of development.

A large number of Bengalis were already around enjoying the *Puja* vacation and moving along with their families to different places of interest. In fact, during this time it was difficult to find a suitable place to live, unless prior arrangement had been made.

We stayed in a small lodge away from the town, which was richly blessed with natural scenery all around. Indeed, this place and its surroundings provided the much needed relief and relaxation that was so badly needed by one who had spent time in the crowded, noisy and much polluted Calcutta.

We found the same greenery, peace and tranquility in the several miles of area we travelled. This was indeed a wonderful land of the poor tribesmen who deserved better care. I thought that their land with imagination could be turned into one of the finest tourist spots in the country, which would also bring prosperity to this area as well as the much-needed financial help to the tribals.

Another thing that struck me was the presence of a large number of Punjabis. Most of them were refugees from West Pakistan, who had lost everything and after staying for the minimum possible time in various refugee camps had ventured to even such remote parts of the country.

After learning about the opportunities available in remote parts of Bihar, where the Bokaro steel plant was just commissioned, several of them had tried their luck to find jobs. Others had taken to more challenging opportunities of contractors to execute several works needed in this major steel plant.

Still others had opened wayside *dhabas* (restaurants) and teashops and more enterprising ones had set up medium-sized hotels, which provided facilities of food and night stay at a reasonable budget. Quite a few of them had entered into the transport business, which was in good demand. And so on.

In fact, they had entered into all sorts of areas, where opportunities were available, and did not mind the inconvenience and hard work that these activities demanded. With their rich, enterprising spirit, they were soon on the road to prosperity.

I often compared these people with their counterpart Bengali refugees, who too had been driven out from their homeland in East Pakistan almost at the same time, but had failed to move out of Calcutta and its surroundings. In fact, when I first landed at the Howrah railway station after my posting in Calcutta, I found they had virtually seized the railway station and occupied every conceivable space, thus turning it into a big refugee camp.

The vast entrance to the railway station would drive away the visitors, because of its stinking smell, and the crowd of refugees was so thick that it was a big job to move to a particular platform to catch the train. The railway authorities appeared to be completely helpless and dared not disturb the refugees for fear of inviting their wrath. They were also scared of the several organizations shouting daily for the early rehabilitation of these refugees in Calcutta itself.

That was sheer nonsense. How could Calcutta, already highly crowded, take these refugees, whose numbers kept on swelling everyday? The pity was that while the Hindu refugees were being thrown out indiscriminately from their homeland in East Pakistan, there was hardly any counter movement from Muslim families in Calcutta. Rather, under the garb of refugees, quite a few Muslim refugees too had moved to Calcutta.

This situation was so different from that found in the North-western areas where, barring Sindh, there was a complete evacuation of Hindus from West Pakistan to East Punjab and surrounding areas and of Muslims from Indian Punjab and surrounding areas to Pakistan. Remarkably, within a few months, around five million refugees from either side had crossed the border.

This also facilitated an early rehabilitation of refugees, to a large extent. Further, unlike Bengali migrants, Punjabi migrants had been spread over a large number of camps at different destinations and they had also vacated these camps as soon as they could find alternative places to settle down. They did not mind going to any corner of this country.

It was so different in the case of Bengali refugees, who wanted to be settled down in and around Calcutta only. All efforts made to rehabilitate them in other areas proved abortive.

They were highly sentimental about their stay in Calcutta and around, and unlike Punjabi refugees lacked the spirit of mobility. The result was that soon Calcutta and its surroundings were overcrowded beyond capacity. Most of the empty areas had been virtually occupied by the refugees.

Even Calcutta's vast Maidan area—the biggest green belt in Calcutta opposite the posh Chowringhee—was not spared and soon several refugee markets had appeared on this land. The footpaths of Calcutta too were crowded with refugee hawkers. Several hawkers did brisk business much to the annoyance and inconvenience of shopkeepers and pedestrians.

TRADITION AND *BHADRALOK*

In Calcutta, certain things are difficult to change. Take the example of trams. They were introduced in the country first in this city by the British for the benefit of commuters and they continue to be the most popular mode of transport. On the contrary, in other metropolitan cities these were introduced later and they were discarded soon as they proved to be a hindrance to the growth of traffic.

It appears that Bengali *bhadralok* have a special fascination for tradition and are so sentimental about it that they would not like to change, despite the enormous harm it might cause to the healthy growth of the city. On a personal note, however, I may add, that in the early 1950s while I was in Calcutta, I found travel by the trams to be the best mode of travel. They had a comfortable seating arrangement with the cool air of the fan overhead, which is missing in other modes of transport. Passing by leisurely, one could enjoy the full view of a bazaar, or a street, or a green patch in south Calcutta, especially when it moved through the long stretch of the Maidan.

Another thing that struck me during that period was, cleaning of roads in the early morning with liberal amounts of the Hooghly water. That was the best way of getting rid of the past 24 hours of dirt and filth that had polluted the roads and, sent some coolness into the surrounding areas.

HOME OF ANGLO-INDIANS

Calcutta also had a fairly large number of Anglo-Indians, perhaps the largest in the country, who considered themselves next to the English people, though it was well known that the British did not share their view. So, it was, unfortunately a one-sided loyalty. But, it was a fact that Anglo-Indians were preferred by the British for most of the intermediate types of jobs, whether in the police, or in the railways, or in other similar areas. The Anglo-Indian girls had an easy access to foreign firms, and a large number of which had their offices in Calcutta. They flourished in these firms at the intermediate levels of jobs like personal secretaries, typists, receptionists and even sales girls in stores.

After the British left, their economic situation started deteriorating, as the usual avenues in which they dominated were no longer available to them. Further, since most of them were dropouts from schools and convents and did not go in for higher education, it became quite difficult for them to get alternative jobs.

In fact, in the 1950s and 1960s, quite a large number of them had planned to migrate to Britain, which they had always considered to be their home. They were hardly successful in their mission for various reasons, including the hard fact that the British themselves did not show an interest in such a move. Thus, despite their efforts, they continued to be Indian nationals.

Gradually, they too began to realize the hard realities of the changed times and started identifying themselves with the local population. This is a subject of much interest—how far this change has occurred and what are its implications. One wishes that researchers, particularly some among the Anglo-Indians, should undertake such a job, and compare their slow identification with the changed realities vis-a-vis Christians who, though in much larger number compared to Anglo-Indians, did not enjoy a special status under the British regime as did the Anglo-Indians, mainly because of their complexion.

Transfer to Delhi

I had been posted in Calcutta for a little less than three years when I was served the marching orders to Delhi on a transfer. I was not quite prepared for this, for in the meantime, I had taken admission at Calcutta University for a law degree, and there were yet two more years to go. I, however, sacrificed this and moved to Delhi, which also happened to be near Chandigarh, where my family had settled down, after the High Court had moved to this place from Simla.

It is surprising that unlike Simla where I had devoted so much time and attention to fiction writing, I failed to even have a relook at my works or improve the writings to bring them possibly to the publication stage, though in Calcutta I had far more opportunities than in Simla. Rather I do not recollect even reading through my half-completed works.

Fiction writing was a hobby for me rather than a serious business. Otherwise, I would not have behaved in this casual manner.

Did I continue with this hobby in Calcutta, when I had plenty of time and was not weighed down with any family responsibility, being a bachelor? Partly yes and partly no. Partly yes, because I did open my mind to new writings. Unfortunately, these lacked the vision and zeal that I was so abundantly endowed with in Simla. I attempted small writing exercises, but they did not have either a climax or a logical ending. The Calcutta writings remained half-baked, half-finished.

It was unfortunate that my mind should have remained empty and non-functioning in a city like Calcutta where fiction-writing is in the blood of an average writer. I never attended any writers' workshop or meeting and never interacted with another writer, which would have been far easier to do in Calcutta.

Perhaps it was due to the language barrier. But I think it was more due to lack of interest, having taken to an easygoing life that lacked the seriousness and concentration that such type of work required.

Did I do well in my profession from where I drew my salary? I do not think. In the past seven years—from 1948-end when I joined my office in Simla to1955, when I moved to Delhi—I had hardly done any solid work in the interesting area of industrial development, where I had first-hand access to information on the growth of large industries in India and the behaviour of various key factors connected with their growth or downfall. I barely went beyond mechanically compiling the information (data) as per the set instructions and drafting some routine introductory notes. I thought my job was over the moment I compiled the data in the routine tables, for final publication in the annual report of a government department.

I never sat down to seriously think about the subject from the angle of research nor did I realize my special advantage compared to other scholars. So it remained an untapped exercise.

Subsequently, after a few years, when I was a changed man, I was baffled how I had behaved like this. I had neither moulded into a fiction writer (where, of course, I was not professionally trained), nor tapped my talents for the profession I had joined and which did open before me various vistas for further research and drafting papers for serious journals.

LIFE IN DELHI

My office in Delhi was located in one of the hutments (temporary structures), raised during World War II and continued to be used long after for housing the large number of offices that had mushroomed after Independence.

Frequent shifts also involved the problem of accommodation and adjustment to a new environment, which though was not so problematic in my case, being a bachelor. I hired a flat in New Rajindra Nagar, a new colony emerging around Shanker Road, and it was just a few kilometres from my office. In those days (1955) accommodation was not a problem as several new flats had been constructed in different colonies. Of course, most of these flats were without basic facilities.

The flat that I hired was, likewise, sans facilities. Electricity was yet not available. So there was no question of having a fan during the hot weather, when one had to bear the sweat for most of the time. This reminded me of the early days in Calcutta, when we did not have electricity. But here it was a different situation, the wait was much longer. We had to make do with candles and kerosene lanterns.

Similar was the state of water supply. It had to be fetched from the public hydrant, and there was just one for a row of flats. Thus, it was a cumbersome and time-consuming process, which caused much hardship during the summer period. Flush toilets did not exist. We had to be satisfied with the traditional system of dry latrines.

The bicycle was the most popular mode of travel. While going to the office, one came across a virtual caravan of bicycles, crowding all sides of the road. Very few scooters, mobikes and automobiles were seen. Thus, for most of the time, roads in Luten's New Delhi used to be empty.

This scene, however, changed soon and so dramatically that within the next few years these empty roads got so thickly crowded with vehicles of all sorts that they cried for extra lanes. Despite the heavy flow of refugees during the post-Independence period, Delhi was peaceful and hardly faced any traffic hassle. Thanks to its vast empty areas, even at the peak of inflow of refugees from Pakistan, there was never overcrowding, though immigrants had to face several other problems for their rehabilitation, the major ones being those of housing and employment.

Even these were solved within the minimum time frame. Thanks to the favourable response from the government, it accorded top priority to the construction of rows after rows of generally two-roomed tenements in several nagars that emerged almost overnight.

Even private builders did not lag. In fact, a large number of them were from among the refugees themselves, who found it the best way for their own rehabilitation. Several other expatriates too found jobs in this construction boom, which in turn created several other related jobs.

Thus, several opportunities were available now in laying down new roads and other infrastructure facilities that came with the construction boom.

REHABILITATION OF REFUGEES

When I had visited Delhi in September 1947, I had seen the Chandni Chowk area, which was then the city's biggest market as Connaught Place developed later. I remember the pavements hummed with crowds of refugee hawkers, who sold whatever they could in that condition of penury. They would settle down to their jobs early morning and not leave before late evening.

Their presence was highly objected to by the regular shopkeepers whose business was affected. But then I found that they could not do much about it or dislodge these pavement sellers, who were one and united. The cohesiveness sprouted from their struggle to survive, after having lost everything in Pakistan.

However, within the next few months most of these pavements had been cleared as several of these hawkers had shifted to alternative areas where they were allotted independent shops. It was a remarkable way of rehabilitating these people.

And after so many years of presence in Delhi, these people have now not only moved to top slots in business, but also in several other areas, and practically dominate in all areas of this metropolitan city, leaving the local people far behind.

So, multiple forces worked to quicken the pace of resettlement of lakhs of refugees, who had reached Delhi after Independence virtually in rags. The scene had dramatically changed. Much of it was also due to the grit, hard effort and determination of these refugees themselves. Interestingly, quite a few pavement hawkers had also purchased the very shops in front of which they sat at one time as pavement hawkers.

I had found similar happenings in Calcutta. Quite a few refugees from the Pakistan Punjab, who were settled here, had entered into trades of their liking and experience, but as they were short of funds, they had to be content with selling on pavements.

And before long, I was amused to learn that quite a few of them had purchased the very shops in front of which they once sold their wares. Thus, venturing into an independent life has been their forte, which has helped them stand on their own and in due course create more wealth and income than was possible through paid jobs.

FROM RAISINA ROAD TO JANPATH

Soon from the Raisina Road hutments, I shifted to hutments on Janpath, when I got selected to the new office of the Central Statistical Organisation (CSO), which as the very name suggests was set up to centralize the country's statistics. Till now, statistics were collected by different ministries and remained scattered, as there was no centralized organization to coordinate them.

The statistics were now well organized and collected under one roof to facilitate the publication of the national reports on statistics, "Statistical Abstract of India", where the latest data of each sector of the economy was available.

My parent office, the Directorate of Industrial Statistics, subsequently became the Industrial Statistics Wing of the CSO and industrial data now gathered was far more comprehensive as a large number of industries were added. Thus, the work of the CSO became quite comprehensive as well as complex, with a number of new activities added to improve the collection and collation of different kinds of statistics.

Another important wing of the CSO has been the National Sample Survey (NSS), the preliminary work of which was started in 1950 under the aegis of the Directorate of Industrial Statistics. Earlier, it was exclusively confined to the collection of statistics of large industries and small units had been left out. Soon, it was realized that a proper report on the industrial statistics would be incomplete if it ignored small industries, which in fact constituted India's bulwark of industrial development.

But then the question arose how this gigantic task was to be accomplished, as it involved the survey of a very large number of units scattered all over the country. A comprehensive survey was virtually impossible with the resources available and it would also be a time-consuming process.

It was ultimately decided that while a comprehensive survey should be confined to large industries, in the case of small industries, the task needed to be performed only through a sample survey for which preliminary work had already been done by the Indian Statistical Institute, Calcutta, which had gained a global name in the field of sample surveys.

Gradually, the National Sample Survey gained far more importance than the Annual Survey of Large Industries. In fact, the importance that the latter had enjoyed in its heyday in the 1940s was diluted when the NSS gained supremacy. Also, as the task of the CSO was to complete the data of all sectors of the economy in a comprehensive manner and publish it annually in its statistical abstract, it was soon widely consulted by planners, policy makers, researchers and other scholars and agencies.

When I joined the CSO in 1955, it was in its infancy and functioned from the war-time built army hutments, close to Connaught Place. It subsequently shifted to a spacious and modern building near the Planning Commission and became the prestigious headquarters of national statistics. Soon both the CSO and Planning Commission developed into important centres for national planning.

I did not stay for long with the CSO. In fact, my tenure here was just for a few months, as in September 1956 I moved to London to join the London School of Economics (LSE) as a research student. As I had been allowed leave for this period, my services were reverted to my parent office in Calcutta.

Ship Journey

The London visit had been on my mind for quite a long time, but it somehow could not materialize earlier. I looked forward to studying at the prestigious London School of Economics. Fortunately, my accommodation problem had been solved as I was allotted a shared room in the LSE Hall of Residence—Passfield Hall—that happened to be within walking distance from the school.

I carried four boxes packed with heavy woollen clothes and other dresses to protect myself from the long cold spell of London. This later proved to be a sheer waste of time and energy because on reaching there I realized I had overlooked to carry possible literature, reports, data and other serious material. This proved to be my blunder number one.

In fact, during my eight-year tenure with the government, I was mostly wrapped up in routine jobs and had also cut myself away from the main academic stream. Temperamentally also, as spelt out earlier, I had indulged in areas that had nothing to do with my academic pursuits. Under these circumstances, I was quite ill-prepared for a research degree at this reputed institute, which demanded high academic standards.

Unfortunately, these thoughts did not occur to me in India as my mind was so occupied with extraneous things, and there was little room for academic thinking.

I dreamt of London and other cities in Europe, which I looked forward to visiting and experiencing a new life personally. These thoughts occupied my mind far more than serious things, little realizing the pains I would have to undergo for being so casual about my actual mission.

My passage to London had been booked in the P&O ocean liner 'Strathmore', a prestigious ship which originated from Australia and had the capacity to carry over 1,000 passengers in its first and tourist class cabins. I had been allotted a berth in a twin-bedded cabin. The fare of this air-conditioned and luxury travel was around Rs. 950, which in today's reckoning would be unbelievable.

But in those days, the Indian rupee had a lot of value and was deemed as one of the few currencies close to the dollar and pound. It was also the time when the value of other European currencies was low.

As mentioned earlier, I carried four suitcases, which were packed to the brim with a lot of junk, including a good part of my fiction writing, which I hoped to encash in London. While I had carried one small case to the cabin, the rest were dumped in the box room of the ship.

'Strathmore' carried a large number of English nationals (Australians mainly) and South Asians (mostly from Sri Lanka and India). It was a four/five-storey liner with arrays of cabins on each floor. Luxury and first class suites were separately located on the top floor. It had a crew of 500, including a large number of Goanese nationals.

We had a day-long busy schedule. The morning bed tea comprising fruits and beverage was followed by a sumptuous breakfast. Then there was pre-lunch ice cream and coffee break around 11 a.m., leading to an elaborate lunch and afternoon tea with a variety of snacks. Every evening there used to be some social programme, where ballroom dance was the most favourite item among the Europeans mainly, where the special ship orchestra was in attendance.

This was followed by dinner, which like lunch was elaborate. As if this was not enough, late evening coffee and sandwiches were served before the passengers retired late in the night.

To cope with a large number of passengers, both lunch and supper were served in two shifts. The dining hall had enormous space to accommodate a large number of passengers with enough legroom for movement and service. It was tastefully decorated and very well managed. The service was prompt and courteous.

While the food served was gourmet for the non-vegetarians, there was little choice for the vegetarians and that pinched most of them. They partly compensated for this by sharing Indian items that some thoughtful passengers from India had carried, especially those who were married.

I was pleasantly surprised to find that quite a few fellow passengers were also headed for the LSE and other universities. Soon, I noticed that unlike me almost everyone was carrying heavy loads of research material, including books, articles, notes, reports, etc., which they looked forward to consulting in their academic pursuit.

My cabin-mate, who was a teacher in geography at Benaras Hindu University, too carried stacks of books, reprints and maps and other material for his research project. In fact, much of the space in the big box he had carried to the cabin was filled with it. Thus, it was quite obvious that people already had a complete notion of the work they were going to do in the foreign universities and were keen to qualify for their degree within the minimum time.

As hinted earlier, it was all so different in my case. I was completely unsure of the area I was going to work upon. It was broadly "Economic development with special reference to the problems of underdeveloped countries" which at that time was a new area of study and research. And possibly because I volunteered to take up this challenge, the members of the committee, who reviewed my application for admission at the LSE, had recommended my case.

But frankly, at that time I had the least notion about this field. I had hardly read any worthwhile material on it. I had just thought about it casually and hoped that with an open mind and ability to write a good draft, I would be able to produce a good research piece, without realizing the numerous pitfalls I was exposing myself to.

While I could have done a good job in the area of India's industrialization in the post-Independence era, for which I had access to first hand material, normally not available to others and produced a first rate work, I had unfortunately closed my mind on it. An almost total non-serious attitude had got hold of me. I was overcome by a wave of shocks when I saw the other research students on the ship so well equipped with materials of study.

But then, it was too late to think of all this. I decided to face the situation at the LSE and not be disturbed by such thoughts for the present and enjoy this opportunity to the best possible extent.

The long stay on the ship, where we met fellow travellers frequently, also helped to cement our friendship. In fact, we started knowing each other so closely that it seemed we had been friends for a long time.

It was, however, quite difficult to strike friendship with the Australians who moved within their own circle. An exception to this were the Anglo-Indians, who were quite a few on the boat and actively mixed with the foreigners; especially young girls who often shared their evenings with them, participating in dances and visiting the bar and giving them company for late hours.

In fact, at the table that I was allotted in the dining hall, all other members were of an Anglo-Indian family migrating to the UK. Soon I found it difficult to cope with them and had to ask the dining hall manager to shift my seat to another table, which was allowed. This was a good riddance from the snobbish behaviour and false sense of superiority displayed by the Anglo-Indian family in whose company I had never relished my food.

Evenings, as said, used to be packed with social programmes. Quite a few Indian cultural programmes too were organized by some enterprising Indians travelling on the ship and provided us with a good change.

In fact, there used to be such a long schedule of eating and cultural activities the whole day that by the time we retired to our cabins, we used to be quite tired and slept soundly despite the fully loaded stomachs.

After a few days of our journey, an urgent message was received by the ship authorities from the headquarters to divert the ship via South Africa, as the Suez Canal crisis had deepened and the British personnel who guided the passage of ships through the canal had resigned. The Egyptian leader, Nasser, had taken over the management of the canal.

This message was flashed on the ship through its public address system. A written message in bold letters too had been prominently displayed outside their main office.

The management deeply regretted the inconvenience caused to the passengers because of this sudden change in the route, which meant a longer stay on the ship, almost two more weeks than of the normal schedule for reaching London. Besides, it caused a great inconvenience to passengers who had to disembark en route for the Middle East and other destinations.

The management especially regretted for these passengers and had assured them that they would be air-flown to their destinations soon after reaching the first port for disembarkation. But that itself was an almost seven-day journey. It also disturbed our schedule of joining the universities, where we would now be late by a fortnight. We intimated the institutions of our new schedule. I also requested the warden of the Passfield Hall in London to keep my place, as now in view of the changed schedule I would be late by a fortnight.

Though the new schedule put a high pressure on the resources and management of the ship, they in no way lowered the quality of their services, or food served, or evening programmes organized. Rather, they were quite apologetic for this inconvenience. This is what touched me greatly and brought out the quality of the British character, who even in an emergent situation kept their banner high.

While some passengers were concerned about this delay, it was quite the opposite for most of the Australian tourists and Anglo-Indian families, who were already in a holiday mood. This opportunity proved to be a blessing for them as they could now enjoy the five-star hotel hospitality for a fortnight more at zero cost.

DURBAN OFFSHORE VISIT

The weather at the first port of disembarkation—Durban—was quite cool, as September in this region happens to be a part of the winter season, when we have summer in India. We had to change into woollen clothing for the daylong trip in Durban.

As at that time India did not have any diplomatic relations with the South African government because it followed the policy of apartheid, it was indeed a golden opportunity to visit this land which normally we would not have got. We were also keen to visit the land from where Mahatma Gandhi had started his experiment of fighting with non-violence the forces of oppression let loose by the British settlers on the native population.

As it was after a very long time that a passenger liner carrying so many Indian nationals had disembarked here, a large crowd of South Africans and Indian settlers had crowded the place to welcome us. The local press too mobbed the Indian passengers and took a large number of photographs as well as spoke to many of us.

The afternoon edition of leading newspapers flashed the front-page headline about the landing for the first time of a large number of Indians, including turbaned and bearded members. The presence of Sikhs in our group had particularly fascinated them, for most of them had not come across them earlier.

Before disembarkation, identity slips had been issued and we were specially reminded about the law of this place where whites and non-whites could not mix. So it was emphasized that those who did not like this policy should not disembark. But who would have missed the rare opportunity of exploring this land? Also, after such a long travel on sea, we wanted this change badly and being tired of the ship food, we looked forward to typical Indian food to satisfy our palate and taste buds.

There were separate tourist coaches for the Europeans and non-Europeans. Exceptions were only made in the case of Japanese. This showed that the Japanese, even after their humiliating defeat during World War II, commanded a place of respect in the Western World.

An interesting episode happened. Some Anglo-Indian girls, who had developed intimate relations with the Australians on the ship, had dared to board a coach meant for the Europeans. But when their passports were examined, they were politely told to travel in non-European coaches. So, with great humiliation they came to these buses.

The Indians settled in this city who had come to welcome us were very happy to meet such a large number of their countrymen. They insisted that on our return journey from the daylong excursion tour, we meet them at a particular place and they would take us in their vehicles to meet other members of our community.

They also guided us to an exclusive Indian restaurant of high repute. Strong smell of the Indian biryani and other preparations overtook our senses. We virtually mobbed this restaurant and had our full of this tasty food.

After the meals I took a small walk in the nearby park. Here I came across a middle-aged African who was basking in the sun. He greeted me warmly and enquired whether I was from India. When I confirmed, he was very happy in adding: "From the land of Gandhi!?" He further added: "We would soon throw away the British from our land, which we would free."

And his dream came true after a few years when Nelson Mandela, who had spent the best part of his life rotting in prison, was released and he soon took over the administration of this land.

I also had the taste of the apartheid policy, when our bus stopped at the post office to facilitate us in posting mail. There were two counters. One for the Europeans and the other for the local natives. As there was a long queue in front of the native counter, I went to the other counter where a young lady was dozing in the absence of any customer. But before I could make it, the driver of the bus came rushing and politely reminded me that that counter was meant for Europeans only. However, he volunteered to buy stamps for me and told me not to wait in the queue.

A similar situation could be seen in public parks, where benches were marked for the Europeans and non-Europeans. I thought it was a very humiliating practice and I abhorred it from the depth of my heart.

The bus journey was long, extending over several miles. In the end, it took us to the sanctuary of a Zulu chief who stayed in the wilderness in makeshift huts with a large family of his wives and children. This was, as we could make out, just eyewash to bring home to the outsiders the fact that the natives were yet uncivilized people and it would take sufficient time to tame them. Thus, they stood to benefit from the white man's regime.

On our return, we found the members of the Indian community, whom we had met in the morning, waiting for us at the appointed place. We disembarked from the buses and were taken in their vehicles to a community centre where we were introduced to other people of our clan. When we told them that we were going to different universities to pursue higher studies, they were indeed quite happy and wished us all success.

At the same time, they lamented that such opportunities were not available to their children, because of the discriminatory policy of the local government. Among them, we found a majority were Gujaratis, who were doing fairly well as they ran lucrative businesses and owned multi-storeyed business complexes. They appeared to be quite contented. Later, they took us around the city and saw us off at the port area where the ship was anchored.

VISIT TO CAPE TOWN

Our next destination was Cape Town, a voyage of full two days. However, because of the highly rough sea, this journey turned out to be a major nightmare.

Due to the stormy sea, the ship tilted frequently, disturbing the mood of passengers. Quite a large number of them failed to turn up at the dining hall the next day. We were told that because of the continuous disturbance, a large number of crockery items had also crashed.

There was a heavy demand for paper bags because the passengers vomited frequently and some of them had to be medically treated.

To avoid the turmoil, which was felt the maximum in the cabins located lower down the ship and which also affected me and my colleague, we spent much of the time in the large open deck, which was able to absorb the maximum number of shocks of the tidal turbulence.

On touching the Cape Town harbour, we heaved a sigh of relief and most of the passengers who had suffered for the last two days preferred to recoup quietly, while the others took this opportunity to explore yet another important landmark in the southern end of South Africa.

It was a comparatively smaller city than Durban but more neat and clean. We took a bus ride to the major marketing centre and some other areas of tourist interest. I recall distinctly the fantastic journey by the cable car over a vast stretch of a deep gorge connecting one side of this gorge to the top of the opposite hill, where we explored the surroundings, before returning to the base. It was indeed a memorable event.

We were greatly impressed by the fact that some smart English ladies ran the buses. This was not anticipated, in this apartheid land. Not only did the young ladies manage the buses efficiently, they were also very polite and answered our queries. In fact, realizing that this was our first trip to this city, they helped us visit places of top interest, which we could have never done otherwise within the time at our disposal.

Some of them even alighted from the bus and accompanied us to show the correct route to be followed. This was indeed a great help and we thanked them immensely for their courtesy and cooperation, on which they smiled pleasantly and wished us a good time.

We found that both the cities we visited in South Africa had a large European population. They were well built, neat and clean with well-maintained roads and other services. Though this may be primarily due to the European factor, it was praiseworthy, and reflected their taste to live well and with dignity, something which needed to be kept in mind while planning cities in the fast growing developing world.

A REFRESHING SPANISH RESORT

From Cape Town, after covering a major part of the West Coast of Africa—in fact, right from Cape Town the West Coast begins—our destination was Las Palmas, a thriving tourist spot in part of the Canary Island, which was under Spanish control.

It was an enchanting resort visited by a large number of tourists, mainly from Europe, rich in Spanish culture, music and dances, food and drinks and entertainment. We had a trip through this area in arranged coaches. We were pleased to meet some Indians (Sindhis) settled there and doing flourishing business. One of the gentlemen we met in a curio shop had a Spanish wife. We learnt that quite a few Sindhis had settled down both in the eastern and western coasts of Africa and were doing well. Hats off to these enterprising people and, of course, to Gujaratis who dared to settle down in the distant and even difficult areas of this continent and were earning handsomely.

We were now gradually moving closer to Southampton in Britain. Here the weather changed enormously and it got quite cold during the daytime as we neared our destination. It was a full one month of travel in the company of a large number of passengers, who had by now become so familiar with each other that some of us were even able to trace close links with at least a few of them.

The parting was sad. Now each of us would be travelling separately to our respective destinations.

DESTINATION LONDON

After checking out the baggage we boarded the waiting train, which took us to London. The train finally terminated at Victoria, the local station of London, after a couple of hours. I looked for a young man who was supposed to receive me at this place and guide me.

When I had met his mother in Chandigarh before leaving, she insisted that I carry a small tin of *dhesi ghee* (clarified butter), which her son would have been missing. I was, however, spared of this hardship when her husband intervened, saying that the British butter was far more nutritious and acceptable. Of course, I carried other items that her son had written about.

It took the gentleman quite some time to locate me in the crowd. He helped me to a waiting taxi and soon I was at my destination, Passfield Hall.

Thus, this long journey in the ship was a memorable one for its rare experience, covering such a vast area of the Arabian Sea and, Indian and Atlantic Oceans, apart from several islands and took us to different destinations en route, particularly South and West Africa which we could not have visited otherwise. It was a unique opportunity created because of the Suez crisis.

London and LSE

After dumping my luggage in the room allotted to me, I told my Indian friend that I would like to visit the London School of Economics (LSE) if it was not far from this place, as it would help to acquaint myself with the area. Fortunately, it was not far and I preferred to walk than take a bus ride as it would enable me to know the route. Also I wanted to warm up my limbs in that unusual cold.

Within about half an hour we had neared the school, which I had all along imagined to be a prestigious and imposing structure with excellent surroundings. On the other hand, it did not look any better than an old commercial building with its grey exterior, obviously affected by a thick coating of smog. It was located on the edge of a small street.

However, soon my friend dispelled my impression, explaining that in that country people did not bother about the exterior of buildings, which could not escape the harsh impact of weather. They were far more concerned with their warm and cosy interiors, where they had to spend most of the time.

He was correct. As we slipped inside this unimposing structure, we noticed what a contrast it provided to the exterior look. The walls were carefully done with an eye-soothing distemper and it was a great pleasure to move through its spacious corridors oozing warmth. As the whole building was centrally heated, there was no possibility of any cold air entering its premises.

We had a leisurely walk through its several floors. I was familiarizing myself with its prime locations like refractory (lunch/dining hall), cafeteria for snacks and beverages and library. We went inside the library moving through its two storeys packed with books and journals, and also visited the Research Students Common Room located on the top floor. We also saw some lecture halls.

Students were hanging around in large numbers, chatting and discussing, which I could hardly make out, because of their low voices to avoid disturbing the atmosphere. It was also remarkable that a large number of students were absorbed in consulting material from journals and books for their assignments.

It was a very interesting experience and I looked forward to making the best of my London stay.

I hurried back to the hostel, for suppertime was 6.30 p.m.—a time which would yet be the tea time in India, with dinner following much later.

LIFE AT PASSFIELD HALL

It was my first evening at this new place but I had already picked up friendship with a couple of Indian residents who also helped me become familiar with its surroundings and informed me in case I wanted to be a vegetarian I had to make a special application to the warden, as there was hardly any vegetarian at this place and further, vegetarians had a fixed menu of rice and some preparation made with the help of Indian curry powder that was quite popular then.

They also gave me some tips to make my stay comfortable in this hostel where over 80 per cent students happened to be British nationals. I was very particular about my early morning bath, which I did not want to miss. Fortunately, good arrangements existed for a hot shower bath in the basement, which I rarely missed subsequently.

Another place I rarely missed was the Quiet Room, a common centrally heated room where tables and chairs were spread around for studies and writing assignments.

I was quite restless on my first night in these unfamiliar foreign surroundings, when I was alone in the room as my room partner, an American national, was away. The place was extremely quiet and except for the loud bang of a public clock across the road every hour, there was no life around.

I kept awake for long, much beyond midnight. I would often wonder when the street clock would strike six in the morning, when I could walk to the shower room. Soon I had made it and the bath was so refreshing that my fatigue disappeared and I got over the previous night's hangover. The long corridor, though empty, was well lighted and the cleaners were already on their job, scrubbing and dry washing the floors much before the boarders woke up. I was greeted by them with a good morning and also by others who happened to meet me. This was my first lesson that I never forgot later.

At the shower room, except for me and a lone African resident who also happened to be particular about the morning bath, like me, there was none else. I rarely came across another resident in these early hours and least an English boy. Going to bed quite late, after they had coffee late in the night, which I invariably avoided, and staying late in the lounge, was a routine with them.

In the morning, most of them hurriedly washed their faces and virtually dashed to the dining hall lest they miss the breakfast. The same I observed in the case of both my room mates. While the first was an American gentleman, later it was a Scottish young man, who shared accommodation with me. They would be deep in sleep, when I woke up early morning. I would get ready without disturbing them. They would generally wake up after the ringing of the breakfast bell.

I often shared my breakfast with boarders from Ghana, Nigeria and Arab countries and very frequently with a colleague from Japan—Kei Wakaizumi—who also happened to be mature in age and behaviour and we soon became very close friends, sharing several programmes and visits together. Our friendship even lasted later and I met him again when I visited Japan a few years on.

In fact, non-British students—mostly African, Arab and Indian nationals—were the first to reach the tables and thus enjoyed the pleasure of eating steaming hot breakfast with plenty of milk, butter, cereals, bacon, eggs and other preparations, along with hot and crispy toasts. There was often a change in the menu to break its dullness. Every item was available aplenty and there was no restriction on how much one ate.

It was often observed that the British boys, after eating a hearty breakfast with liberal help of almost all items, would not hesitate to stuff the pockets of their trousers with the maximum number of toasts with butter and jam to help them as their mid-day meal and thus, avoided visiting the refractory during the lunch time.

Most of us could not do the same. In fact, the breakfast was so substantial that it lasted for hours. We preferred to have a light lunch, which also helped to concentrate more on our library assignments.

In fact, though there was plenty of room for readers in the spacious library, it was often difficult to find a vacant seat. This showed how deeply an average student was concerned with the library use. The students sat in the library for hours at a stretch, completing their assignments.

This was so unlike in our country where libraries, though housed in spacious buildings, fail to attract any readers, except during the exam period when students would be busy memorizing from cheap texts. In fact, even teachers fail to patronize the libraries.

Here in the LSE library, even the 80-plus retired director of this institution would be often seen climbing up the stairs to hunt for material for his writing. Faculty members and researchers who had been consulting the library for several years were also regular visitors.

Even more surprising was the fact that they would often sit next to an undergraduate student, without any sort of assistance from the library staff. They would themselves hunt for the material they wanted to consult and even return it to its proper place so that their seat could be vacated for the other users.

Such devotion to the library culture, which occupied the central place in their educational system needs to be carefully nurtured in our educational system also, and both teachers and students should regularly consult and value the libraries. Like in Britain, this habit should begin from the school level. In fact, the school is the right place to instill library culture.

BRUSH WITH SUPERVISOR

When for the first time I met my guide, A.D. Knox, a Canadian national expert in the area of economic development with special reference to the problems of underdeveloped countries, it turned out to be a pleasant meeting and most of my earlier misgivings about him had to be cast off. We had a frank discussion in the area I proposed to work on during my stay here.

He spoke little, mostly keeping mum and allowed me to talk. In the end, he asked me to visit the library and prepare a draft of my proposed work and meet him when it was ready. He did not say anything about the material I should consult or how I should proceed with the draft. He left this to my discretion, indicating that I was to think of it myself. Though this puzzled me, I did not conceive it wise to press the matter further with him.

Of course, later as I sat in the library, his behaviour and silence left me dumbfounded. I was honestly filled with apprehension. I consulted other Indian scholars who were already registered for research work. They told me that under the system prevailing here and other universities of this country, the guides left much of this task to the students, who were expected to slog in the library for hours thinking about their research scheme and the supervisor's role was to read the final draft and make comments.

Thus, I struggled with the draft of my project. I used all my diligence and patience in preparing it, consulting material I could find here or elsewhere, especially in the India House library. I put in a virtually round-the-clock effort, including several hours of sitting in the Quiet Room of my hostel.

It took me a fortnight to produce a meaningful draft. Though still filled with misgivings, I sought an appointment with the supervisor.

When I met him finally, he greeted me warmly and had a look at the small note I had prepared. He carefully scanned my scheme of work, as well as the bibliography. He seemed to be pleased and returned it to me with the remark that while it appeared to be all right, more would be revealed as I proceeded with my writing. He advised me to prepare a draft of the introductory chapter and send him its copy and wait for the next appointment.

When we met after around four weeks, he again greeted me warmly and went through the draft. His only comment was that though it was interesting, it was just a sort of historical account. To make it acceptable it needed to be honed. He advised me to cut down its size and added that the shape of my research work was more important than this introduction. He was of the view that I should do more reading and planning before I sent him another draft of the introductory chapter.

Thus, I could sense that this sort of approach would not fit into my research project and I needed to be more careful while revising the draft. He had some queries here and there that required to be closely looked into while preparing the next draft.

Hitherto, I had thought that any historical narrative called for a big dose of facts and figures and minimum analysis but now I realized that this was not so. My writing invited several awkward interventions from the supervisor and needed further clarification and investigation of statements, before it could be considered relevant.

I was, thus, pushed into the corner and had to frame quite a few drafts on each of my writings and yet the supervisor was not satisfied. He only appeared to tear off my drafts. Frankly, after some time I became doubtful of the motive of my supervisor; whether he was bent on throwing me out of the LSE, though I was told by my senior colleagues that such a situation was often encountered by students from developing countries who had to struggle a lot to meet with the standards expected here.

VERA ANSTEY

I was, however, fortunate to have another supervisor as well, Vera Anstey, a senior and much respected lady who understood the problems of Indian students well for her husband had been at one time the Principal of a college in Bombay and she herself had been in contact with the Indian students at the LSE. Since I was under the joint supervision of both A.D. Knox and Vera Anstey, I thought it would work in my favour. Further, Anstey had done pioneering work on Indian economic development which had gained high reputation among the academic circles and was considered to be the most authentic work on Indian economic development under the British rule.

So I consulted her and told her about the awkward problem I was facing in the progress of my work. But I found she was not in anyway prepared to go against A.D. Knox. Ultimately, it was decided that I should get registered for the masters (M.Sc.) degree and start attending regular lectures of some faculty members, as well as participate in seminars and spend more time in the library consulting journals and books in my area and also write small assignments.

This was, of course, a big jolt for me. But there appeared to be no escape from it, if I wanted to have a degree from this institution. Accordingly, I started preparing myself for the exam, though my mind was filled with dubiousness whether I would emerge successful in the exam on the foreign soil. Further, I had not taken any exam at home for the past several years. These apprehensions took a strong hold of me and I was often troubled by them.

In fact, when I joined the LSE I had never thought of facing any exam and felt confident that with an M.A. degree from a reputed Indian university, I would be able to earn my doctorate.

The present negative development had started weighing psychologically on me and I was uncertain of my own capability to do justice to the exam. No matter how hard I tried to overcome, this feeling, it somehow, stayed firm. But I resolved to not let this interfere with my stay in London and make it a happy experience.

INDIA HOUSE LIBRARY

While in London I used to spend a good part of my time in the library of India House in the Aldwych area, which happened to be close to the LSE. Often, when I felt bored I would walk to this place and relax in its cosy atmosphere and share the company of senior scholars from different universities in India busy with their project studies. The library was a rich wealth of rare books mostly contributed by British scholars, old reports, monograms and documents, which had been preserved with much care by one of its longest serving librarians, W.K. Thorne. She was also a very considerate and helpful lady and soon we got to know each other so well that she treated me almost like her family member.

Later, during her visits to India, she would also come down to Chandigarh and invariably stayed with us. She was carefully looked after by my wife who would make her stay quite comfortable and to her liking.

The India House cafeteria also served lunch and other snacks and beverages at concessional rates and I frequently had my lunch here. It mostly consisted of rice and prawn curry, which provided me with a good change.

It was a great pleasure to walk through the corridors of the multi-storey building of India House. It was an imposing structure, stoutly built by the British during their Raj. It had one of the largest contingents of Indian employees and at that time Vijaylakshmi Pandit, sister of Jawaharlal Nehru, was India's High Commissioner. She was a graceful lady who enjoyed a good reputation among the local politicians as well as in social circles, and took an active part in the local life.

The entire building was centrally heated. In fact, almost all buildings in London were centrally heated. This had become the major factor for the high pollution of London environment, with thick smog often hanging low for most of the time. It led to poor visibility and, at times, the sun would disappear for days together.

SMOG, SNOW AND LAKE DISTRICT

Smog was injurious for children and senior persons and particularly affected those suffering from breathing problems. Several deaths were caused as a result and a large number of victims had to be hospitalised. It also was a major reason of accidents, often fatal ones. Thus, smog took a big toll.

Later, with the shift to alternative fuel in place of steam coal, the situation improved to a large extent. But it still continued to be the biggest hazard during winter.

Being a lover of snow, I certainly looked forward to the winter with interest. Unfortunately, London did not have the thick blanket of snow that I had witnessed in Simla. Here it was a rare event and even when it snowed, it would soon melt, without providing an opportunity to children to have the fun of making a snowman.

In fact, snowing would soon turn into an unhappy experience with slush all around, making it difficult to move about. However, it was so very different in the North of England where it snowed more frequently and in rich abundance and stayed for weeks, especially in parks and other open spaces.

Soon I had the opportunity to join a trip to Lake District in the North. It was arranged by the British Council. This Council took a special interest in the care of the overseas students and often arranged subsidized trips for them to different destinations, as well as provided them an opportunity to enjoy a part of the Christmas holidays with British families. We used to be treated as special guests and our hosts would arrange special dinners and other programmes for us, which provided a refreshing change, besides allowing us to familiarize ourselves with the local customs, traditions and food as well as social life. We were taken around for picnics and visits to the neighbourhood, and evenings were generally spent in watching some special entertainment programme.

Thus, these visits were eagerly looked forward to and most foreign students availed of them. Such a trip was arranged for me and another Indian student who was also a research student at the LSE. The particulars of the family that would act as our host during this stay were provided to us, as well as details of contacting them in case they failed to pick us up.

As the family we had to stay with happened to be close to Lake District, we had dovetailed this visit with our trip to Lake District. We, a group of overseas students from different countries, were taken in a coach from London. It was my first visit to this place, rather to any distant place outside London. Soon we were passing through the British countryside. It presented a panoramic view with greenery and mini lakes here and there. It wore such a contrast to the dull and ugly atmosphere of London.

We were also thrilled to see snow-covered fields extending over a vast area. It stirred in me memories of snow on the hills of Simla when we would be on our toes with snowshoes and caps donning our heads to protect them from falling snowflakes. Though we could not do the same here, we enjoyed feasting our eyes on the breathtaking spectacle, from our cosy seats in the centrally heated coach, which moved cautiously through the snowy stretches.

En route we moved through some villages, which we found to be so very different from our own in India. Their houses were comparable to any urban area and possessed all possible modern facilities. We also came across a shopping centre with stores, grocery shops, pubs and other facilities. Villages were well connected with the surrounding areas by modern means of communication and farmers owned vehicles to move around.

In fact, there was hardly any difference here from the urban life. Rather, this life was preferred, for it provided much relief from the maddening crowds and an absolute freedom was available from the nasty smog. The village life ensured a quiet and peaceful stay and helped one to be away from the stress and disease-prone surroundings of urban areas and thereby added extra years to one's life.

It is so very unfortunate that in India, despite efforts made over the decades, we have failed to improve the living conditions in the rural areas where even elementary facilities are lacking. We should pick up lessons from the advanced countries and try to make the rural atmosphere more friendly. This, of course, calls for a determined effort, which is generally lacking in our leaders, policy makers as well as bureaucrats.

At our destination, we were lodged in a spacious building that at one time was owned by a business baron who successfully controlled a vast textile empire, which had helped the tycoon and his likes to amass fabulous wealth.

Subsequently, this place had been acquired and converted into a tourist resort. It was centrally heated. All around it was the breathtaking view of the vast lake area, which at that time of severe winter was completely frozen. So much so that one could walk on it without getting wet. Of course, with snow spread everywhere it was risky to walk unless one could maintain balance, which was indeed a Herculean task.

Most of us, however, in sheer excitement would undertake such a risk but had to return without going far. Poets have immortalized the beauty and scenery of this place and they are quite justified, even though the winter scenario was not as picturesque as it was during the summer.

A warm welcome awaited us on the evening of our arrival. A group of local country dancers dressed in all white had been called. They virtually forced each one of us to dance with them, which was a rare treat and honour especially in the company of the young damsels who were expert in Scottish dance. With the local music being played and drinks served, the full warmth and thrill of these dances was soon experienced. Even those who hesitated and felt shy to dance, joined in the revelry and soon one wished that this saga would continue the whole night.

ENGLISH HOSPITALITY

After the trip was over, I and my Indian friend bade farewell to our colleagues and boarded the coach to visit our host family, where we were to spend the next couple of days before returning to London. As they had been already informed about our arrival date and time, we did not anticipate any difficulty. In fact, as our coach arrived at the destination, we found the hosts already waiting for us.

They extended warm greetings and welcomed us to the place, which they hoped would give us an opportunity to see something of the English life as well as the countryside.

And so it was. After we had a wash and settled down in our room, we were taken to the family's sitting room, where we stretched ourselves around the fire to warm our limbs and feel relaxed.

The family consisted of a middle-aged couple and their only son, who too had come to spend the Christmas break with his parents. As was customary, we exchanged gifts with the family that we had brought with us and the family also offered some gifts in return. In the absence of their son who had gone to meet his friends, both husband and wife helped each other in bringing different items of food from the kitchen, steaming hot, to the dining table. In fact, we were told that the husband had cooked the turkey, a job which was very well done, and showed how the husband and wife shared the kitchen work without burdening a single partner.

Two hectic days followed when we were taken around to different places. In the early morning we visited the surrounding forest, where a crowd had already gathered, to witness fox hunting. On Christmas Day, fox hunting was looked forward to with eagerness. Some liveried gentlemen were riding horses and controlling a team of hounds, specially trained for the occasion. Soon they were let loose to hunt down foxes from the interior of the forest. The owners of the dogs who were successful in this game were given special prizes and the dogs too were appropriately honoured. While this provided a great deal of excitement to the crowd, personally I did not relish this barbaric custom.

We were subsequently taken to the most popular pub in this town. We leisurely enjoyed the specially brewed drinks, along with snacks in that cosy and warm environment, which also helped us to warm our limbs that had almost gone numb in the icy cold atmosphere of the forest area.

We also went around sightseeing landmarks, including the well-maintained parks. I liked the parks immensely which showed a high sense of awareness of the local population in maintaining their environment. After lunch and relaxation, we were escorted to witness a Russian circus which was packed to capacity. It was a large crowd-pulling occasion with the majority being children.

The next day again from forenoon onwards, we had another busy schedule, and the visit to the Town Hall was a major attraction. We were received by the Mayor of that place, who welcomed us warmly and showed us around and explained the functioning of the local Municipal Corporation. He also attended to our queries and we marked our visit in a register meant for distinguished visitors. So we got the distinguished visitors' status and felt highly elated.

We had spent a memorable time in the homely environment of this family to be cherished later.

BACK TO PASSFIELD HALL

Back to work after a short holiday. By now, my roommate in Passfield Hall had changed. While earlier it was an American, this time it was a Scottish gentleman who held a government job. He was working on trade unions and was at the LSE on a short assignment, where he had to attend some lectures and write a couple of papers.

He was comparatively more open and friendly than an average British student residing in this place. In fact, I could also notice his dislike for the English people as they considered themselves to be superior to the Scottish. I noticed the English considered themselves superior even to an average Welsh.

As mentioned, this man was more open. We would often discuss issues of academic as well as social interest and he was eager to know more about India. Thus, with him the room atmosphere became livelier and its earlier dullness was broken. Not that the American, was less friendly or open; he was out for most of the time. We hardly spent time together or got the opportunity to engage in a serious discussion.

My meetings with the supervisor were fewer now. However, I had begun attending lectures as advised and often met Vera Anstey who, was quite a sympathetic and helpful lady. How I wished I had been put exclusively under her charge, right from the beginning. That would have undoubtedly helped me make far better progress in my research work and ultimately perhaps fulfill my mission.

But, it was too late to think of it now. I was completely under the control of the other supervisor, who had the major say in the matter. My initial mistake was to engage myself in the area of 'Economic development with reference to problems of underdeveloped countries'. This being his area of specialisation, he had straightaway given his consent. Had I shown interest in an area related to India, Vera Anstey was the natural choice for its supervision.

I also attended seminars, especially those organized by A.D. Knox, which used to be well-participated. Seven or eight weekly programmes had been organized on the most sought-after publication on economic development by Arthur Lewis, who was a native of the West Indies and occupied the Professor's chair at the University of Manchester.

It was through these over two-month long weekly seminars that we covered the whole text. Indeed, it was a very comprehensive seminar. I also read Lewis' interesting publication on the growth theory which was written in a simple and lucid style, and could even be followed by a layman. In fact, Lewis has a remarkable style of putting forth his ideas in a logical and consistent manner, which instantly arouses the curiosity of a reader. His being the pioneering work in this newly coming up area on economic development in the early 1950s, it became an instant success and was adopted as a text by universities all over the world. In fact, in newly developing economies where the subject of economic development was introduced for the first time, this book by Arthur Lewis, "A Theory of Economic Growth", was indispensable and became a standard reading.

The other seminars that I attended were organized by Vera Anstey. Being an expert on Indian economy, these seminars were invariably devoted to India, where major topics were covered and discussed widely. These seminars naturally had the maximum participation of Indian students. Incidentally, during those days of 1950s and even 1960s, Indians were the maximum admission-seekers at the LSE, both in the graduate and undergraduate courses as well for Ph.D.

The Indian universities also accorded a high priority to degrees from the LSE and thus, a candidate who was LSE-qualified was sure to find a suitable academic placement, though quite a few also opted for non-teaching areas like research institutes, Planning Commission, central ministries (particularly in their economic wings) and also in the private sector where, of course, suitable openings were limited.

There was thus little surprise that the first priority for the admission-seekers for a social sciences degree in foreign countries was the LSE. The benign presence of Vera Anstey, who acted as godmother to an average Indian student, was an additional attraction.

VACATION IN BIRMINGHAM

During the first summer vacation, I decided to spend some time in Birmingham with a couple whom I had met on the ship, where during the month-long stay together, we had developed a close friendship. In fact, we had traced some common family links, which had further cemented our bond.

After parting company at Southampton, we had kept track of each other through correspondence. Rattan had been registered for a Ph.D. degree in chemistry with Birmingham University. His wife, though a housewife, was socially active and played an important role in the social side of the Indian community settled in Birmingham.

They were married just a few days before coming to Britain and were trying to adjust to their new life. It was no mean task for most of us not accustomed to the British system of education and research. Besides, they had to cope with their new set of family and marital adjustments simultaneously.

It was remarkable that back home in India, we would be hardly prepared to spend long hours on research projects and degrees were easier to earn for they did not call for too much rigour or the deep probe invariably insisted upon by reputed foreign universities, where each draft had to be written with utmost care and even then it often failed to be accepted by the supervisor. But we adjusted well to these challenges in foreign countries.

When I was in Birmingham, spending a part of my summer vacation, I found that Rattan had very little time to spare from his commitment to the research project. Often his wife and I would visit him and find him so engrossed that he would heave a sigh of relief at our sight, as he then got the needed break wherein he could engage in *gupshup* in Punjabi and also enjoy *paronthas* and vegetables prepared in the Punjabi style, with some Indian pickle.

We would share *paronthas* with his colleagues, who found them very tasty and thanked the lady for having made some extra for them.

After we had finished the late lunch, Rattan would wind up the day's work and get ready to join us for sight-seeing, or a visit to the market, or even call on some Indian families and we returned home late in the evening.

Knowing that Rattan was yet a long way to go in his research work, though he was anxious to complete it within the minimum period, we did not much disturb his day's routine.

A few more Punjabi families also stayed in their neighbourhood. Thus, we had a happy time together in a homely environment, speaking our language, sharing experiences and particularly enjoyed jokes about the peculiar behaviour of the local people. I also had a good opportunity to eat home-cooked food, which I had been denied since I moved to London. *Paronthas* and *chapattis,* in particular, our staple food, were sorely missed.

I ate them with relish, knowing too well that back in London I would miss them. In London, apart from the India House cafeteria, we also got subsidized Indian food at the Indian YMCA as well as at Indian Students Hostel, the latter run by the government. I occasionally visited these places, which fortunately happened to be close to my hostel, for a change. Though *paronthas* and *chapattis* were not prepared at these places, I relished the rice and other Indian preparations that were served.

We had taken a day off to visit Stratford-on-Avon, the world-renowned place where Shakespeare was born and wrote his classical plays. The place was, therefore, like Mecca for Shakespeare lovers. During summer particularly, a large number of tourists would converge here to witness Shakespeare's plays as well as enjoy its picturesque view and hear the music played by the Scottish highlanders dressed in their typical national dress.

ANOTHER YEAR IN PASSFIELD HALL

After a few days in Birmingham, I returned to my nest in London. During the summer vacation, all British students had to vacate their rooms. Only the foreign students were allowed to stay back, except for a fortnight, when this place had to be completely vacated for renewals, repairs etc. The vacated accommodation was thrown open to foreign tourists for a short stay. Most of them were visitors from western Europe who had to pay quite a high tariff for board and lodging. The extra income thus earned was used for meeting the maintenance expenses of this place.

At the start of the next session, I was allotted a single room to myself. Now, there was no longer the sharing headache, though personally I did not face any trouble on this account. Even so, I preferred independent accommodation. The new place was just across my earlier room, so I was already familiar with the location and had developed a liking for it.

Another major advantage was that it was protected against cold or draft. I had earlier been highly uncomfortable, for the rooms were not centrally heated, though one could get the heating arrangement in every room by inserting coins. Also, being next to the lounge, it was convenient to watch TV programmes occasionally and to relax and read newspapers.

Like my earlier room, it was close to the dining hall, as well as Quiet Room, both located on the ground floor. It was a room where I could concentrate on my studies and relax when I liked.

On the weekends, the place was agog with fun, drinks and music, all of which flowed in abundance. The venue was the basement where the bar was located, though often it spilled over to the upper floor, including the lounge. Students danced with their girlfriends and boyfriends till late in the night.

There was much merrymaking, with over-drunk boys and girls often creating ugly scenes. It appeared that during the weekends, a complete licence was given to the boarders to spend this time entirely the way they liked. Though when the situation got completely out of control, the warden would intervene to restore normalcy, which was not an easy job.

Interestingly, once a week a hairdresser, a Jewish gentleman, visited the LSE. We could get our hair trimmed at concessional rates from him. He operated from a particular place and was on the premises from morning till afternoon. A diary was kept on a table where the schedule for different sittings was entered and the students who wanted a haircut would select a vacant slot and come exactly at that time. It took around 15 minutes for one cut.

There was a heavy demand for his services as getting a haircut here was convenient and cheaper than the market salons. Naturally, students who failed to reach in time would be disappointed and had to wait for his next visit. I would invariably have my haircut here and was usually the first to make it.

I was all praise for how well the services were managed in this country. The dining hall of Passfield Hall was extremely well managed by just six women, who attended to the job with a high degree of efficiency and responsibility. The kitchen catered to around 130 boarders and yet this handful of ladies managed the enormous load of crockery used to serve soup, the main items of food, plus vegetables and dessert. This three-course dinner entailed the washing of hundreds of items of crockery, maintaining a high standard of hygiene, drying them and keeping them in order for the next service. And this job was performed remarkably well within the time frame.

The ladies who cooked food were equally praiseworthy. Apart from preparing several dishes, they maintained a high state of cleanliness and quality. It was indeed a commendable job. In fact, I could hardly believe that just a dozen or so ladies could manage this enormous job so well. I never heard of anybody complaining about the quality of food or service.

I have often wondered why after years of freedom we in India have so completely failed to improve our services. In fact, they leave much to be desired and one is often disgusted by the way they are rendered. Take the case of our hostels, where we continue to follow the archaic system of management, cooking food, washing the crockery and serving food to the boarders.

Rather, the situation is deteriorating and unfortunately the victims are the students. There is certainly much to be learnt from the British example, where kitchen management as well as services and allied tasks are handled by middle-aged ladies, helped by younger colleagues in a satisfactory manner. Changes in the overall cleanliness, washing of crockery and other utensils, cooking under hygienic conditions and several other areas too are desired. Under the current system, an army of male servants is employed to do the jobs and their unhygienic ways of functioning and gross carelessness are too well known.

EXAM BLUES

My preparation for the M.Sc. degree was not proceeding satisfactorily. Partly it was due to the load of lectures and seminars I had to attend and partly because I had to write and rewrite quite a few assignments because of my lack of sufficient concentration. I was in the dark about what should be read and what not. Though I was quite aware of the broad contours of my courses, I did not know the specific areas that I should concentrate upon.

I wrote a number of assignments which I generally handed over to Vera Anstey, who took pains in correcting them. Later, I tried to improve them on the lines suggested.

I did not want to stay in London longer as it was a costly place. The Indian government had made only a partial contribution towards my stay, only up to the extent of paid leave I was entitled to while the rest of the period was treated as extraordinary leave without pay. So I was mainly dependent on the support from my father which I wanted to cut down to the minimum.

I had, therefore, filled in the application form for appearing in the exam at the first available opportunity, which was in May 1958, after a little less than two years at the LSE.

It would, of course, be heroic if I cleared the exam. However, I kept up my confidence and hoped that any lapse in the written answers would be compensated during the viva voce test that followed.

The exam was held as scheduled and I thought I had done reasonably well. However, that was not so. It was at the time of viva that I committed serious errors and failed to provide satisfactory replies to the volley of questions put to me by the committee of examiners. They made a negative recommendation in my case. But, they informed me that in case I wanted to avail myself of another chance I could do so during the next exam in December.

Highly dejected over the outcome and torn between conflicts, I ultimately decided, after consulting my colleagues, that I should avail myself of the second opportunity instead of going back to India without a degree.

I also considered that it was the lure of such a degree, which had propelled me to undertake such a costly risk. I had not only lost my salary that I would have otherwise earned during this period, but worse, I was a parasite on my family who had supported my London stay. Thus, there was no going back without a degree from the LSE.

Soon I wrote home about my failure, owning the entire responsibility. I also thought of undertaking some part-time job to support my extended stay. But on second thoughts, I found it would only be at the cost of my studies and preparation for the next exam.

Baujee expressed his full sympathy. He cheered me up and promptly asked me to extend my stay without worrying about the financial involvement.

Though it was a great relief and encouragement, inwardly it injured me for being a burden on him.

PRIVATE ACCOMMODATION

Soon my permitted stay in Passfield Hall came to an end. I decided to shift to a modest place where I could cut down on my cost of stay. I found a room on Holloway Road, no longer within walking distance of the LSE. I got a monthly pass issued for travel by the underground railway authorities at a concessional price.

Hitherto, I had avoided underground travel, as I would invariably walk to my school. But now after shifting to this suburb I became quite accustomed to such travel. It was very convenient, as within a short time one was able to cover a long distance. Since these trains ran to time and were so comfortable, I developed a great liking for them. It also improved my mobility, as I could travel to different destinations without facing any problem.

I am sure had these trains not been built in time, it would have been a tremendous, rather impossible job for the lakhs of commuters to travel to their different destinations. Further, when they were developed, it was easier to reach the underground area for laying down the track because of the thinness of population and plenty of open land all over. And then these tubes had a rich coverage, linking practically all destinations in the four corners of this megacity and one could reach any part conveniently.

In India, like our slow progress in other vital areas of services, we have utterly failed to develop this efficient mode of travel, at least in our mega cities, which are invariably crying for an efficient city transport system.

Delhi, the capital of our country, which is already nearing London's population, has a highly inefficient system of local transport, causing much inconvenience to lakhs of commuters who have to reach their workplace in the morning.

Why did the administration not think of developing an underground rail system at a time when Delhi was sparsely populated and it would have been easier to execute this project and that too on a low budget? While the country had given priority to creating public sector industries, where several hundred crores of rupees were spent in the crucial decades of 1950s and 1960s, little thought was given to the most important service areas, like power and transport. The negligence in developing an efficient city transport system today gives us the maximum headache. If resources had been spent in developing an underground transport system in Delhi in the 1950s itself, when it was so thinly populated, compared to the pressure on it during the last three decades, we would today not have been facing such a serious transport muddle.

The same holds equally true for other fast growing cities. Except, of course, Calcutta which has an underground railway system. But even after 30 years of effort, it just covers a part of the vast spread of this metropolis. The longer we delay this system, the more difficult it becomes to execute it.

Fortunately, a good beginning was made in this respect in Delhi recently, and it is hoped that the city does not face the problems of Calcutta.

My new place on Holloway Road cost me just about half of what I had been paying at Passfield Hall. Here there was no arrangement for breakfast and evening supper. I had to prepare my meals. Though initially I was not used to cooking, gradually, I coped with the job.

My landlady, who was a Polish national, was a very kind and sympathetic lady. She often shared her preparations with me. She also took care of cleaning and dusting my room as well as arranging things in order and even attended to other deficiencies that she noticed. Thus, she was a great help and a source of relief and my stay here was even more comfortable than in Passfield Hall.

There were two more tenants in the house. In the room next to mine lived a young Spanish lady who was working in an office. She was married and her husband was working in another city. The other tenant was a middle-aged English couple who stayed on the first floor, while the landlady and her husband stayed on the ground floor. The house had a small garden in the backyard, which was carefully tended to by the husband of the landlady. They did not have any child, nor did the English couple. Thus the place was very quiet, though it was close to the main road.

There was a single toilet-cum-wash place for us three tenants. To avoid inconvenience, I would get up in the early hours, much before the others woke up and even took my bath almost daily, managing it with a small supply of hot water that I would boil in my room. Thus, I did not find any difficulty in adjusting to the new surroundings even though some facilities so abundantly available at Passfield Hall, were conspicuously missing here.

There was hardly any contact with the other tenants except wishing each other when we met. Of course, it was so different with the landlady. She would visit my room, especially on weekends, and spend hours talking about her country Poland, which I had the opportunity to visit later. She told me how they had to leave it after the Germans occupied it and the several hardships they had to face before reaching here. On weekends, she would bake cakes or prepare sweets and share them with me. She would also bring some special dish she had prepared.

Her husband, though equally accommodating, had some difficulty in speaking English while his wife was fluent.

I began spending longer hours in the library and returned to my room quite late. I would prepare a hurried dinner of some packed vegetables. Sometimes when time permitted, I would prepare soup from a packet and drink it with a couple of bread pieces. This became my routine, though occasionally for a change I would cook rice and even try my hand at preparing *paronthas,* where, of course, I generally ended up a failure.

It was later when Rattan and his wife moved to London, after Rattan completed his degree and had a job here, that I could relish *paronthas* more frequently and even carry a few along with me to supplement my breakfast.

ANOTHER FUTILE ATTEMPT

In December, 1958, I sat for the exam again and hoped that this time, with better preparation, I would be able to make the grade and finally clear this hurdle before I returning to India. But even this attempt proved to be yet another futile exercise. The committee was still not satisfied with my performance in both the written test as well as the oral one. But they had added that in view of the great improvement over the previous attempt, they would recommend yet another chance for me after one year so that I had enough time to prepare for it.

This was again a big bolt from the blue. Frankly, I did not know how to face this second consecutive failure. The worst aspect was that it meant extended hardship for another full one year, though I had cut down my expenditure drastically and accumulated some bank balance meanwhile.

I had to not only collect sufficient courage to break this sad news to my family, but also deal with my office as my leave had expired and I did not know whether they would extend it further for a year. When I wrote to them they replied that this could be considered only if I produced documentary proof from my supervisor explaining the need for such a long leave. This was, of course, complied with and I was granted extraordinary leave without pay for another year, with a stricture that under no circumstances would the leave be further extended.

Thus, I was caught in a vicious circle from which it was difficult to escape. It was again the lure of a degree for which I had struggled hard that kept me going even as success eluded me.

What if the story repeated itself, I asked myself. But I found no answer to my predicament and no one else could help me either. It had frankly become a big gamble. Something I was unable to understand. The only thing I avoided was putting my mind under heavy pressure. Instead, I sat longer hours in the library daily, which provided me a great help in adjusting to my failure.

Also, at this late stage, it would be a tough job to find admission elsewhere. And even if I changed my course, I argued, what was the guarantee that the situation would improve. Also, it involved a heavy fresh expenditure. So, I reasoned that it was better to stay put here and take another chance.

Meanwhile, there was also the full support from *Baujee*. He counselled me affectionately and told me not to be disheartened by the repeated failures. He advised me not to neglect myself but eat well and live comfortably and not bother about the additional expenditure. Though I had decided to live on the minimum expenses, further support from him encouraged me immensely.

JOB IN A POST OFFICE

That Christmas I took up a temporary job in the local post office as a recruit to help in the clearance of the large Christmas mail. It was my first experience. I had to clear a small aptitude test in the shape of feeding the mail correctly into the various pigeonholes of the postal box. I enjoyed this experience of a fortnight or so and also earned liberal pocket money. It also provided me with the desirable change, after my failure in the exam.

What struck me here was the smooth functioning of the postal services, where every job was performed with efficiency and speed and hardly anything was kept pending for the following day. The triple-storey building presented a graceful look. It was well lighted and had clean surroundings. The central heating further added to the work efficiency. It was a pleasure to work in such an environment where nobody behaved like a boss. Officers would get matters settled with their juniors by visiting them.

Complete discipline was maintained and everybody was engrossed with his or her allotted job. Complaints were rarely voiced, while the multiple tasks were completed within the scheduled time and often even earlier. The mail—quite a bulk—was received, arranged and distributed in time and to the satisfaction of the public.

I watched this feature closely with absorbed interest during my brief stay and it got stuck in my memory. I also had the opportunity to deliver mail to the nearby addressees in the company of another temporary helper. And what a joy it was to work even as a delivery man where one was welcomed with a smile and wishes of good day and thanks were exchanged when the mail was delivered. The etiquette of the residents is worth remembering and emulating.

I have a word of special admiration for the cafe on the first floor of the post office. It was open even during the late hours and one could get hot snacks at highly subsidized rates and enjoy a cup of steaming hot tea. Its clean surroundings were also appreciable.

I avoided taking up a regular job, even a part-time one, for that would make a heavy demand on my time and affect my studies, especially writing tutorial assignments.

TRIP TO THE CONTINENT

During this period, I took a trip to the Continent. It was arranged by the Indian chapter of the YMCA. The main attraction was the first ever International Industrial Fair held in Brussels. For most of us, this was the first visit to the capital of Belgium as well as to an international fair.

Arrangements for our stay had been made on the fair premises. There was a big island of temporary tents at one corner, complete with all modern facilities. It was a remarkable way of accommodating such a large crowd of visitors where comfortable beds, clean toilets and shower baths had been set up and there was complete security for the baggage and other articles.

The exhibition area itself was so vast that it was impossible to cover even a part of it on foot. The tourist vehicles and other arrangements made for transport were insufficient to cope with the unexpected rush. Thus, we could only cover important segments during our three-day stay.

India was conspicuous by its absence. We realized when we had met a group of Russians who spotted us in the crowd and greeted us warmly but added ruefully about the absence of India in this fair.

The central attraction in the fair was the Atomium. It was a tall structure, rising to the sky. At its top was a revolving cafeteria, which could be reached by a lift. It presented a fascinating view of Brussels city. One could spot the scars of the German attack during the Second World War in and around the city.

Incidentally, even in London, which was heavily bombed during the war, tonnes of debris of the shattered buildings could be seen in Central London. In fact, there was a vast destroyed area close to the LSE which presented a very ugly sight. Such areas still existed, reminding one of the horrors that the city had endured during the height of the war.

After three days in Brussels, we spent an equal number of days in Paris, a mega city brimming with tourists. The city's social life would come alive with colourful fountains sparkling at night. Brightly lit areas held a special attraction for visitors who would throng them to satisfy their lust and curiosity.

In fact, tickets for the nightlife programmes were sold out much in advance, especially during the summer rush. A large crowd of American tourists, mostly in the middle age groups, who had booked seats for these entertainments, thronged the tourist sites.

We also tried our luck at a popular nightclub and were told that only limited seats were available in the standing space circle, which too was heavily crowded despite a very high tariff. The Americans had occupied the almost entire sitting space and were watching the nude show of young damsels from different countries.

We covered most of the tourist spots, including the famous palace of Louis XIV at Versailles. Spread over a vast area, it was rich in art and boasted of a collection of rare paintings. Several other items of historical importance were also on display. Though we devoted a long time to cover important segments of this place, a lot remained unexplored for it would take several days to do justice to this historical place.

The underground rail network in Paris was far more confusing than London and we often got lost. Unfortunately, a majority of French people whom we asked for guidance in English feigned ignorance of the language. This was indeed shocking, for we were under the impression that an average Frenchman spoke better English than us.

Later, we learnt that even those who knew English pretended to not know it, just to maintain the superiority of their language. I had also noticed that most of the Continental people who stayed in Passfield Hall during the summer holidays, often struggled hard with their English. It amused us a lot.

This visit to the Continent showed that English was rarely spoken after one crossed the English Channel, a distance of barely 30 miles.

In Paris, I was surprised to find small shops using gunny bags, like in India, for storing grocery items and even vegetables. Further, unlike London, where I rarely came across a beggar, I found quite a few beggars in Paris and some even sleeping in the open space close to the underground stations.

I noticed a similar phenomenon in Dublin where it was common to see small girls begging. Unlike Britain, Ireland suffered a high population pressure with a large number of members in an average family and little prospects of employment. Under such circumstances, one could well understand the pressure on a typical family. But what surprised me was that being next door to Britain why did this country not change the way Britain had? In fact, I found a large number of Irish citizens working in London and other places. On the contrary, one rarely came across an Englishman in Ireland.

Though our hotel in Paris was modest, we found it quite comfortable with excellent room service as well as breakfast and dinner. I noticed that visitors in the hotel rarely drank water. Instead, they found it more convenient to drink red wine brewed from grapes, which was quite inexpensive. We also tried this and indeed enjoyed the flavour.

With us on the trip was I.S. Johar, famous film actor and producer of those days. He was much fascinated by the French damsels. One morning, while I was sharing a breakfast table with a couple of them, he joined us and introduced himself to these young ladies, adding loudly that he was looking for young foreign faces for his forthcoming films. He handed to them his richly embossed visiting card, wanting to know whether they would be interested.

These girls were, of course, not interested in his talk and soon excusing themselves, left the table. I wore a mischievous smile, though Johar appeared to be least affected.

I recall another interesting incident that happened in Passfield Hall. Among the summer visitors during 1957or 1958 after the Commonwealth Games were held, one award-winning Indian player who had later became quite popular, also stayed here for some time. One morning at the breakfast table that he happened to share with me, on seeing young ladies from Italy sitting across the table with bare legs, he remarked in Punjabi, *"Inhan dian tanga bahria hee sonia hain* (their legs are very beautiful).

Another interesting trait about this guest was that he only wanted fruits, much to the amusement of the table attendant.

The point is, most of us Indians are attracted to the white skin, especially when it is exposed during the summer season. A lot of Indian students too get lost in winning the friendship of these ladies and feel excited and superior when they are in their company, especially during dances. During my hostel days, I observed that many Indian students would not only take the advantage of coming close to these women, but also try to make unethical advances, which were hardly encouraged by these ladies.

In Paris, I came across a young lady, who, when questioned about the naked display of young girls in their fun shows, remarked that hardly any local girl participated in these shows. Only girls from other countries performed in the shows. She added that the local population hardly cared for these shows and seldom visited them. The shows were mainly patronised by tourists alone, which enabled the country to earn rich revenue and there was nothing wrong about it.

I completely agreed with what she said and my estimation of their culture, morals and clean family life rose further. In fact, I also learnt that like in India, they took care of their elder family members.

FINAL DISAPPOINTMENT IN LSE

Much of this forced year-long stay in London was spent in the library, where I read a large number of articles. I tried to brush up my earlier pieces which were later published in academic journals, and this ultimately helped me shake off my desk job in the government and move to the university, which was my long-cherished goal.

There was hardly any perceptible change both in my performance as well as the rigid views formed by my supervisors. All this became apparent in the end result of my extended stay, when I faced yet another failure. This shook me completely and left me in a state of deep shock. I do not know how I bore the repeated jolts, especially the final one. Possibly, my inner strength and determination were largely responsible for it.

Vera Anstey gave me a big parting hand-written note, expressing her disappointment at my performance and advising me to concentrate on my present position in the government, where I would make better progress, than join an academic institution for which I was not cut out both by temperament as well as by my long stint in the civil service. She had written similar comments to the university in Chandigarh, where I was a candidate for the position of a lecturer. That was certainly sufficient enough to not consider me for this position.

VISIT TO DUBLIN

Before returning to India I made a trip to Dublin in Ireland to try for a possible admission for the M.Litt. degree, which I was told could be earned in one year exclusively on the basis of written dissertation. Further, the faculty members there were comparatively more sympathetic and cooperative. Though reluctant to stay longer and also worried about the financial problem as well as the possibility of losing my job in India, I still decided to visit Dublin.

This visit also provided me with a much-needed change, particularly when I was under so much mental pressure. I found that the Irish people were far more cooperative and helpful than the British and they had in particular a soft corner for India, for both the countries had struggled hard through difficult times to earn freedom. I learnt that Mahatma Gandhi was a popular name in that country. His preaching of non-violence to gain freedom was much appreciated by the local people.

After an overnight steamer journey, I landed in Dublin early the next morning. It was too early to disturb my friend. So, first I went to a restaurant across the road and ordered some snacks and tea. Here I also gathered details of the location of my friend's place as well as the bus I should take.

My friend was waiting for me and made me feel comfortable. He introduced me to the landlady, who was happy to welcome me. Soon I found that the Irish, like the Indians, believed in extended families, where a large number of members stayed together. And a majority of them being Roman Catholics, they did not believe in family planning. One came across families with a large number of children, which was so unlike the British.

Being Sunday, the day was spent in looking around the city. The next day, we went to the university and got in touch with the professor in charge of the programme who gave me a patient hearing. But he frankly told me that it was very late in seeking admission and also pointed out some technical and procedural hurdles. Thus, ultimately I decided against any further stay abroad and made up my mind to book the earliest available berth in a ship sailing to India.

Journey Homeward

This time I boarded a French boat, 'Laos', from Marseilles, after a day and night long journey from London through France. This ship was quite modest compared to the 'Strathmore' in which I had travelled from Bombay to London. The passengers were mostly Asian, with just a few Europeans. This was in a way a blessing, for we could be more friendly and social, unlike the earlier experience.

As we reached the other end of the Suez Canal, a large contingent of Gujarati families joined us in Eden. In fact, soon we were in a typical Asian environment and we almost felt as if we were moving in a bazaar of Bombay with a large number of ladies and children shouting at each other and children running around freely. In fact, a typical Middle East environment had started making its presence felt the moment we entered the Suez Canal, after the journey through the Mediterranean Sea.

We took a journey through the city of Alexandria in Egypt where we had stopped over. It had crowded bazaars, houses with open windows and loud music blaring. In fact, it made me feel that I was very much at home, after the stilted environment of London where these things were completely missing. They were two different worlds with their typical cultures, behaviour, food, and social life.

At Eden where foreign consumer goods were easily available and at much cheaper prices, though I wondered how that could be, most of us made purchases from a large number of street sellers who did brisk business. In fact, the bargains were struck so quickly that one hardly bothered to check how genuine these products were. Also, the clever sellers would soon vanish after collecting the money.

I bought one Parker fountain pen and a wristwatch of a well-known Swiss make and like my other friends, also felt that I had struck gold by paying only silvers. It was only when I presented these to my younger brother at home that I realized the items were fake and worthless.

After we entered the Arabian Sea from the Suez Canal, it took us just couple of days to reach Bombay. Though it was the month of January, the day temperature was pretty high and the atmosphere was hot with full blazing sun. Also the crowd that we had to cope with now appeared to affect the temperature.

BOMBAY SUNSHINE

At long last, after a full three and a quarter years in London, I was back home, the sweet home, amidst my people, enjoying the weather which wore such a striking contrast to the ruthlessly cold, rainy and smog-filled London.

I was reminded of the Parsi lady who worked in the India House library and was married to an Englishman. She used to often reminisce about her home in Bombay and dreamt of basking in the sun as she was totally fed up of London's uncompromising cold climate, as well as its people and environment.

I certainly felt the same when I reached the shores of India. It was back to the familiar environment and its people.

As I did not expect anyone to receive me here, I hastened to move out. Unlike in the West, there was no problem of carrying luggage with a horde of porters descending on the ship soon after it was anchored. I quickly managed my luggage and hired a taxi to the railway station, where I was fortunate to reach in time to catch a train leaving for Delhi soon.

The compartment was packed and some passengers had uncharitably blocked the sitting space by spreading themselves and no one wanted to enter into an argument with them. Here, two co-passengers I had met on the ship journey joined me. They were Italians—a young girl who spoke English well and her boyfriend. They had come for a sight-seeing tour of India as well as to take photographs, for the young man was a professional photographer. They were heading to the industrial fair being held at Pragati Maidan in Delhi.

So I had their company and learnt a lot about their country and family life. I also familiarized them about India and guided them about the tourist spots they should visit. They were already quite familiar with its geography and carried literature and notes to facilitate their movement.

The next evening the train reached Delhi. I learnt that a connecting train for Chandigarh was leaving around midnight. As there was sufficient time and I was burdened with a lot of luggage and felt unsafe to leave it on the platform, or even deposit it in the cloakroom, which was a cumbersome and time-consuming process, I decided to straightaway board the compartment that was to be attached to the Chandigarh train. I made sure about it from the porters as well as passengers who were also travelling to Chandigarh. It, was then in the yard and though pitch dark, I made myself comfortable after arranging my luggage with the help of a porter and heaved a sigh of relief.

NON-STOP TO CHANDIGARH

After the strenuous and non-stop journey from Bombay, my badly aching limbs got some relief.

It was quite early the next morning when the train reached Chandigarh, a small railway station, ill-lit and with just a few porters on the platform. I hired a *rickshaw* to my place which was at a distance of about 15 km. There was a chill in the early morning air, but nothing compared even to London's day temperature. Here the air was fresh and crisp and I was quite happy to breathe in it after three years.

Soon clear twilight broke on the eastern horizon, surrounding the nearby Shivalik hills, and made a fascinating presence. It was daylight and one could hear the chirping of birds from the surrounding trees. As the *rickshaw* rolled cautiously on the narrow road without any light, I could not spot any human being for over a good distance. The city was just waking up. It would take quite sometime before it took its shape and came to be recognized as one of the top destinations, not only in this country, even globally.

As I neared my home in Sector 3, hidden behind thick bushes and trees, I could spot some life—early morning walkers, milk vendors, labourers and others. I sprung a big surprise on my family members when I rang the doorbell. They were still sleeping.

I enjoyed home-cooked food, my favourite vegetables and dal fried in *desi ghee* and crisp *chapattis*. Also, I had a good time savouring all sorts of *paronthas*—my favourite breakfast that I had missed sorely all these years.

ACADEMIC AND OFFICIAL ROOTS

I often visited the Panjab University campus, which was gradually taking its shape. Of course, it was the Department of Economics, which was my main attraction, and it had just shifted from its camp building in Hoshiarpur, where a large number of other university departments were located in the Government College.

I participated in the programmes of the department, particularly in their weekly seminars and was happy to find that economic development was the main topic of discussion. I was offered the post of research assistant, which was an ad hoc position. However, I did not accept it. I preferred to join my office in Calcutta, where I held a permanent position.

KNOCKING AT PLACES

However, before joining my parent office in Calcutta as a last resort, I decided to make a hectic visit to the economic wings of Central Government offices, Planning Commission and research institutes in Delhi, for greener pastures, during my couple of weeks' leave that was still to my credit. I met those who mattered. All this, however, proved a futile exercise. None was prepared to take me seriously unless I had the LSE degree, though some did shed crocodile tears on my sad experience, which I least liked or cared for.

10

Back to Calcutta

As my leave was drawing to an end, I boarded the train to Calcutta and looked forward to meeting my old colleagues, who were also happy to have me in their midst after a gap of more than eight years. There had hardly been any change here except that it had lost its former independent identity and was now a wing of the CSO. As I settled down, my colleagues would consult me on several matters, as they did earlier, and requested me to take the lead in the office cultural and recreational activity. I was its president for a number of years before leaving Calcutta and also of the Office Union which too had started functioning before my leaving Calcutta.

Just a few days later, there was a call for an all-India strike by Central government employees for fulfilling a charter of their demands. To ascertain that our office did not lag in this important matter, its employees had with one voice, requested me to take the lead, though frankly I did not like to get involved in trouble.

But pressure was put on me from different quarters, which I found difficult to ignore. So a meeting was held under my chairmanship and a unanimous resolution was passed to absent ourselves en mass on the day of the strike. Leaders from other local organizations were also present. In my speech I lent full support to the cause and exhorted the members to be unanimous in observing *hartal* (strike,).

On the day of the *hartal*, I sat in the library of Calcutta University and wrote an article on "Income, output and employment in the Third Plan" as this plan was being discussed that time. I drafted a good part of this writing and was happy it had come up well. Later, it was published in an important weekly journal, 'Commerce'. It then was a highly respected journal on current economic and financial matters.

This is how I determined to turn my unsuccessful sojourn in London to a success, through my writings, and ultimately make an exit from government service to an academic career. Before I left London, people would often ask how I had found my stay abroad and what I proposed to do after returning to India. Without hesitation I would answer that it had been a highly rewarding visit where I had got several new ideas, which would help to shape my career in India.

This is what I found myself doing in the next three years—interestingly a period equivalent to that I had spent at the LSE. My mind was totally engrossed in finalizing drafts of the papers written earlier, which I tried to bring to the standard of publication in serious journals.

PREPARING FOR CHANGE

My initial foundation for this had interestingly been laid in the library of Calcutta University, thanks to the strike, which provided me an opportunity for this. I was soon lost in the academic world. I reworked on my old writings, with much labour and thought and got them accepted for publication in the country's reputed academic journals. Gradually, I made an encouraging progress.

Fortunately, my office work did not interfere with my research work. Rather, being of a technical nature, mainly addressed to the compilation and study of India's large industries, it provided me an opportunity for further research. Soon I was able to produce some first rate papers based on the information available on several aspects of the growth of Indian industries and got them published.

I sent the reprints of some of the published papers to my supervisor, A.D. Knox, who had, meanwhile, shifted from the LSE to the World Bank. He was quite pleased to read them and wrote back to say that I was doing very well. I was happy that at long last I had succeeded in changing his opinion about me.

Soon, I rented a room close to the National Library, the biggest library in this country housed in a spacious building, which at one time was the residence of India's Governor-General with several acres of grassy area. It was a nice place for leisurely walks as well as for quiet thinking. I spent my spare time in a quiet corner of this library from where I could access journals and books of my interest easily. It provided a nice view of flowers and verdant lawns which I found very inspiring.

Now I began to spend late evenings as well as holidays in this library and concentrate more effectively on my work. I also enjoyed my favourite snacks of Bengali dishes in a nearby restaurant, which made my late sittings easier.

BRIDE HUNTING

I was around 39 when I started hunting for a bride, as I did not want to end a bachelor. If I postponed beyond this date, I would certainly become a life-long bachelor. Already I was late for a suitable match as per my concept of marrying a young and beautiful belle.

This was exactly what I looked for when I was younger but did not honour any proposal for an arranged marriage, though quite a few of them came from high and well-settled families and the girls happened to be beautiful, slim and graceful. But I did not yield. The idea of an arranged marriage did not go with my thinking. Perhaps if I had had an opportunity for a love marriage where I could mix up with my partner and know her well, I might have yielded. But that unfortunately did not happen. It was to avoid chronic bachelorhood that I agreed to an arranged marriage.

I started a serious hunt for my bride in 1962 after the marriage of my younger brother.

Interestingly, around a dozen years had lapsed since my unsuccessful love affair in Simla, and I again became so concerned about my marriage. Meanwhile, I had stayed for a good part in Calcutta, Delhi and London. I had not had another adventure into the domain of love life. Perhaps it was due to my mature age.

Even in London, where I had stayed for over three years and there were a good many opportunities, I did not indulge in such activity. Possibly I was not as sure of a British girl or any other foreign national as I was of our own women who had a different concept of life and were faithful, homely, pliable and less troublesome. Also, age certainly brings out a different outlook on life, when practicality takes precedence over romance.

It was a tough task to find a dream girl at this age, when one is written off from the young brides' market and is labeled as fit for marriage to a senior lady. I faced this in my quest too. I visited quite a few possible partners, wherever suggested. It was an interesting experience and I enjoyed it. But wherever I would give my assent for marriage, it would not work-out for some reason or the other. Of course, the age factor was the most disturbing. Also, not holding an alluring job went against me and I was summarily rejected.

An interesting incident occurred when I visited a prospective family in Delhi. The father of the girl was the son of our family physician in Lahore and was possibly a doctor himself. His daughter was young, healthy and attractive but tall. So the main concern of the family was the height of the future groom, who they felt should be a little taller than the girl, otherwise they would make an awkward couple. I called on them to see the girl. I talked to her and enjoyed snacks and cold drinks with her (it was summer season). Later, her father requested me to stand against the wall and carefully measured my height. I do not know whether he expressed any regret for this unusual stop. That was left for me to judge after I had parted.

At another place in Delhi, I was taken to the official flat of a lady doctor by my relative. I was quite impressed by the location, size and maintenance of the flat in the posh area of this city. But all my dreams were crushed when I came face to face with the lady doctor who soon got into *gup-shup* with the ladies who had accompanied me. Obviously, she was close to them and was looking for a partner who could be roped in through her professional and living affluence. At least, I could not be.

Her younger sister was sitting nearby, busy with some repair work of her dress. She was an airhostess and had quite an impressive personality. She presented a big contrast to her elder sister. While there, most of the time I was thinking of her and not her elder sister.

We left after tea. It was during the return journey that my opinion was sought about marrying her. I could hardly agree. I wished they had asked about her younger sister where I would have agreed instantly. But then I am sure she would have outrightly rejected me. So this is the tragedy of life.

There was a proposal even in Chandigarh. The lady was a teacher in a school and quite attractive. She did appeal to me and I was prepared to accept her. But both my age and job did not appeal to her as she preferred a professionally qualified husband.

I had also rushed to Simla where I had been again suggested a schoolteacher. But that visit too proved futile and I returned, promising myself not to indulge any more in this exercise of bride hunting.

NATURE'S HELP

However, simultaneously Nature had been working in my favour. A good family friend was settled in Ropar (close to Chandigarh). He was a freedom fighter and reputed lawyer. He was looking for a match for his sister-in-law's daughter settled in Lucknow and knew about me. In fact, during the marriage of my brother in 1962, he and his wife had visited Chandigarh with the specific purpose of having a close look at me.

They sat in the family drawing room along with me and enquired about my profession and views on marriage. They were quite satisfied and wrote to Lucknow about my programme of dropping there for a day or so in the house of my uncle (younger brother of my father). They suggested that this opportunity should not be missed, and I should be allowed to see the proposed bride before I left for Calcutta to join my job.

In Lucknow, they came in the forenoon to meet my uncle and me and fixed a convenient time for a meeting with the girl in a hotel close to the place where we stayed.

We got ready for the appointment in the hotel. My uncle and a cousin accompanied me. My cousin was quite enthusiastic to meet his future *bhabi* (sister-in-law) and promised to provide all possible details about her. At the meeting, my cousin was more vociferous while I was reserved and spoke little. We later moved to a nearby park to have a closer look at each other.

When we returned home my uncle wanted my opinion about this match. As far as he was concerned everything was fine.

However, I kept mum and insisted on another meeting before I left for Calcutta by the afternoon train. Uncle thus got another meeting arranged in the forenoon when we all met at a nearby place. Here we could have a close look at each other. We both appeared to be satisfied. So after this short meeting, I gave my approval of the match to my uncle and he conveyed this message to Chandigarh immediately.

A NEW TWIST

However, after I reached Calcutta pressure was put on me for marriage with another girl who stayed close to my uncle's house and her mother and my aunt were friends. She had somehow come to know that I was yet not married and was looking for a bride. In fact, I knew the girl well. She was quite smart and fair-skinned with an impressive personality. Already she was in my mind, though I was not sure about the response from her family.

This time strangely the offer had come from their side and the mother of the girl was pressing my aunt hard to get this match fixed. I had received a letter to this effect, I don't remember whether it was written by my uncle or cousin on behalf of my aunt. I was thus in a double mind now. Had the proposal come earlier, I would have most probably accepted this match. Thus, torn between conflicts, I could not come to any final decision.

The gentleman who had taken the initiative for negotiating my Lucknow match was quite upset when I did not reply to his letter, wherein he had mentioned how upset Baujee was when he learnt of another proposal, as the matter had been already settled. He strongly emphasized that once having committed, one should not go back on one's word.

Thus I finally made up my mind, and wrote back that I would stick to my earlier decision. And that settled the matter.

Then followed a small period of courtship, when I received quite a few long letters from my fiancee Santosh written in chaste Hindi and in beautiful handwriting, often camouflaged in romantic poetry. She had to take permission from her elders before she entered into correspondence with me, a practice usually followed by the middle class families during those days. Invariably, I replied in English, as I was poor in writing in Hindi.

However, I wrote in simple English, which she was able to follow. It was after marriage that she developed a fairly good command over English and had no hesitation in conversing in this language even with strangers. Thus, she had the inclination to pick up new languages. She was already well versed in Bengali, which was also her optional paper in college. Since there were quite a few Bengalis in her neighbourhood, she picked up fluency in spoken Bengali. This facility later came to her great help when, while staying in Calcutta we faced domestic helpers who spoke only Bengali. In fact, just before marriage she was also appearing in her graduation degree exam.

TYING THE NUPTIAL KNOT

We got married on May 10, 1963. The marriage was performed in Chandigarh, where my family had settled down. There was a big gathering of a number of relatives.

I remember the excitement I felt when at midnight after the ceremony we were driven back to our house to consummate our marriage in a room specially prepared for this purpose. When we reached there, some ceremonies were performed, welcoming the bride to her new life. Soon we were virtually pushed to the special room by my sisters-in-law.

There were three of them and it was Sudershan who was most active and vocal. She had also put her ears to the closed door to listen to our conversation, and conscious about this, we spoke in a low volume, almost a whisper. I wonder how much they could hear us. Anyway in the excitement of the first *suhag* (marriage) night, I was little bothered about what went around. I was determined to enjoy this time to the utmost.

It was after the sunny rays had penetrated into the room that I woke up in the morning. There had already been repeated knocks at the door. My wife Santosh, had woken up, while it took me quite some time to get ready. Meanwhile, she had opened the door and soon ladies and children trooped in a highly jovial mood. They mobbed me with several pleasant and unpleasant queries, which I found difficult to attend to. Here I must admit it was Santosh who came to my rescue and saved me from several awkward situations.

ANOTHER MARRIAGE

That day there was another wedding in the family. This time it was my younger brother, Amrit, who was getting married in the evening. The ladies soon left and got busy with the next marriage.

Soon we also got ready to see my wife's relatives who had been housed in a place not far from ours. We were told that it was unusually cold that night, most unexpected for the month of May. Despite the blankets, some of them were not feeling well.

They were packing to return to their homes. We bade them goodbye. A few very close family members called on Baujee to express their full satisfaction about the arrangements made for the marriage and that evening they also wished my younger brother's marriage a success and wished the couple a happy life.

Since Amrit's in-laws stayed in Chandigarh itself, it was far easier for them to arrange the marriage, while it was so different in the case of my in-laws who had came all the way from Lucknow.

That night we had to vacate the room in favour of my younger brother who had to consummate his marriage now. With the arrival of the new bride, Santosh felt somewhat neglected, as did I. But we did not have much to feel sorry for, since we had already had the taste of the first nuptial night. That night we slept in the open verandah and prepared ourselves for the quick honeymoon in the nearby hills, as we also planned to visit Delhi and Lucknow before returning to Calcutta.

We spent a short time in Kasauli and Chail hill stations. Most of the time we were outdoors, almost chasing each other on the beautiful hills, and preferring to visit lonely roads and woods. Both of us had unbound energy and we must have walked miles and miles, unmindful of several slopes.

Every time we returned to the hotel, our appetite would be whetted and we enjoyed hot soups and food which were served in the room. I remember how almost at a stretch we walked to Sanawar the next day. The famous public school here was closed that day, but we were able to visit most of its area and enjoyed its wonderful surroundings. We hoped to visit it again, perhaps this time for the admission of our son, yet to be born. We learnt there was a long waiting list for admissions and parents sought berths in the school even for their yet unborn children. There was a virtual craze with many parents to get their sons educated here.

We had one very interesting experience around here. While we were returning, we walked into a place managed by the British/American Charity Association, which was looking after orphaned infants. They were the Tibetan children whose parents were either killed during the takeover of Tibet by the Chinese or who had been abandoned by their parents who were unable to take care of them.

The moment we entered the place, Santosh was virtually mobbed by a number of chubby children from all directions and she tenderly picked up as many as she could manage, though every child wanted to be fondled.

It was a pathetic sight and showed that the children longed for the love of their parents. Of course, we could not afford to spend much time here, as we had a long distance to cover before we reached our hotel. Thus reluctantly, we bid good bye to the children and missionaries engaged in such a noble cause.

VISIT TO CHAIL

The next day we moved to Chail and entered a hotel, without prior reservation. Even modest hotels were not to be found here those days. The porter at the bus stand carrying our luggage guided us to a government rest house. The chowkidar there expressed his helplessness to accommodate us. He, however, did not disappoint us. He made available to us a modest accommodation attached to the rest house, where he made arrangements for a comfortable bed, hot water and other facilities.

We agreed to it, as we had to just spend a day or so and most of the time we would be on the move, exploring that lovely place. That guest house presented a breath-taking view under enchanting surroundings with soothing sunshine.

We visited the bazaar, where we had a late lunch, and then walked around its surroundings going as far as we could. Indeed, we discovered that we had covered a good part of the area and should not go further as it had become dusky. So we hastened back to our modest honeymoon villa. Soon it got quite cold but with plenty of warmth stored in us we moved still faster.

The next afternoon we planned to return by the last bus which left around midday. Before this we climbed up to the highest cricket ground of the world. Here we spent quite some time looking down at the surrounding hills and valleys on the four sides. It was the most enchanting scene where one could never feel tired of lingering for hours. We, however, could not take this liberty, as we did not want to miss the bus.

This way, within the short time at our disposal, we enjoyed the maximum and it turned out to be a memorable visit, before returning to the hot and sultry atmosphere of Calcutta.

CALCUTTA LIFE

In Calcutta we occupied a two-room accommodation in an old building in the crowded Bhowanipore area. While we had a makeshift kitchen arrangement, we were denied certain independent facilities. We had to share the toilet and wash facilities with two more families who stayed on the same floor. The toilet was old-fashioned without the flush facility. In fact, there was no water tap on the first floor that we occupied. It had to be fetched from the ground floor from a common tap, which was shared by a couple of more families.

Thus, one can imagine the pressure on this single tap with around a dozen members sharing it. Yet, it was managed well with the cooperation of families. We woke up early to store water for the day when the water pressure was also at the maximum.

For domestic help, we had engaged a Bengali lady who did not speak Hindi. Fortunately, Santosh was quite conversant with this language. She spoke excellent Bengali, much to the pleasure of our maid who would often tease my wife for marrying a Punjabi, little knowing that she too was a Punjabi.

During the evenings, I would accompany Santosh to the vegetable market, which was spread over a vast covered area and not far from our place. Here we would purchase our needs leisurely. While my wife spoke good Bengali and could strike quite a few favourable bargains with the sellers, I found that with my speaking in Hindi, they would invariably quote higher prices.

There was a rich choice of vegetables and fruits and, of course, fish, which we did not eat. We came across a number of new exotic vegetables, which we would try and explore their taste and flavour. Some of them became our favourites later and we missed them when we left Calcutta. Thus, visits to this market were not devoid of novel experiences and I took pleasure in them, especially after a busy day.

It was surprising that despite staying in these surroundings, which formed a part of the old 19th century world without modern facilities, we did not have any cause to grumble. Rather, our stay was quite enjoyable and refreshing and we found the people were extremely warm-hearted and invited us to their local festivals. We mixed freely with our neighbours, which was indeed comforting for Santosh as she could share her time and problems with the young ladies, while I was away to the office and even took the liberty of staying a little late. My visits to the National Library were fewer now. Fortunately, our place was also not far from the library.

Interestingly, throughout our stay here we exclusively depended on the municipal water supply for drinking, cooking and all our domestic needs. It was never filtered or boiled to destroy possible germs, in spite of the fact that we often read news in the press about living and dead insects and even small snakes being found in the tap water in our area. This area was also notorious for its highly unsanitary streets and backyards. Yet, we survived and hardly faced any trouble. Probably, our system had got acclimatized to the municipal tap water.

In winters, our area would get wrapped in a thick blanket of smoke, much akin to the London smog. But it was far more dangerous for it was mainly the deadly smoke from steam coal being burnt by a large number of households. Later, with the shift to kerosene and gas, the situation improved.

In early 1964, Santosh started complaining about giddiness and often vomited. She was in the family way and I had to cut down my late sittings in the office and return home early. Thankfully, the ladies in the neighbourhood took good care of her in my absence. Also, the Bengali maid was of great help. She purchased our daily needs and thus, lessened my burden, particularly when my wife knew I was not used to visiting the market alone with a shopping bag.

As she entered the advanced stage of pregnancy, she needed greater care and often I had to spend sleepless nights, which began to tell on my health. Ultimately, this problem was resolved as my mother-in-law came to take care of her.

RECOGNITION FOR WORK

Meanwhile, an interesting thing had happened. After my marriage I had hardly made any tangible progress in my academic life. It all rested on my earlier publications of well-considered papers, which, as I have mentioned, had also received a word of warm appreciation from a person like A.D. Knox, my guide at the LSE who had failed me thrice. He was indeed a hard nut to crack and one found it difficult to meet with his expectations.

My work was also recognized in other quarters. I also earned a word of praise from the Head of the Department of Economics at Panjab University, Chandigarh, where I was earlier a candidate for the post of lecturer in 1959. However, it had fizzled out later in the light of negative recommendations by my supervisor who had also advised me to concentrate on a non-academic job where I would do better.

I was soon to prove my supervisor wrong, when in 1964 my name was suggested to the Planning Commission for a top post in the Regional Transport Survey being conducted by the Panjab University's Department of Economics. The Head of Department who had read my work did not hesitate to accept the proposal. This was the start of my break from civil service to the university, albeit through a project when I was sent on deputation to the university for a year.

Initially I hesitated to take up the offer, for I was not quite sure how I would fit into the new environment. Of course, my failure at the LSE was the main reason for my doubt. But following a discussion with a close friend, I realized that I should not miss the opportunity to fulfil my dream of an academic career. Also the fact that I was going to Chandigarh, my hometown, where my father at that time was in poor health, strengthened my resolve.

This meant a complete shifting of the house and items collected with great care over the last one year of marriage, had to be disposed of. Further, in the absence of Santosh, who had gone to Lucknow with her mother to deliver the baby, I gave away these goods at whatever price I was offered, which meant a considerable loss. It spoiled my wife's mood after she returned with our newborn son Rajeev.

I received urgent communication from the Department of Economics to join my new position at the earliest as work was suffering. The long journey to Chandigarh in the cold weather of December, especially with the newborn baby, was tough. However, we were spared much of this hardship again when my mother-in-law and brother-in-law agreed to accompany us right up to Chandigarh.

My first child, a son, was born early October 1964 and I had to join my new job early December. My wife and our baby joined me in Calcutta only a few days before our departure for Chandigarh. We had a difficult time with the infant, who could not be properly looked after under the circumstances when we were busy packing and the whole house was completely upset. Also, by this time most items of furniture had been disposed of and the house looked practically bare. We had to sleep on the floor, which was not considered safe in that old house when often unsuspecting creatures could crawl up through the rain pipe. In fact, Santosh was also quite weak in her post-delivery state and needed more time and care to be her normal self.

Rajeev too demanded a lot of attention and care. Here again, thanks to the neighbours, who looked after Rajeev and saw to it that he was kept in good mood, Santosh could concentrate on our move to Chandigarh.

Both my mother-in-law and brother-in-law had come when we were ready to leave. I was greatly moved to see the ladies in the neighbourhood and young children virtually crying at our departure, especially of my wife with whom they had developed a deep affection and attachment within a short period.

END OF STAY IN CALCUTTA

Thus ended my nearly five-year stay in Calcutta, which proved to be quite fruitful, particularly after the over three years of disillusionment with the much-hyped visit to London. In Calcutta, I was able to work up my way to an academic career in a determined manner. In this endeavour, my work in London was a good starting point. I had thus lived up to my promise of a safe passage to an alternative job in a university. It looked that I was close to it.

I had also at long last got married and broken my prolonged bachelorhood. Now I had support from my strong-willed and intelligent wife, who was a great help to me.

This also reminds me of my meeting a palmist who was a senior officer in the Government of India and a colleague of my close friend. Both of them had visited Calcutta during the early 1960s. My friend had asked him to study my hand. Though an amateur palmist, he was known for making accurate predictions and even some high-ups in the government as well as in politics, would consult him frequently.

He took a measurement of the lines on my right palm and said he would comment the next day after a close study. Accordingly, I visited him the next day and wanted straight answers to my queries, which I had already posed.

He revealed some very interesting and extraordinary things. He had predicted my early marriage, which had somehow evaded my attention so far. And to my great surprise, he also foresaw a change in my career in the not-too-distant future. And the most interesting thing he had read was that I would make higher progress in life after my retirement.

Though I did not give much credence to what he had said, later as time passed I noticed that all his forecasts had come true. I do not know whether one should have faith in the science of palmistry. But the way the situation turned out in my case, I could hardly doubt it veracity.

Life in Chandigarh

Baujee was in frail health, after suffering a paralytic attack. He was quite pleased to see us by his side and especially the new grandchild.

I had a tough job in handling the transport project for which I had been especially recruited and brought all the way from Calcutta. Rangnekar, Head of the Department of Economics, was its honorary director and I had to assist him in this survey. An inter-departmental team of three teachers of the university, including Rangnekar, constituted this group and managed the project. Thus decisions were taken jointly, within the guidelines laid down by the Planning Commission, though the job of project implementation, execution of field work, recruitment of field staff and day-to-day matters was left entirely to Rangnekar and the latter to a large extent depended on me for this job.

Managing the field surveys spread over a vast territory of North-West India, which included Punjab (including the present Haryana and a part of Himachal Pradesh), Delhi and surrounding areas, entailed a lot of hard work.

A large geographical canvas was covered at selected traffic points, where round-the-clock surveys were conducted by intercepting all goods carriers and subjecting them to the gruelling task of answering a large number of questions posed by a team of our field investigators.

The field job meant my being away from Chandigarh quite frequently. Visits to most of the places of survey were held with the cooperation of the public works and transport departments.

MULTIPLE PROBLEMS

I had grossly underestimated how hectic my new job would be at the time of leaving Calcutta. Further, with the accommodation problem in our family house, where already the families of four of my brothers were staying, our worries multiplied. Santosh had to virtually squeeze in a corner of the drawing room with the baby. Though the house was quite spacious, it did not have enough covered space for five families, besides Baujee.

To compound the problem, it was the first winter of Rajeev, barely a couple of months old, who often ran into health problems, which again Santosh had to take care of for most of the time. Even when I returned to Chandigarh after a strenuous time in the field, I had to spend long hours in the department for sorting out several aspects of the next phase of the survey as well as instruct the data tabulators about the tables to be generated from our field record for the final report.

While we had recruited field investigators, most of them were raw and untrained and had to be briefed and guided about the field work. All this was time-consuming and demanded long hours in the department. Further, the director of the programme was a hard task master and would often enter into lengthy discussions and hold meetings lasting till late evenings.

Thus, by the time I returned home it used to be pitch dark and I would be dead tired and needed complete rest, which unfortunately was just not possible in the crowded drawing-room atmosphere, where other family members were having *gup-shup*. Also, this place was devoid of any privacy. In those difficult days I was often reminded of the line scribbled boldly in a Ramakrishna charitable homeopathy dispensary near our house in Lahore, which read: 'This will also pass.' Of course, the reference was that the ailment one was suffering from would soon end, and the person would once again enjoy good health. This aptly applied to my plight during those days and recalling it provided a great relief.

A further hardship that I had to face was depending on a bicycle, which was the most common mode of transport during those days, for travel to the university early morning and returning home late. Quite a good distance had to be covered in the freezing temperature of winter. Especially my return journey would be miserable as by then I was tired and had little energy to cycle back home on roads which were narrow, poorly lit and not well maintained. Chandigarh was just coming up in the 1960s and most of its area was uninhabited.

Soon, the major survey work of this project was over with a mind-boggling number of schedules having piled up in the office. Now a fresh team of data processors was recruited to help process these schedules and bring out meaningful results. This again meant my further involvement, when I had to look into a number of aspects of this data for the purpose of providing the final report to the Planning Commission on the lines they wanted. Here I often ran into difficulty with the director where we found it hard to agree to a common programme.

He had his own ideas which I found difficult to accept. Often, these differences were ironed out when his programme was found difficult to execute. A sort of compromise was drawn, but not before much time was needlessly wasted.

To escape the messy environment in the house, where there was no privacy and no room for rest, I preferred to stay longer in the department. This also helped expedite the survey work.

LONG-CHERISHED GOAL MET

Within the next couple of months, a very desirable development seemed to be on its way. There were vacancies of faculty members in the department and my name had been included in it, after consulting me. Thus at long last, there were signs of fulfillment of my cherished dream and I wanted to prove to my guide at the LSE how wrong she was in writing me off from the teaching job in the university.

Within the next few days, a list of the candidates for interview had been finalized and my name figured among them. This ultimately ended in a happy outcome, when I was selected and asked to join my post soon.

I was asked to start lecturing to MA (previous) pupils. While I felt elated at this development, it imposed on me a high responsibility, as I had to do the teaching work along with the project work, which was now at its advanced stage.

Further, I had been out of touch with the academic life for a long time and had to brush up my knowledge before delivering lectures on areas assigned to me. This meant burning the midnight oil and further missing much of my already disturbed sleep.

Indeed, it was a chilling task, though there was one redeeming feature. We had, meanwhile, shifted from the main family drawing room and settled in the small annexe of the house, which though lacking in basic facilities and in need of repairs, was still a great relief. I had a small room where I could plan my work according to my needs and most importantly, I could relax undisturbed.

Santosh, appreciating my added responsibility, single-handedly took good care of Rajeev and much of the household work. Thus, due to her care and cooperation, much of my tension and mental load was diffused. She too was under high pressure since she had not only to manage the infant, but also see that this annexe became more livable, and she did most of the renovation herself.

Thus, I was able to make a tolerable beginning in my teaching career where I needed more time to brush up my knowledge to come up to the expectations of intelligent students.

SNAGS IN APPOINTMENT

In my zeal for the university teaching assignment, for which a regular appointment letter too had been issued, I had completely overlooked the fact that I was on deputation from the government and could change my job only after obtaining due permission from the government. This aspect somehow had been overlooked by the university also, when they treated my appointment as a fresh one.

Soon as my deputation period of one year drew to a close, my department in Calcutta wrote a letter to the Vice-Chancellor seeking my return where, meanwhile, they had also promoted me to a higher position. A telegram followed soon, stating a final date of my joining the office in Calcutta.

It created a peculiar situation. If I had to stay in the university, I would have to break all links with the government, which also meant losing the new position offered by the government as well as my pension benefits, when I had already put in some 16 years of service. In fact, my wife had never compromised with my leaving Calcutta and joining the university even on deputation. She was quite content and happy with the life in that city and further did not want me to lose the benefit of the long service already rendered, which would be counted for pension, whereas the same was not the case with the university job. In fact, there was no pension here.

TORN BETWEEN CONFLICTS

Thus, I was torn between conflicts and ultimately decided to go back to Calcutta and join my new position. But the major hurdle remained yet unresolved—how could I have joined a regular position in the university without my first seeking permission from my parent department? And in this respect, the university had written that the matter had to be resolved between my department and me.

In fact, not satisfied with my version, the Planning Commission had written a strong letter to the Vice-Chancellor to explain about these irregularities committed, knowing well that I had been sent on deputation. Ultimately, I had to shoulder the entire burden of this unpleasant development and tender a written apology to the Planning Commission as well as to the CSO, my employer. In the end, though the matter was resolved happily, I could not go back to Calcutta, as in the meantime the government had accepted my resignation.

Thus, it was a matter of chance that under these unusual circumstances, I stayed on in the university and spent the next 18 years here before my retirement in 1984.

How it all happened is quite difficult to explain, particularly when I had finally decided to quit my job and go back to Calcutta. Perhaps it was the intervention of Nature or some such invisible power, which did not want me to give up the teaching opportunity for which I had been waiting anxiously for the past over eight years. First, I had spent three years at the LSE, and then in the subsequent five years at Calcutta, I had made frantic efforts to rebuild myself for winning an academic position after suffering failure at the LSE. This was despite the allurement of a higher position in the government as well as pension benefits.

Thus, inscrutable are the ways of Nature which intervenes to force us to follow the much-cherished goal even when entrapped in attractive options.

Had I stayed on in the government job, I would have at the most retired as a middle range officer at 58, without much advancement in career and possibly been little known outside that small circle of friends and colleagues. Also, I would have gained little academically or hardly been invited to national and global programmes, thus not extending my horizons far and wide as I was destined to do later. It was indeed a positive and long-term gain, which could not have been earned on a government job where there were gross limitations, unlike in an academic career.

My second year in the department was a great improvement. I was able to achieve a firm grasp over my lectures, which were delivered with greater force and clarity and gained more confidence of the students who also took a greater interest now.

That year, the work load too had also suddenly risen with the introduction of the additional programme of Honours School in Economics in the department, almost parallel to the LSE programme. Also, this department was among the very few of its kind in the country. This course used the new tools in economics, which called for a specialized knowledge as well as expertise to deliver lectures to a select number of students.

Apart from these new teaching programmes, the department had also introduced an ambitious programme of regular tutorials in both MA streams. Under such teaching and tutorial system, the functioning of the department was extended to the whole afternoon which now became as busy as the morning.

All this added a heavy burden on each faculty member since further recruitment of teachers had to wait.

Under these circumstances, I could not give sufficient attention to the transport project work. In fact, to cope with it I would extend my late sittings in the department and even wake up quite early to clear the backlog.

MANMOHAN, A UNIQUE PERSON

In the context of surveys, I must make a special mention of

my acquaintance with the unique and talented Manmohan Singh, who rose to such prestigious positions as the Governor of the Reserve bank of India and Finance Minister of the country before being handpicked by Sonia Gandhi for the highest office of the Prime Minister.

In 1966, soon after the Indo-Pak war, Dr. Manmohan Singh, who was then a professor in economics at Panjab University, was commissioned by the Punjab government to make an on-the-spot assessment of the loss suffered by the industry in the border districts and give suggestions about the help that should be rendered. Manmohan took me along with him for the tour.

He reached my residence at the appointed time and, in fact, had to wait in the verandah of our house as I took little longer to get ready. We sat in the rear seats of the car and during the journey discussed several issues pertaining to planning and Punjab economy. He was quick-witted and we often had a lively debate. He would doze off during the journey and seemed to enjoy these occasional breaks.

We visited Batala which was a foundry business centre with a large number engineering units. Without wasting time, Manmohan went straight to the business and acquainted himself with the traders' problems. Copious notes were taken.

Next we moved to Amritsar where again a large number of local businessmen were waiting for us. Manmohan first of all expressed his regret for keeping them waiting. The next morning we went to Jalandhar and Ludhiana—the two mega industrial towns equally affected by the war—before returning to Chandigarh.

By this time Manmohan had a full mental picture of the problems faced by these towns and what kind of help was most feasible under the circumstances.

That was Manmohan Singh. Within a short period not only did he meet the industrialists of the four important industrial destinations, but also sorted out their specific problems and developed the strategy to stabilize the industry in difficult periods.

Manmohan was a teacher par excellence. His favourite area was international trade. He would deliver lectures in a simple easy-to-follow language and in a logical manner. Little surprise that these were well attended. He would spend time in his room preparing his lectures or attending to research.

In departmental meetings, he was forthright and would not even spare the Head of the Department, Dr. S.B. Rangnekar who was also his teacher, in case he felt that his decision was arbitrary. He did not even show any hesitation in putting in his resignation letter if he felt the Vice-Chancellor's decision was not in the interest of the university. He was a daring teacher.

He has held many a challenging position in the UNCTAD, Planning Commission and the RBI, discharging his duties with full confidence and honour.

The rest is all well known—his being a highly successful Finance Minister (1991-96), the Leader of Opposition in the Rajya Sabha and now the Prime Minister.

Manmohan's has been a rare career graph. I think there has been no other like him. It is a rare honour for a person belonging to a humble family.

ANOTHER RESEARCH PROJECT

Incidentally, apart from this project, the department had another project on "The linkages between small and large industries", based on the Ludhiana field studies. Though it had started much before I joined the department, its progress was slow due to certain technical and operational problems, despite the Planning Commission having often extended its time schedule.

Now they were not prepared to extend it further and pressed for a very early submission of its report. Since I had an intimate knowledge of the large industries, I too had been made an integral part of this project and was deputed to draft a part of its final report. During its last phase we had to spend the whole night virtually in the department. Thus with cooperative effort, the report of this project was completed well within the extended period.

But my being virtually absent from the house meant a great hardship for Santosh. For long hours, she would be alone, as the annexe where we lived was cut off from the main house. Further, in the absence of a partition wall at the back boundary wall, it was exposed to a long stretch of uninhabited area.

In fact, anything could have happened and in such a case, the inmates in the main house would not know of it. Since Rajeev was barely two years old, often she had to keep awake and miss her sleep.

While fortunately no untoward incident occurred, I had to pay a high price for my total involvement with academic and project work. Soon she was again in the family way and could not take care of the unborn child which was born in November 1966.

A DAUGHTER BORN

I recall my first reaction when I learnt it was a daughter. I had inwardly desired for a son again. It took awhile to reconcile with the fact. I remember Jyotsana was born during the wee hours of a cold morning in hospital. I had a class that morning. Though tired and not well prepared for the lecture, I did not want to miss it and disappoint over 60 pupils. I came home, hurriedly changed my clothes and, without eating anything, rushed to the department, making it just in time.

But my mind was yet not at peace and I could not do justice to my lecture. I terminated it 15 minutes before the scheduled time and promised to compensate the students for this the next day.

It took me some time to reconcile my mind to the reality. This shows how the psyche of even a well-educated person can function. Soon, of course, I fully reconciled and gave Jyotsana even more affection than to Rajeev. In fact, she was so close to me that she would often plead for the cause of her brother, who felt shy talking to me straight.

In my own family of five brothers where I am the eldest, three of us have one son and one daughter each, one did not have any child, while the fifth one, the youngest, is blessed with daughters alone. In fact, in his desire for a male heir, he ended up with four daughters. All of them are well qualified and settled. On the other hand, in comparison, the boys in the family have generally not done as well. And yet our mind is unfortunately glued to a male child.

LATE MARRIAGE BLUES

Late marriage does have its problems. When my son was born I was almost 42 and at my daughter's birth I was 44. So it was a long wait before they could settle down in life, much after my retirement. But I never allowed this problem to worry me though it was often different with Santosh. I believed the situation would take its own course and some solution would emerge when the time came.

For the post-retirement period, although I had pinned hopes on my wife who was some 15 years younger to me and well qualified with a Ph.D. and a first class degree in library science, she failed to settle down on a good job. And neither was she interested in one that did not come up to her expectations. Instead, she decided to devote herself to the care of both children, who were growing up and needed her full attention.

And this care soon proved a great blessing, for the children were saved from falling into bad company. Fortunately, both of them were frank enough to discuss all problems with their mother and thus were counselled wisely if they were going wrong and this helped them to move to the right path.

MAKING TEACHING INTERESTING

Let me recapture how I was able to convert dull and uninteresting teaching into a purposeful and interesting one.

I must admit that when I joined the university I initially found it quite difficult to cope up with this task, which I found beyond my comprehension. I often longed for the comparatively easy life of a government official to which I had become accustomed to for several years. But simultaneously, I would argue with myself that teaching was a challenging profession, which brought out new ideas and new thoughts. One now had ample time to read new texts, articles and research papers. A teacher could frame his mental attitude in the mould that he chose, which later would also facilitate in writing and absorbing articles and research pieces, bringing to fore his best and raising his stature in the academic world.

Thus, in due course of time I was able to raise my position to a new promising future. My mind now would be often occupied with new areas of thinking for my class lectures instead of blindly sticking to what was said in the texts. I used such reading to tailor my own approach, which also fitted well in the classroom lectures and no longer did I feel puzzled.

I developed self-confidence, and it cemented further when I put to practice the ideas that struck me during teaching or seminars and similar other programmes, to make them more interesting. In fact, after initial failure I saw a new light emerge in my whole self.

Rarely did I experience any pressure on my mind later. I delivered lectures slowly, in a simple but forceful language, each word flowing one after another, in a continuous fluid succession. There was also the required clarity and seldom did a line of thought suffer from any ambiguity. The style of the meaningful delivery was such that students followed what was being said.

With the shortage of faculty in the beginning and the rising burden of new courses introduced, we had to share a number of courses. This necessitated an added load of teaching. However, we did our best to distribute this burden equitably. Still, we were under high pressure and could not do justice to the new courses. The situation improved soon with the induction of new faculty members.

Personally, this additional burden helped me to teach myself the new courses, and even when pressure had declined, I did not give up my interest in these streams. In fact, sometimes I was able to contribute writings in these areas or participate effectively in seminars.

On the whole, my experience is that if one is determined, there is no reason why classroom lectures cannot be made more interesting and arouse the curiosity of students and broaden their thinking power. Much depends on a teacher's approach and commitment. In fact, several new ideas have emerged from my classroom teaching and tutorials. It can happen equally so with others too.

Campus Life

A lot of good things happened after we moved to a spacious house on the campus in 1970, after almost six years in the annexe. When I look back I find that the 14 years on the campus, before I retired, were perhaps the best part of my life. This long stretch is full of happy memories.

The hassle of projects, which consumed much of my time and energy in the early part of my university career, also interestingly coincided with my stay in the family house. It was also the period when I had to burn the midnight oil to prepare for my lectures, especially during the initial couple of years. Now, free from the projects, I could devote more time for my family as well as research work, which had received a big jolt in the later years of the 1960s when I was busy establishing myself in the new career. All that zeal and time devoted in constructing new ideas for writing papers in journals that I had cultivated so abundantly in Calcutta was now almost missing.

I began reviving my research interest and here I gave a special place to the library, where I would now sit for late hours, brooding, engrossed in reading, searching new thoughts and weaving these into writings. Even in the department, whenever I found time, I would indulge in writing and thinking.

I would scribble down the main points that emerged from my daily lectures in order to improve them further. This exercise would at times also help conceive new ideas and make my lectures more thought-provoking and interesting in a well-knit and coherently argued out route.

In turn, it helped boost my self-confidence and considerably improved my delivery system, as well as helped me participate in the seminars and other academic programmes more effectively.

I would not hesitate to address problems of my students during lectures. But this practice could not be encouraged beyond a certain level in a lecture theatre.

Keeping in view the overall interest of students, I would advise students to visit me later in my room where we could discuss in more detail the issues raised by them. And happily, quite a few of them would visit me and we would have detailed discussions.

Close contacts with students were also built during the afternoon tutorials and the occasional seminars that I encouraged select students, who constituted the core group in the class, to participate in.

This helped students to be drawn closer to me and the gulf that usually divided a student and teacher was narrowed. I even welcomed students to my residence on the campus where we could sort out specific issues over a cup of tea.

SOCIAL ACTIVITIES AND EDUCATIONAL TRIPS

Over a long period, I had been a social activist and was interested in encouraging social life. It proved to be of much help while dealing with the department's student society, where I found ample opportunity to encourage both short and long visits to various places. This provided a healthy change from the routine life, as well as opportunities for learning and gaining from new surroundings.

While day trips were easier to arrange and manage, particularly when the faculty members were also accompanying, it was different with long-distance trips where a long rail travel was involved. There was also the problem of accommodation at the new place, particularly when a mixed group of young boys and girls would be staying together. Also in a long trip, usually only one teacher accompanied them and thus the entire responsibility of the safety of students and their conduct would fall on him.

During the quite a few long-distance trips involving both boys and girls, I rarely let my mind be occupied with questions like what would happen if this or that problem arose and how would it be tackled. I would remain cool and let the situation decide for itself. And this magic did work well during all my long-distance trips, often punctuated by some visits to spots not listed on the schedule.

In fact, my philosophy is that once a decision to go to a far-off place has been taken, stop worrying and make the best of it, enjoy and learn from the experience and do not miss visiting spots of special interest. At the same time, avoid wasting time in visiting very distant areas as well as those of little significance. Early in the morning we would prepare a definite sight-seeing plan and spend the maximum time outdoors and have our snacks, lunches and dinners wherever convenient.

We hardly faced any accommodation problem, even in a city like Bombay, and stayed at well-protected and convenient places on reasonable budgets. In some places we were accommodated in educational places for which we paid very nominal charges. Most arrangements were made in advance so that time was not wasted when we reached the place.

My experience is that the more you try to discipline the students, the more you alienate yourself from them. My practice of leaving them alone to sort out their problems has worked well and it seldom created any adverse situation. When a student goes wrong, the right approach and proper counselling, makes him realize his mistake.

One of the advantages of accompanying students to such trips is that if you are a little pushing and energetic you can build a good rapport with teachers elsewhere, who would come to your help during emergent situations.

Apart from having a wonderful change by visiting new places, these trips also helped me renew my friendship with teachers and learn of new developments in their institutions. I utilized the free time for this purpose, while the students visited their friends and relatives or did shopping.

All this worked well and we rarely faced any black sheep in the group. Students, in fact, behaved in a responsible manner and rarely created any awkward situation. If visiting relatives or friends, they would return in time. They would also be at the railway station well on time to catch the train for our next destination. So, all these trips ended well, and we returned to Chandigarh by the date and train already intimated, to anxiously awaiting relatives, especially of girl students.

This sort of mix of academic and social life, which I had encouraged during my stay on the campus, bore a fruitful outcome.

VISITS TO LIBRARY

My visits to the library became a matter of routine. Whenever I had free time in the department I would, instead of indulging in gossips and campus politics, visit the library and spend time there chiseling my earlier writing or shaping a new one.

I must acknowledge my debt to the LSE, which had to a large extent helped me learn the priceless gift of scientific reasoning, which alone helped me reach the correct route in research. I had picked up the logic of correct thinking, scientific development of thought and bringing it to a meaningful conclusion the hard way and painstakingly at the LSE, and it had stayed on in the deep recesses of my mind. I put the rigorous training to productive use by developing my writings into long essays for publication. This was also the starting stage of shaping my writings for publication in book form. In other words, some of these long essays were soon shaped into meaningful chapters of a book.

This is in reference to my essay on "Socialistic Pattern in India —An Assessment" which had earlier appeared in a journal. Now when I sat down in the library during the long summer break, I developed it into a book of the same title by adding a large amount of additional material after consulting several reports, documents and books. When it was duly supported by tables and references, I got it typed and sent a copy each to two experts for their comments so that if need be it could be revised accordingly. It took me over a year to bring it to its final shape. Several long sittings followed in the library to fashion its draft and scan the logic of several statements.

Since it was my first attempt in book publication, I was not quite sure how it would fare with the publisher; whether it would be accepted, and if published, whether it would be received well by the readers and critics.

A sad incident also happened meanwhile. I had decided to request P.C. Mahalanobis, whom I considered my guru for introducing scientific planning in India, to write its foreword. But before the letter of request could be posted, I got the sad news of his death. So this idea had to be dropped and I decided to dedicate the volume to his memory.

Another development also happened around this time. While I was busy completing the draft of the above book, a deep crisis had occurred in the international monetary system, when the dollar was no longer freely convertible into gold at a fixed rate. I was approached by a popular competition journal for writing a comprehensive paper on the dollar crisis. I agreed but keeping in view the requirement of the target readers, I had to write in a simple style and language. It turned out to be a pretty long write-up, with all background details that had prompted this crisis, its possible consequences and how it would affect the economies of developing countries in particular. In typed form, it turned out to be full 32 pages and I was not quite sure whether it would be acceptable.

Fortunately, the editor of the journal liked it and published its full length after minimum editing. In fact, it was projected as the front-page story of the journal. He had forwarded its reprints and paid a handsome royalty, which I had not anticipated.

Even more interesting was the fact that the publication of this paper opened before me a new vista of publishing a small volume on current international issues against the backdrop of the prevailing world economy.

PUBLISHED WORK

In the same pattern as the piece on the dollar crisis, I wrote essays on the UNCTAD as well as European Common Market and a couple of other issues, which were in the limelight around that time. Ultimately, this lot of around half a dozen essays of nearly 170 typed pages formed the matter for my second publication.

Simultaneously, I was approached by another national publisher who had heard of my name for a book on the current Indian economic problems. While I had already developed the contours of such a script earlier, now I was required to put in them sufficient flesh by going through a fresh study of the latest government reports and journals. So, I readily agreed to write it also, though for the time being it was put in the pipeline as my hands were full.

It was wintertime but fortunately I had the heating facility in my room in the department. Also, it turned out to be a comparatively lean academic period. I took full advantage of this opportunity and started staying back as long as I could in my room, scanning through reports and other documents and soon made good progress in my commitments. Interestingly, while the other two volumes were slim and almost ready, needing only last-minute touches before being sent to the publisher, it was the third volume which, when worked upon turned out to be a voluminous one. I had to invest the maximum time on it, and it came to around 500 typed pages. It had a befitting title of 'Planning, Development and Economic Policy in India' and became quite popular.

Interestingly, all three of my initial attempts were published in the same year, 1973, though completed at different points of time. It was sheer coincidence, but was of great significance for me. I had grown richer monetarily, as well as become a known author by these three publications in a single year.

That these volumes had been well received by critics became duly evident from a good number of reviews that appeared in the press as well as journals. I was completely satisfied that I had proved both my LSE supervisors wrong, who had written me off from the world of academics.

Thus the year 1973, when I was around 50, was a landmark one in my life when my kitty of published work, papers, articles, book reviews, essays and books fast bulged.

This shows that if one is determined to face life's failures with will power and effort, one can certainly make it. My climb to the academic life was painstakingly slow, full of thorns and several pitfalls, but with determined effort I finally reached where I wanted to be. Had I continued with the government job, I could not have had the time and possibly the inclination to write these works.

However, I did not rest on these laurels. I took them as a very modest starting point in my academic career wherein I felt I had a lot of ground to cover yet, especially in my favourite areas of economic development and international economy and also on the

Indian economy that had lately become a subject of great fascination for me.

Though my sittings in the library were less frequent, I spent a good part of the time in my room in the department and in my study at home. I had converted one room on the first floor of our house for this purpose. Here, I worked late in the evenings as well as on holidays.

Between 1973 and 1978, besides the above three volumes, I could credit my writings with three more published volumes. All of these were slim volumes. One of them was based on my classroom lectures on the Japanese economic development model which I tried to fit into the Indian planning model. Another was based on international financial issues and the third one dealt with my own attempt in constructing a new theory on economic development.

These were also carefully scrutinized by critics who gave a mixed response to my works. However, I always attached a great value to sincere attempts of a reviewer even if the comments were negative. But I strongly abhor a reviewer who makes remarks after just a superficial study of the book. I remember pulling up one critic who had reviewed my book on Japan just after studying the blurb and having a cursory glance at the contents and introductory chapter. I had proved his views wrong and my rebuttal was published in the paper where the review had appeared.

The late 1970s also saw the publication of another slim volume on various aspects of economic development. It was a collection of my earlier papers that had appeared in journals which had been redone and brought to a specific order.

During the early 1980s, the second edition of my book on "Planning, Development and Economic Policy in India" was published after a revision. Subsequently, I confined myself mainly to the edited volumes and those based on the Indian economic development.

It was also during this period (1970s) that I was actively involved in reviewing books, which were published in journals as well as leading daily newspapers. In fact, my collection of reviews during this decade was large enough to feed a full-length volume published in the early 1980s.

CAMPUS TEACHERS' ASSOCIATION

The period of 1970s saw my keen participation in other areas as well. I started taking an interest in the activities of the Panjab University Teachers Association (PUTA). It was the only body for protecting the rights of the teachers and it was quite powerful as it had say in the matters affecting the interest of the academic community. I was elected twice to its executive committee as a member and once as its vice-president.

On all three occasions, I took an active part in its activities, at the same time guarding myself against undue indulgence in unhealthy politics unlike some other members. I concentrated mainly on those aspects of the campus life which needed an improvement or a fresh thinking, especially those related to academics and the general welfare of teachers and students. This limited participation, though not liked by some teachers, by and large worked well for me and also did not tax my time. And this was one important reason for my being accepted by various groups.

The involvement with the teachers' association brought me close to the faculty members, especially in the science stream whom I would possibly not have known otherwise and they constituted the major chunk of the total strength of teachers. I was happy to get acquainted with a number of teachers on the campus.

ACADEMIC CONFERENCES

By shifting to the campus, both my academic and social horizons expanded enormously. It was also due to my regular participation in academic conferences that my interest widened whereas earlier I had practically avoided such participation. In 1975 for the first time, I attended the conference of the Indian Economic Association held in Mysore. Interestingly, I had attended its conference in 1945 also, when I was a postgraduate student of Economics at Panjab University, Lahore. Thus, there was a long gap of almost three decades between the two conferences of this association that I participated in.

I took an active interest in its deliberations and presented my papers as well as attended to the queries of critics. Besides, I got elected as a member of its executive committee for the next three years. It brought me close to the activities of this association as well as several teachers from other universities with whom I was able to cultivate good relations.

I made it a point to participate in almost all its conferences held subsequently. This helped me visit varied destinations in the country, which would have perhaps been not possible otherwise.

Soon, I found myself attending global economic conferences and seminars. How it began has an interesting background. In 1978, I visited Warsaw on a three-month programme, under the Indo-Polish Cultural Exchange Programme through the UGC. Here, towards the end of my stay, a Round-Table Conference of world economists was held to discuss certain issues of economic theory. It was a one-week long (five days) programme held under the aegis of the International Economic Association where select economists had been invited. A volume based on the deliberations of this programme was later published.

It was a unique opportunity to interact with these few select economists. There was ample time to interact with some of them. I approached the coordinator of this programme in the Warsaw Economic Association for permission to participate. I already knew the gentleman and was allowed entry with the status of an observer.

I went through the schedule of this week-long programme and the list of participants, which helped me know about their background. I was pleasantly surprised to find the name of Meghnad Desai from the LSE among the participants. This assumed significance as after Warsaw, I was going to London for a couple of weeks on an invitation from the British Council, which had already arranged my meeting with Desai. I would be going to the LSE after a long gap of 18 years and was looking forward to reviving my memories of this global institute, though now in a different capacity.

Incidentally, Desai was later elevated to the position of Lord Meghnad Desai. There were quite a few others in the Warsaw Round-Table whose names and works I was familiar with, but had not had the opportunity to meet personally.

So I imagined that this visit would prove quite significant and possibly open my entry into the activities of the World Economic Congress, which was the only global body of economists and held a very prominent place in the field. I decided to attend all its sessions, in which there were just a few local participants and a couple of observers. In those five days of the programme, I was able to strike cordial relations with some participants and also found a good opportunity to discuss some issues that emerged from the programme. At times, the interactions turned out to be quite lively and rewarding.

On the last day of the Round Table, I presented my views on the areas discussed and elicited a good response from the economists of socialist countries in particular.

Thus, this participation proved to be a good beginning for gaining a foothold in the global programmes of this association.

HOME-COMING TO LONDON

After Warsaw, I landed in London which appeared to me like home-coming after three months of *banwas* (stay in jungle) in the socialist world where I was confronted with both language and food problems. In fact, when I landed in Warsaw in early April 1978 it was bitterly cold. The snowfall in that month had plummeted the temperature to near freezing point.

Apart from the language problem since hardly anyone spoke English, I faced an acute food problem. There was not a single Indian restaurant. In fact, Indian food was practically unknown there and I had to be content with the local food, though in the evening sometimes I would cook rice for a change.

I would also request the members of the Indian Embassy to invite me on the weekends for a change to Indian food. Apart from this, I could also speak Hindi/English with the family members and thus feel at home. So, I looked forward to visiting London, with which I was so well acquainted during my long stay earlier. I could freely converse in English and enjoy Indian food, particularly as I stayed with an Indian family.

While in Warsaw, I had taken sufficient care to get visa endorsements for my possible visits to other destinations and it saved me a lot of time and possible harassment in London. An official from the British Council had come to receive me at the airport in London and guided me to the place where I had planned to stay. He also handed over a letter of my itinerary during my stay in Britain, including a visit to the LSE library, for which a temporary card was handed over to me. I also looked forward to meeting the director of the LSE and some faculty members in case they were available, including of course, Meghnad Desai whom I had met recently in Warsaw.

I had also expressed my desire to visit Oxford to meet some faculty members and this too had been arranged. In fact, the very next day after collecting 50 per cent of my grant, I left for Oxford. I was at the British Council at the appointed time and was greeted by the official in charge for the overseas visitors. He accompanied me to the railway station where the ticket for my travel to Oxford was given to me. I was also apprised of the particulars of my hotel stay.

VISIT TO OXFORD

As I relaxed in the train, enjoying the scene of the lovely British countryside, I was happily surprised to find that the ticket checker was an Indian gentleman. I had come across similar situations during my earlier visit also. I noticed that gradually more Indians as well as nationals from the West Indies were being employed on responsible jobs. These people had at long last moved out of their earlier factory-worker status. The new generation was educated, unlike their ancestors, and frequently mixed with the local people, a trait that was earlier completely missing, especially among the Asians.

In Oxford, as I moved from the station to the street, I encountered a young lady from East Asia who greeted me with a smile and guided me to my hotel. As the weather was quite pleasant after a drizzle, I took a leisurely walk to my hotel studying en route the new surroundings with great interest, most of which happened to be educational sites housed mainly in ancient buildings, which were well maintained, with lots of greenery and flowers. The whole atmosphere was quiet and peaceful.

I felt exhilarated by this short walk to the hotel. In fact, most places in Oxford and Cambridge are easily accessible on foot. This is the one reason why bikes, despite the craze for automobiles and mobikes, are still quite popular here. I walked to almost all the locations in Oxford, including the renowned Bodleian library, one of the largest and oldest libraries in the world with a huge collection of books and manuscripts. I felt deeply honoured when

I was offered its life membership card and spent quite sometime in its corridors, where one needed strong legs and stamina to cover its vast area.

Among the meetings with the faculty members of different colleges, the most memorable one was one with the renowned economist, John Hicks. In fact, Hicks was no stranger to India and even Chandigarh. He was planning to visit Chandigarh again during the ensuing winter season along with his equally talented wife, Ursula Hicks. This was good news, especially as he would be visiting our department to deliver a lecture. I mentioned to him my proposed visit to New York. Incidentally, this visit, though very well thought of earlier, matured only after I was able to save a reasonable amount from the British Council grant.

He suggested that I contact one of his senior colleagues at Columbia University who also happened to be his former student. I took down his address and other particulars in my diary.

Incidentally, this three-week stay in London proved far more productive than the earlier more than three years of stay in this country. In fact, one of my colleagues at the LSE sarcastically remarked once that he had never seen a smile on my face, much less laughter. Though I was alarmed to hear this remark, I knew very well that it was a correct observation. It was the result of the sickening mood I had developed in those prolonged unpleasant times I had encountered.

It was unfortunately contrary to what I had decided before I left India. Although I was determined to make the best of the opportunity, that was not to be. Instead, I had developed a morose and stiff attitude since my mind was obsessed with obtaining a degree from the LSE, and I had turned out to be an introvert, little realizing that the more I worried about this degree mania the more I was distancing myself from it. And that was what had ultimately happened.

Fortunately, this time I was in quite a different mood. I meant to make the best of the opportunity and enjoy myself to the full, meet as many people as I could and strike a note of cordial friendship with them. I did exactly that, and later this proved to be a great help professionally. In London, I covered several places of interest and participated in its rich cultural life, which I had missed earlier.

The most exciting part of the London visit was a long cruise through the river Thames, where I could feel the pulse of old London and its past. It was a completely fascinating and highly rewarding event and reminded me of our river Hooghly in Calcutta with its long cluster of factories and warehouses created by the British on its banks. In London too, on the banks of the Thames one comes across its rich past. I had never undertaken this kind of journey earlier, nor even thought of it.

So, by the time I left for New York, I had made good the several gaps I had left during my earlier stay in London.

VISIT TO THE USA

Fortunately, I was able to buy a standby ticket costing just half the usual fare. This was a big saving for me as I was financially tight and now with this windfall I could finance my internal travel in the USA, to a few select places.

My first priority after reaching New York was to contact the gentleman Hicks had mentioned. He was very pleased to hear from me and invited me to meet him the next day at the university.

The first thing he did was to make my presence at Columbia University into a recognized capacity by according me the status of a Visiting Scholar, for the period of my stay in the USA. It indeed, gave me a sense of importance to be accepted as a scholar in that prestigious university. He also advised me to visit the UN library, which was well stocked with latest books and reports compiled by its members as well as other scholars. This I gladly did and also became a member of the library with the help of the Indian Mission.

I was happy to find that our diplomatic missions and embassies in foreign countries did a wonderful job and took full care of the Indian nationals abroad. This was so unlike the experience that one had about the functioning of our government offices within the country.

After a couple of days in New York, I thought it prudent to explore at least a tiny part of this vast country, over three times the size of India. I started by first visiting Princeton University, which was not far from New York. It was another prestigious place about which Hicks as well as another senior faculty member, who was an expert in international finance, had mentioned.

Though I had taken care to ring the particular faculty member here, he was not quite sure whether he would be available as this was vacation time, but he advised me not to miss the beautiful campus where I would certainly find some other colleague in the department who would be of equal help. So I took this chance. The day turned out to be quite pleasant and I enjoyed the travel through the countryside when the bus moved at a high speed through a maze of highways with several lanes and bypasses. It was quite an experience to watch the smooth movement of traffic over different lanes.

I leisurely walked to the campus which was close to the bus terminal. In fact, this university wore a close resemblance to Oxford and Cambridge. Soon I found myself knocking on the door of the professor I wanted to meet. Unfortunately, he had gone out on a fishing excursion.

Nevertheless, his colleague took full care of me and we discussed several areas of finance, and my knowledge about a number of fresh developments was updated. I gathered some latest literature in this area and learnt about the current work being done by the department and looked forward to a close association with them.

He also invited me to lunch on the campus where I was happy to find a young Indian lady helper. I was told that students there could earn pocket money and often much more by running errands on the campus and thus partly finance their education.

It turned out to be a productive visit. After lunch, I sought leave and thanked him for his help as well as the sumptuous lunch. Before boarding the bus for New York, I had a round of this beautiful and green campus, where life was so peaceful and quiet, compared to the noisy and highly polluted New York.

AT THE WORLD BANK

Next, I visited Washington, again not far from New York. Here I was keen to meet Paul Streeten at the World Bank headquarters, with whom I had developed a good rapport during the Warsaw Round-Table Conference. I had spoken to him about my visit. On reaching Washington, I learnt that there was a strike of the public transport. So I had to walk down the distance to the World Bank building.

It was luckily, not very far. In fact, I found that one great advantage of Washington, also the capital of the USA, was that it had a small population and was easily accessible.

However, Streeten was busy at a meeting and I waited for him in his office. I did not mind the delay, for I had travelled all the way to meet him and to know about his work at this most powerful world financial institution, which controlled the destiny of the newly developing economies in particular. Meanwhile, I gathered information about the fresh activities of the bank and also collected some latest literature.

Streeten apologized for keeping me waiting and well remembered how at Warsaw we had interacted on financial and developmental issues facing the newly developing countries. He also had a deep interest in India's development and when I posed him the issue of the contribution of Indians to this bank, he took out a list of employees holding responsible positions in the bank and added smilingly: "See how many of your countrymen are doing so well". I was certainly pleased to find a large number of Indian scholars holding responsible positions.

I spent much of the afternoon in moving around on foot. Being the headquarters of the American government, Washington housed all the important government buildings, though I could see only some of them during my brief stay. I spent some time at the President's residence, the White House—indeed a very imposing structure covering a vast area. A large number of tourists could be seen around this place.

When in the USA, I could not afford to miss the Niagara Falls, though it involved a whole night journey by coach. Early the next morning, we were in Buffalo city from where the Niagara Falls was close, on the border of the USA and Canada. Incidentally, the night-long journey helped to freshen up my tired limbs through a sound and undisturbed sleep. I was now ready to undertake this trip to the Niagara Falls where tons of water poured from precipitous heights on the Canadian border to produce electricity. The speed at which the waters moved as well as the quantum of waters released was indeed so terrific, that one dared not risk going near them.

We had been supplied with raincoats and strong caps to save our clothes from being drenched as the boat carrying us quickly circled around the falls. It was a very majestic but nerve-twisting experience and soon we were bundled out, which was a big relief. There was a big crowd of visitors and I walked along the quieter areas where the canals carrying waters moved slowly.

I purchased some mementos before returning to Buffalo. While relaxing before my return journey to New York, I came across an Iranian national who was a taxi driver. He told me that he hardly missed an opportunity to visit the USA to spend his holidays, for which he would save sufficient money. It was of course, 1978 when Iran was ruled by a liberal government. I wondered whether he was able to continue with his US holidays when the Shah had been deposed and sent in exile and the country was ruled by religious fanatics.

Also while in New York, I made the best of my stay, despite the heat and humidity which were at the peak. Like me, there were crowds of visitors who moved around in their light clothes. Every place of interest was packed with visitors, including shops, stores, and restaurants. There was a virtual invasion by the tourists—young, old, children.

Here, I used my Indian connections with the global social organizations. I was a life member of the Indian Federation of the UN Associations as well as the founder-member of the Lions Club of Panchkula. Like in India, the UN organizations chapters existed in practically all major destinations and so was the case with the Lions Clubs. Both these organizations helped to widen my contacts with local people during this trip, whether in socialist countries (where of course only the UN clubs existed and not the Lions Clubs) or capitalist nations. The building of the UN Association in New York was close to the UN headquarters itself.

It was indeed a great experience to visit the UN Headquarters in the Manhattan area, which I was shown around by the Secretary-General of the UN Association of New York. A tall, multistorey building, it presented a unique view. He treated me to lunch here in the members' dining hall. A formal dress was essential for this, a jacket and necktie, which I was provided with.

Similarly, the Lions Club of Central New York hosted a dinner for me in a posh and popular Japanese restaurant, where hot preparations were served in a few courses. The restaurant had a typical oriental environment with soothing music. After dinner I was shown around the city to enjoy the glamour of the late evening tour. The organization presented me with a memento as a token of my visit and also some literature.

It was quite late in the night when they dropped me back at my host's flat. By then I was feeling quite drowsy as a result of the Japanese drink, and it appears that I had had excess of it. Of course, my friends had realized it. But I did not need any help. I thanked them profusely for the wonderful dinner and equally wonderful drive in the city and promised to write to them after reaching India. It was a memorable evening and I often recalled it with fondness even later.

The Manhattan area is thickly crowded with tall buildings. Most of them are several storeys high. In fact, it appears that each building vies with the other to reach to the sky. The State Empire Building, which had been the tallest for a long time was much later matched by the still taller towers of the World Trade Center. On September 11, 2001, the twin towers of the WTC fell to the terrorists' attack.

The State Empire building continues to steal the show and is a favourite with visitors who can go right up to the top with its two lifts and enjoy a panoramic view of this city. While I had the opportunity to go to its top, I missed it in case of the WTC.

I also undertook a boat journey through the Hudson river, which took us close to the Statue of Liberty—a marvelous structure rising like a firm rock amidst the turbulent waters. A series of bridges, spanning the river frequently, present a fantastic view of bright colourful lights shining against the backdrop of the approaching dusk.

After around 16 days, I had to wind up my visit to the USA. Incidentally, it also reminds me of a funny incident which could have as well turned out into an awkward situation. When I landed at the Kennedy International Airport, late in the evening after my flight from London, I had completely failed to notice the grim face of the lady to whom I had been sent to get my entry papers cleared.

She had a close look at my passport, where in the endorsement column the passport officer in Warsaw had clearly stated that it was valid for six months. It appeared that she did not relish this and asked me how many dollars I was carrying. In those days, due to strict foreign exchange restriction, every traveller from India visiting the foreign country was allotted 500 dollars. I had carried more dollars after encashing quite a few British pounds saved from my British Council allowance.

But the lady was not convinced with the amount of cash I was carrying and felt that it was not quite sufficient for a long stay in that country. She cut down my stay period in the USA to one month, despite my protestations that I had already paid for the return journey and that in New York I would be staying with a relative. Anyway, knowing that I would not have been there for more than this period, I did not press the matter. But the situation could have been quite awkward in case I had planned to stay longer.

BACK TO LONDON

I returned to London after nearly two weeks to face a planned hectic programme of visits to Paris, Geneva and Moscow. However, time was becoming a major constraint. Originally I had been permitted three months of leave, the period equivalent to my official stay in Warsaw under the exchange programme. I had planned to spend it at the Central School of Planning and Statistics in Warsaw, which happened to be the world's biggest institution on Central Planning. In addition, I could avail myself of a few more days of leave because of the intervening summer vacation, before my department opened in the middle of July.

However, I found that it was not possible to cover all visits within this time frame and had applied for an extension of leave by one month to the Vice-Chancellor of Panjab University from Warsaw. The application was routed to the Department of Economics for comments, for it was only after a positive recommendation of the Head of the Department that the leave could be sanctioned. A colleague of mine was at that time acting as the head.

The acting head, however, on petty considerations, put an obstacle in my itinerary by making a negative recommendation on the application. But the timely intervention of my wife, who came to know of this development, saved the situation by personally meeting the Vice-Chancellor and explaining the position to him.

Incidentally, the colleague who played this negative role was quite close to us and before his marriage was a regular visitor to our house and we least expected him to behave this way.

My visit to Moscow had been settled while I was in Warsaw, when the UN Friendship Secretariat in Moscow agreed to treat me as an official visitor to Moscow for three days on my return journey to India. This programme, as I was told later, was valid only for the month of July. Subsequently, however, because of my tours to the UK and the USA, the situation turned different.

Under the changed situation, I decided to visit Moscow in August for which I had also moved a fresh application. But there was no positive response from Moscow, even though I had personally called on their London office. I got the pet answer: "Please wait." Nothing was clear. It put me in an embarrassing situation, since, meanwhile, I had finalized my programme of visits to Paris and Geneva and my air ticket had been confirmed.

I had also written to Mr. I.K. Gujral who was then India's Ambassador in Moscow for his intervention. In fact, he was quite aware of my July visit to Moscow. I explained to him the circumstances under which it had been changed and he promised to intervene.

Thus, due to the indifferent attitude of Moscow, I was under a good deal of strain, which, coupled with the highly hectic travels to the USA and UK, resulted in health problems, which could not be got properly treated due to lack of time. Instead, I had taken some quick-relief capsules, which only provided temporary respite.

Incidentally, when I returned to London from the USA, I apprehended harassment at the airport on my re-entry, though it was within the permissible schedule of six months of the validity of the visa. This apprehension was strengthened because of the sad experience at Kennedy airport in the USA. Also around this time Indians were often harassed, discriminated against and even refused entry. But fortunately, the emigration officer turned out to be of a cheerful disposition. When he found that I was a Mahajan, he remarked that he had had an opportunity to stay in the Friends Colony in New Delhi which was so closely associated with the name of Justice Mahajan. And that was all we talked about before he stamped my passport.

THE LONDON UN ASSOCIATION

The London UN Association too was of great help to me. Its headquarters was close to the Whitehall and British Parliament. I had attended a programme organized by it in a committee room of the Parliament. Here I also came in contact with a renowned economist, Hans Singer, who was then attached to a famous development institute in Sussex.

It was a pleasant surprise to be introduced to him. He extended me an invitation for participation in a programme on 'International Economic Order', which was already going on and would continue for a week more. Incidentally, during that decade, 'The Establishment of a New International Economic Order' had caught the thinking of the UN, in which the developed economies were being asked to devote at least one per cent of their national income every year for the economic development of poor countries.

Subsequently, I visited this institute, which was located in Brighton, and spent one full afternoon there, including participation in the seminar. I maintained contact with Singer for quite a few years. He would send comments on my writings, which helped in their improvement.

Thus, I had a happy start with the UN Association in London. I visited it again later and discussed quite a few global and regional issues with its director who was a well-informed scholar and of cooperative nature. In fact, he even guided me about whom I should meet regarding my new project on "Global Finance" and also arranged some meetings with experts.

He allowed me to make use of the telephone from his office, which proved of great help in contacting distant colleagues in particular. When I mentioned to him that I was likely to visit Geneva, especially visit the secretariat of UNCTAD as well as the headquarters of the World UN Associations, and was facing accommodation problem, he promptly suggested that I stay with an English couple who lived in its suburbs. He also spoke to this gentleman, who had recently retired from the ILO and was an active member of the local UNA.

Thus, this contact turned into a double advantage. Not only could I come in contact with a large number of academic and government officials here, I could also explore the possibility of staying with UNA members in their countries. In fact, by staying with the English family in Geneva, I had been saved from a major monetary problem, that had been worrying me in this highly expensive city. Also, there was the language problem as English was yet not quite popular. But staying with this family, I could speak with comfort.

CONTINENTAL AND RUSSIAN VISITS

Geneva is the headquarters of the world's largest number of global associations. I was told that there are around 150 of them.

Among the few in my list, it was UNCTAD that topped, for I had developed close contact with it over several years, and had a special word of praise for Raul Prebisch, a renowned Latin American economist, who had laid its strong foundations in which he was also assisted by the known Indian economist, Manmohan Singh, who later became the Prime Minister of India.

During 1968, at the time of the second international conference of UNCTAD held in Delhi, Raul Prebisch had visited Chandigarh where he was honoured with an honorary doctorate by the University. Later, accompanied by Manmohan Singh, who was formerly on the faculty of the Panjab University Economics Department here, and at that time was attached to UNCTAD, Raul Prebisch, visited the Department of Economics, and our students as well as faculty members were quite happy to have him in their midst.

Thus, this long-cherished visit had its own uniqueness.

While in London, I was also able to exploit my contacts developed during the International Economic Association (IEA) Round-Table held in Warsaw. I got a chance to visit Paris, where the headquarters of the IEA are located.

The IEA had sanctioned funds for my visit as well as made arrangements for my three-day stay in Paris. This was how Paris also emerged in my return journey. Here, apart from the IEA, I also planned to explore other bodies involved in economic development programmes.

During my second visit to London, I refreshed my earlier memories of Birmingham and Manchester. This time I travelled in a car to these places. Driving through the new expressway connecting London with Manchester was indeed an exciting experience. Birmingham, after 19 years, was a totally changed city, especially in its basic services. When we neared Manchester, darkness had descended. We stayed the night with an Indian family, and left for London the next morning after breakfast.

Thus, I had a very busy schedule in London during both visits. A busier schedule awaited me on my return journey, though I had yet to wait for the clearance of my visit to Moscow, which I learnt would be done at the last minute. However, I had given the addresses of both the places I was dropping en route.

So I left for Paris at the scheduled time and stayed in a hotel room there, which had been reserved by the IEA. I conveyed my personal thanks to the IEA for the help they had extended. They also hosted a lunch for me and guided me about my possible queries regarding visits to other places. As it was a holiday period in most of the academic and research institutes, hardly anyone could be contacted.

Even on this second visit to Paris, like earlier, I found it tough to deal with the local people, even young ones, who would refuse to answer any query put in English.

This time, therefore, I took adequate precautions. I persuaded a young Indian, who was staying at the same place as I, to accompany me. We were together for a good part of the day and visited quite a few important tourist spots. Paris, as usual, hummed with visitors and everywhere there were thick crowds.

As mentioned, while in the last lap of the London visit, I had developed a health problem and suffered from a sore throat, which did not permit me to stay outdoors for long periods. So I hastened back to the hotel and took rest.

But the unconfirmed Moscow visit continued to cause me worry. The next morning, I rushed to the Indian Embassy and met its first secretary and requested him to send an urgent fax to his counterpart in Moscow. I had already drafted the fax matter that morning.

But he narrated to me a distressing experience he had encountered recently, when he had sent a fax message at the request of another Indian visitor to some other embassy, which turned out to be a fake one. He, therefore, wanted to look at my passport or some other documentary proof about my identity. Unfortunately, since at that time I was not carrying my passport, I promised to return in the afternoon.

Meanwhile, I happened to enquire from him the name of the university from where he had got his education. To my surprise, it turned to be Panjab University where he was a student of Botany. When I gave reference about a particular gentleman in that department, he said he was his favourite teacher. Again when I told him that he was my colleague, he happily said that there was no need for me to come again and added that the fax message would be sent soon.

It was thus, Nature's help that came to my rescue at this difficult time, when I had little energy left to undertake the second trip. Further, I was sure that this gentleman would take good care about this message, particularly when I told him that the Ambassador in Moscow was my close friend.

The throat problem was getting worse, despite my taking tablets to suppress it. My body had started feeling slightly feverish. Still I tried to put up a brave face and did not let it pull me down.

THE PICTURESQUE LAND OF GENEVA

In Geneva, as mentioned, I was the guest of an English couple. The gentleman had come to receive me at the airport and welcomed me to this place. He straightaway drove to the ILO headquarters, where he had served before retiring and introduced me to some heads of departments, including one Indian.

It was a spacious place where a large number of experts worked. My host took me on a round of this building and showed me in particular its huge library, well stocked with books and journals. I looked forward to coming here again. The librarian was quite pleased to welcome me.

I was indeed much fascinated by Geneva, the land with matchless scenic splendour, wide and well-maintained roads, high cleanliness, natural lakes and forests. Everything looked so tempting and inviting that I wished to spend the maximum time around these surroundings. There could not have been a better place for the location of practically all the global bodies. Still, the place was so quiet and peaceful.

My hosts stayed in a spacious villa mostly done in wood, in an enchanting suburb of Geneva, surrounded by dense forest greenery. It was a highly charming place and so very quiet. Breathing the fresh air of Geneva made me feel greatly relieved of my health problem. I felt a lot better.

The next morning, I went to the United Nations Associations (UNA) headquarters, which was now on the top of my agenda and was greatly relieved to learn that the message had at long last come, clearing my visit to Moscow. I was advised to collect my visa papers form the embassy in Zurich for which I expressed my helplessness. The Secretary-General of the UNA kindly agreed to help me.

During this brief stay in Geneva, I also visited a few more global organizations, including of course UNCTAD, which was high on my list. I spent a couple of hours at this place, meeting a few officials who handed over the latest literature and promised to help me in connection with my work on UNCTAD.

During the last lap of the trip, my health again began to cause concern. But by then I had covered most of my itinerary and now the last visit to Moscow was left, and I was sure I would brave it with equal success.

LAND OF THE IRON CURTAIN

When I flew into Moscow in the almost two-third vacant Russian airbus, Aeroflot, from Geneva airport, my legs were aching. I experienced a great difficulty in walking up to the main lounge of the airport where I had to fill in quite a few documents, meant for all foreigners before entering the city. It was quite a nerve-racking task in my poor health condition. While I was scanning through these papers, luckily the Secretary-General of the Moscow UN Friendship Society spotted me, as I was the only Indian sitting there. After ascertaining my identity, he said there was no need for me to fill in these forms, as there would be automatic clearance in my case.

Another gentleman from the Indian Embassy was also waiting to receive me on behalf of the Ambassador. He was also a great help.

Soon I was out of that suffocating environment and headed towards the hotel where arrangements for my stay had been made. My host informed me that the entire three-day programme for me had been meticulously chalked out to allow me to combine sight-seeing with official visits. They also placed an official car with a chauffeur, as well as an interpreter at my disposal.

This was my first visit to that powerful country. At that time it was as powerful as the USA, but unlike the USA, it was a highly mysterious land and reeked of all sorts of suspicions. I was keen to know more about this country. Ignoring my sickness, I concentrated on meeting people, visiting organizations where my meetings had been fixed and enjoying the sight-seeing. I remember the visit to the famous Red Square which happened to be close to the hotel I was staying in.

The interpreter was a great help. He was with me for most of the time. We even shared breakfast, lunch and dinner on the same table. He explained to me the history of this country, the struggle which the ordinary people had undergone, and how they had succeeded in building a strong welfare state—the first of its kind the world over. Of course, all this was what he had been instructed to acquaint the foreign visitors with. He took me around to see some selected places, which could be shown conveniently in the little time we had.

I made it a point to meet Gujral at his official residence. Incidentally, Gujral and I are products of the same college in Lahore though he was senior to me. While in India we had failed to meet after Independence. Destiny had brought us together on a foreign land after a gap of over three decades and we exchanged views on areas of mutual interest and reminisced old days of college and Lahore.

I was indeed touched when he came to see me off, placing his arm around my neck like an old classmate and waved cheerfully as the car left. I was glad when he later rose to the position of the Prime Minister of India in the nineties.

On the third and the last day of my visit my fever, hitherto suppressed, began to make a visible appearance. However, I did not want the interpreter to have any inkling of it. So, as usual, I got ready and had a small breakfast, though I felt little inclined for this. My indisposition was noticed by the interpreter too, though he kept quiet. I attended the forenoon programme but after returning, I was so completely exhausted that I excused myself from lunch and also requested the interpreter to get my afternoon programme cancelled, as I was not feeling well.

I went straight to my room and rested. I could feel my whole body in the grip of a high fever. Soon, to my surprise, a nurse and a doctor visited my room and seeing my condition the doctor asked the nurse to take down my temperature, which had risen quite high. After doing their work, the two left without saying anything.

Meanwhile, sensing detention, I had contacted the Indian Embassy chief medical officer whom I had met the other day in a party arranged by the first secretary of this embassy and explained the situation to him. He promised to come and see me soon. I had also spoken to the Secretary-General of the local UNA.

Soon a team of doctors and my host called on me and considered my deteriorating health. They thought of shifting me to a sanitarium for a detailed check-up and care. This is what they told to the Secretary-General who in turn explained it to me in English.

Meanwhile, the Indian Embassy doctor had also joined us. I explained to him that I needed to leave Moscow positively by the midnight flight as my family members would be extremely perturbed if I did not turn up. Further, I was already late in joining the department and my leave could not be extended. But all my entreaties fell flat on deaf ears of the visiting Russian doctors. They insisted that I was not in a position to travel and since I was also a state guest, it was the responsibility of the local government to ensure that I returned to India in good health. Their government would also write to the Indian government about this, and so there was no need to worry.

However, the Indian doctor intervened, assuring them that it was a simple case of malaria, a disease with which they were not quite familiar. In such a state the temperature suddenly shoots up, which, with the administration of appropriate medicine would decline perceptibly soon. It was only after he took the responsibility of treating me and bringing the temperature down to normal that they put me under his responsibility and care, but even then only after they were fully satisfied about his credentials. Luckily he also held a degree of medicine from the Russian university, apart from the Indian university, and was at a senior position in the Embassy.

The Russian doctors told him to monitor my health and only when he had certified that I was fit to travel did they issue the necessary certificate for my travel. I became conscious of the fact that their health system was very cumbersome and complicated. The Indian doctor assured me that it was nothing more than malaria. Soon he left and to get the appropriate medicine for my treatment.

I was certainly in a poor state of health. My energy had completely disappeared and the whole body was in the grip of high fever. I rang up Gujral and informed him about my state of health. But I added that despite this, I was determined to catch the midnight flight. He fully agreed with my decision adding that once I reached Delhi the situation would be different.

Nature also helped me. After taking the medicine brought by the Embassy doctor, the temperature had started coming down gradually and the body pain was also lessening. By evening my temperature had almost come down to normal and this message was duly conveyed to the Russian doctors in chaste Russian by the Indian doctor.

Thanks to the timely intervention of the Indian doctor, I was able to escape from the very difficult situation of being sent to a sanitarium about which my family members would have hardly been well informed.

The Secretary-General of the local UNA and his daughter had come to see me off. After obtaining my clearance from the Russian doctors, they took me through a long drive to the airport, which took more than one and a half hours. We reached much ahead of the scheduled departure time. The flight too was delayed by two hours and since it was already late, I bade goodbye to my host in Moscow and his young daughter who spoke fluent English.

After moving to the lounge after the security check, I hardly bothered about the state of my health, for there was no longer the fear of detention or being sent to a sanitarium. It was the most perplexing experience in my life that stayed in my memory.

So the next morning I was at Palam airport. Now I realized there was nothing to compare with the comfort and care of home. Still the ghost that had visited me in Moscow was quite fresh in my memory, though I shuddered to think of the sequence of events. It was indeed a miracle to have escaped from being thrown into a far-off sanitarium where anything could have happened and my family would have been kept in the dark about it.

Gradually with homely care I was soon back to my normal self and all the health problems that had constantly nagged me during the return journey disappeared. I, however, marvelled how Nature had again come to my rescue and did not allow my normal schedule to be disturbed. It was only on the last day that I was actually in the grip of a real health problem, which had immobilized my programme.

It is such experiences that strengthen one's belief in there being some supreme power that comes to your rescue in difficult times.

This four-and-a-half month trip to several destinations abroad was almost akin to a global trip. I have often wondered how it all shaped up and that I never had to face any financial problem. Rather, when I reached home, I had saved enough foreign exchange to help finance another short trip.

And it was not long before another opportunity knocked at my door. And it was again no less than a global visit. Thanks to the International Economic Association (IEA), this time I had been invited as a discussant at the 1980 IEA global conference of world economists, which is held every three years. This time it was being held in Mexico.

AS A BOOK REVIEWER

During the 1970s I also moved to the world of book reviewing, an absolutely new task for me. I found it to be a highly fascinating activity, for I got to read new books which widened my knowledge and also made me aware of what the author was driving at, and whether he had done justice to his work and if he had faltered, where? All this helped me become a balanced critic.

In fact, a decade later, when several reviews penned by me had appeared in various publications, I found the material to be good enough for a book which appeared soon under the title 'Economic Development of India'.

Several of my writings that had appeared in journals, newspapers and periodicals lay scattered about as also quite a few unpublished pieces. I thought that after editing them, they could go into a couple of volumes and thus would be well preserved. And this is exactly what I did subsequently, along with a few more volumes based on the contributions by other scholars, and with long introductory notes written by me. In due course, they added substantially to the collection of my aggregate publications.

Foreign Academic Sojourns

My foreign academic sojourns, where the Warsaw Round-table had proved to be a good start, kept me busy for the next few years.

The next year (1979) itself, another IEA Round-Table was held in India in Poona, where I made an effective participation. At this five-day meeting, I also realized that these programmes, besides providing an opportunity to make your contribution, also helped in building contacts with scholars whose say mattered a lot in the academic horizon.

Not long after the Poona conference, I was pleasantly surprised to receive a long cable from the IEA inviting me to their next global conference of economists being held in Mexico. I could not have asked for more as they were also paying for my air tickets both ways, as well as providing me with hospitality in a five-star hotel for one full week. Here I had to act as a discussant for a paper in the session chaired by Paul Streeten, whom I had met in Warsaw and subsequently in Washington. The local secretary of this conference was Victor Urquidi, whom I had also met in Warsaw.

It was a wonderful opportunity to make a trip to the far-off land of Mexico located in the deep West. So this was like a global ticket and I could thus plan another world round visit—this time through the East, visiting possible destinations where Japan was in my priority list, and returning through the West.

TOUGH OPPOSITION

But, unfortunately, it was not to be. This time I had to face even tougher opposition, when the Head of the Department questioned the very purpose of this visit, since acting as a mere discussant in the conference, in his opinion, did not amount to making any original contribution. It was just a waste of time for several days when I would also be away from the department, especially at a time when the new session was starting and my presence here was far more important.

He had typed out this reply to my leave application, and forwarded it in a secret envelope to the Vice-Chancellor.

When I learnt of this, I was extremely upset. In fact, I could have never imagined that the gentleman, who was quite close to me and had often enjoyed our hospitality before he joined the department, could adopt such a negative and nasty attitude. He always spoke in a meek and sweet language, hardly revealing his true intentions.

He had deliberately sat on this application to the last; even though it had been put up well in time. Whenever I enquired about it, he would just smile mischievously, giving the impression that it would automatically be cleared. But when at the eleventh hour the real truth emerged, there was unfortunately very little time left to contact those persons who carried voice and could speak on my behalf. I ran from pillar to post and even met the Vice-Chancellor, but nothing appeared to work.

Ultimately, when the Vice-Chancellor was sounded that in case I was not allowed to participate in this important conference, where I was invited and which was an honour to the university, the teaching body on the campus would protest; he had second thoughts. A meeting was arranged between a couple of senior members of the syndicate and the Head of my Department. They allowed barely 10 days of leave to me to attend the conference and I was strictly told to return within the stipulated time.

Under these circumstances, I had to skip my global honeymoon and confine the visit to the conference. Apart from sticking to the deadline on leave, I had also to seek assurance from another faculty member that during my absence he would attend to my work schedule apart from his own. Thus, the leave was laced with nasty conditions.

With this minimum time available, I had to rush for my journey reservation, which itself turned out to be a problem, because of the heavy summer rush when all flights were virtually full. As I could not manage any direct flight to Mexico, I had to break my journey in Paris and catch the next morning flight to Mexico.

This caused me further inconvenience, as I was late by one day and missed the coveted opening session in Mexico.

Further, at Delhi airport my baggage had been booked straight to Mexico by mistake, while I was to break the journey in Paris. So after landing in Paris, the very first thing I did was to inform the appropriate authorities to detain my baggage and reload it in my next flight to Mexico. And, soon this was duly confirmed. This way I felt free of the burden of carrying my baggage in Paris for the overnight stay when just a small handbag sufficed.

While I tried to have a good time in Paris, the thought of missing the conference opening session, which I had been looking forward to with great expectations, marred my joy.

The next morning, confident about the reloading of my baggage, I boarded the plane without checking it. It was a day-long flight, with quite a few stopovers en route. By the time we reached Mexico, it was dusk and a welcome band was playing.

Anxious about my baggage, I hastened to find it. But I was shocked to notice that it was not there. I checked and rechecked the baggages around, but there was no trace of my luggage. This made me sullen and all the enthusiasm of participating in this conference disappeared.

Ultimately, there was no alternative except to lodge a complaint with the airline people, who expressed their helplessness in the matter but promised to flash urgent messages to all those places where the baggage was likely to be detained, and inform me at my local address. They gave me a shaving kit to get ready the next morning and also told me that I could buy a new suit for the conference and charge it to the airlines.

It was thus in a highly frustrated mood that I travelled to my hotel and after collecting my keys and without eating any dinner, I hastened to my room and slumped in the bed without even changing my clothes. It proved a highly uncomfortable night with several negative thoughts flashing across my mind, as my baggage carried not only my suits and other garments, but also important documents and literature as well as my foreign exchange. If I failed to locate it, I would have to put up with great inconvenience and would be hardly able to buy anything for my family.

I could hardly have a wink of sleep and kept tossing about, anxiously waiting for the morning to dawn, which appeared to be endlessly delayed. I was compelled to wear the same dress the next day and after a hurried breakfast, travelled in the coach to the conference venue. Here I felt little interest in its proceedings either.

I had a lurking belief that Nature was again testing my patience and would soon rescue me from this mind-boggling imbroglio, which had disturbed my entire schedule. In fact, I had been facing a tough time right from the moment I had put in the leave application for this visit. It was a very difficult period and there hardly appeared to be any relief.

I was lost in my world of frustration and uncertainty when a little before lunchtime a message was flashed at my hotel address about some unclaimed baggage found at the airport, and I was asked to come over and identify whether it belonged to me. I immediately contacted the gentleman in charge of transport and was soon at the airport. Here I was advised to check in the left luggage room where I was shown an unidentified baggage, which luckily was mine. It had arrived a day before I had reached.

Since no one was there to claim it, the baggage had been dumped here. I was indeed very happy to get it at long last. But my happiness soon disappeared when I found that its locks had been tampered with and the brand new suitcase was in a bad shape.

However, when I examined its contents, I found every article, including the foreign exchange intact. When I brought the poor shape of baggage to the notice of the airlines authorities, they promised to replace it with a new one and asked me to collect it the next day from their city office. Of course, this was hardly important since my things were in order.

Perhaps it was Nature again, I felt intuitively, that had listened to my prayers and saved me from further agony. Meanwhile, I had been told distressing tales of lost luggage, which had been traced only after a long wait. I met a Pakistan national who had been visiting this airport for the past few days, enquiring about the fate of his lost baggage. I was perturbed after hearing his tale and could not imagine what would have been my plight if I had to return home without my baggage.

After this, there was such mental relief that words fail me. I could now fully concentrate on the conference and especially on my assignment for which I had travelled all the way from India. I was to present a critical assessment on a paper contributed by a British scholar.

That evening and late night were spent on studying this paper. I carefully read it and spelled out its main issues. Then I examined their validity before providing my own views in detail. I wrote down a couple of drafts and after weeding out the unwanted points, wrote the final draft which ran into about 14 pages of easily readable writing.

Due to the troubled period I had undergone for the last several hours, I was not yet my normal self and was overcome with fatigue and drowsiness. But I pulled up myself with determination and in the morning, enjoyed a hearty breakfast before proceeding to the conference venue, in a caravan of about ten luxurious buses that ferried the delegates. My presentation was in the morning session, after the first paper. There was a fairly good audience, which showed that it was a popular theme.

My presentation, on the whole, proceeded smoothly. I raised quite a few interesting issues in the paper given to me. In the presentation of about half an hour, I intentionally put in a rather slow but clear tone so that the Spanish speaking scholars, who were there in quite a good number, could follow me easily.

While there was, as usual, a mixed response from the critics, it had to a large extent lightened my burden. Now I was in a position to enjoy sound sleep as well as move around the city. Mexico happened to be quite an enchanting metropolis, and enjoyed mild climate even during the summer since it was located at a medium altitude. The hotel where we were lodged had a vantage location from where one could see the long spread of the city on all sides, especially at night time when it was brightly lit and presented a fairyland-like view. Incidentally, at that time Mexico also happened to be the most populous capital in the world.

Despite the local language being Spanish, there was no difficulty in moving around freely as English was understood by several people. I took a trip to the outskirts for which the organizers had provided the transport. I was keen to visit the settlements of the Red Indians who originally lived here, but had been driven northward after the Spanish conquest.

It meant a trip of around 50 km either way but it was quite rewarding as I saw these settlements as well as their places of worship and learnt about their mode of living and culture. There was a good deal of similarity with our tribal mode of living.

It also helped me to see their rich countryside, particularly the growth of agriculture. Incidentally, India had borrowed extensively from their experience in wheat cultivation, leading to the Green Revolution in Punjab and Haryana in the sixties.

Had restrictions not been imposed on my leave, I would have certainly made the best of this rare opportunity and moved around at more ease and visited some new destinations. But I was compelled to report back to Chandigarh within ten days. Consequently, I could barely manage a stopover for a couple of days in London, where I preferred to do shopping for the family.

But, as they say, inscrutable are the ways of Nature and you never know how it would compensate you for the opportunity missed. This aptly applied in my case.

VISIT TO JAPAN

In 1982 another invitation had been extended to me by the IEA for participation in the world energy Round-Table being held in Tokyo where I was required to contribute a paper on the experience of India on the non-conventional sources of energy. Thus, my cherished dream of a visit to the East and particularly Japan had come true. I also wanted to combine this trip with a visit to Manila, to see the functioning of the Asian Development Bank, and possibly visit Vancouver in the extreme western corner of Canada, which I learnt could be combined with this ticket. But again the constraint of time came in my way and I had to content myself with visiting Japan alone. I extended my stay there for a few days beyond the programme period to know more of its local life, culture and society.

Accordingly, after the programme, I moved to the suburb and stayed there with an Indian gentleman, the son of my colleague. He was pursuing Ph.D. at Hitosubhashi University. His fiancee was a Japanese lady and both lived in a small flat, in the traditional mode of living. I was keen to know about it since quite a large section of the society still followed it.

This was a typical oriental living style, which is also followed in several parts of our own country. But the Japanese had improved upon it a lot, unlike us who had made it worse and gradually unacceptable by the modern generation. In the small flat they occupied, there was one big room, which practically served as a complete living space. This room could be converted into two at night time by inserting wooden panels. Thus, without any trouble it was partitioned into two separate bedrooms. A large mattress covered the entire area of the room and on it was spread a spotlessly clean white sheet. In the middle of this was spread a small round table, around which members sat on their haunches for the meals.

I was surprised to learn that the Japanese fiancee of my friend's son was well versed in preparing *paronthas* of different sorts. She promised to treat me to them in the morning. Indeed, it was a very well done job, almost the way we did back home. They were so tasty that I overate. I had missed them during my weeklong stay in the hotel.

The usual Japanese food consisted of rice, steamed vegetables and fish. I was astonished to see that a very large variety of fish was available which was eaten with soya sauce. The Japanese diet was much lighter compared to the Indian one.

What appealed to me most was a high sense of hygiene and cleanliness in an average house. Before entering it, one had to unlace the shoes outside, where other comfortable light pairs of footwear were available for internal movement. Of course, while entering the main room covered with spotlessly clean linen one had to take them off and move around barefoot, which provided an easy access to all corners of the room, including squatting around the central table for food.

At night time the mattresses were taken out from their stacking place and each was covered with linen and supported by a comfortable pillow and soft wool blankets (according to the season). The bed was thus ready for a comfortable sleep. In fact, I enjoyed a far more comfortable sleep here than I did in the five-star hotel. I hardly knew when I slept and when I woke up. This was a unique comfort of the oriental style of sleeping.

In the morning, the mattresses were rolled up again and stacked back in their places. The partition was also removed and the big room was back in its proper place. Is this not wonderful? I appreciated how innovative and forward-looking the Japanese were. Little surprise they have moved to the top position on the development ladder.

Under such a living system, there was also the advantage that a guest or two would pose no problem and even in a small flat was comfortable. The toilet too was an improvement over the Indian style toilet. It was so meticulously planned that when flushed, not a drop of extra water would spill over to the outer space, which remained spick and span like before. Also, thanks to their technology, not only a smaller quantity of water was needed for flushing out the human excreta, but due to the force with which the flush worked, there was hardly any chance of any excreta left, not even the stubborn one.

On the contrary, in India we still stick to large flush tanks, which waste a considerable amount of water and even then fail to give the desired results.

Certainly, this is something to be learnt from that country, where appropriate improvement in technology provides a lot of benefit.

I had a Japanese friend, Kei Wakaizumi, who was a professor at Kyoto University, and I wanted meet him. We were together at the Hall of Residence (Passfield) in London and had developed close friendship. Now, after a gap of several years, there was an opportunity to meet again. I had contacted him from the hotel and we agreed to meet after the programme.

I travelled by a superfast Bullet train. It was my first experience of commuting by a train that moved at a speed of around 180 km per hour and the whole distance of 500 and odd km was covered in three hours only.

The remarkable part of the journey was that one could move with complete ease from one corner to another, while the train was in full motion, without feeling disturbed or experiencing any jerk. All the time it appeared that the train was in a stationary state, while actually it was running at the highest speed. En route, I keenly observed small towns and rural life and was struck by the economic use of its resources by this country. I observed well-demarcated small farms, with small tractors and other farm machinery parked in a corner. Even in large open places in towns, rice was cultivated.

Thus, while only a small percentage of land was available for agriculture—around 15 per cent of the entire area—yet it was put to the most intensive cultivation for growing rice and other crops. Later, I learnt that this small island country was almost self-sufficient in rice, which was also its staple diet.

The train reached its destination exactly at the announced time, such was the punctuality. My friend was waiting at the appointed spot. I went sight seeing in that beautiful city, visiting its cultural and historical places, as well as the university where students were on strike, but unlike our universities it was a peaceful strike, as discipline is an integral part of the Japanese culture. Even major strikes by workers are peaceful and seldom turn violent.

We also made a trip to the nearby port city of Osaka, where I learnt that quite a few Indians, mostly traders, had settled. Here I wanted to buy saris for my wife. Incidentally, in those days there was a craze for Japanese saris, which were known for their beautiful designs as well as strong texture and dyes. But when I enquired about these in Tokyo, hardly any one knew about them. Ultimately, it was the fiancee of my host who informed me that I would get them in Osaka.

We located a store in a corner, which stocked these saris. As its proprietor, a Sikh gentleman, had gone to meet Indian sailors who had arrived around that time to seek patronage to his store, we spent this time in moving around in that business city and had lunch at an Indian restaurant. I was told that there were quite a few Indian restaurants in Osaka, which showed that the city was quite popular with Indians.

When we revisited the store, the owner had returned. On learning that I was also a Punjabi, he spoke in chaste Punjabi with me. He had settled down at Osaka for several years and was married to a Japanese lady. I got to know that he owned a couple of more stores and was doing very well.

Thus, I spent around 12 days in Japan gaining useful experience of this remarkable oriental country, which had gained the top position in industry, technology and commerce.

During my return journey, while waiting at Narita international airport for my flight, I realized that I had left behind my newly purchased umbrella in the coach I had travelled. I did not have the coach particulars and as several coaches reached the airport in a short time, I thought that even if I complained, there was no chance of recovering the lost umbrella. Still I reached out to the customers' assistance desk and lodged a complaint with the minimum particulars I had. I was politely told to contact the desk again after some time.

I made a last-minute effort before going for the security check. And I could not believe when I was told that my umbrella had been retrieved and would soon be handed over to me. Even before this message had been delivered, the umbrella itself was very much there in the same condition I had left it. This strengthened my belief in the efficiency and honesty of the Japanese. Had this happened in India or in several other countries, there would have been scant hope of recovering a lost umbrella.

Another interesting situation worth recalling is my visit to the Tokyo fish market, which I was told is the world's biggest fish market. It was spread over a very large area, and one could not cover it in a single visit. A very large variety of fish had been put up for sale. What struck me most was the absence of any foul smell about which I had been worried on this visit, and had kept a handkerchief ready in my pocket to protect my nose. But there was no need for it as the whole area was highly hygienic, with regular drainage of fish with running water and several other precautions taken.

When I emerged from the market, after spending a good part of the morning, I realized there were surely unique qualities in the Japanese culture and character, which helped them in the maintenance of a high standard of hygiene and cleanliness.

And when we talk of technology, I recall my purchase of a camera as well as a Seiko watch during this visit. Though the camera was lost subsequently, even if a novice handled it, it yielded perfect snaps. The Seiko watch has been ever since giving me high precision in time, even after entering the next millennium. Could there be a better example of perfect technology?

This achievement is more remarkable as in the decade of 1930s, Japan was still struggling hard to establish itself in the world markets, and its goods were considered inferior compared with the British and several other West European countries. The label 'made in Japan' was associated with low quality products.

What a wonderful growth this country has made since. Even after suffering a complete annihilation during the Second World War, it has reached the top position.

No wonder this small island country, deprived of several key natural resources, is a top-runner in the world economy.

HONG KONG

En route, I stopped at Hong Kong, another beautiful island city, which was then a colony of the British and enjoyed a high status in global trade, business and finance, as well as had thriving tourist traffic. With several hours to go in catching the evening flight to Delhi, I moved around the city. Its several high-rise business premises, full of the latest goods, were shimmering under bright lights.

I also took a long boat ride through the blue waters that seemed to surround this port city endlessly. The weather was calm and pleasant, making our cruise all the more enjoyable, and I closely watched the fishing trawlers that we crossed en route. They were laden with the prized catch and we were warmly greeted by the fishermen. We also visited some small islands, strolling in their expanses of rich greenery.

Hong Kong was a major transit airport for several international flights. It was a fascinating sight when the flights took off from the airport. It appeared they were taking off from the surrounding sea itself, sending both a thrill and fright down the spine.

Then Hong Kong was still under British rule, though an agreement had been reached for its surrender to the Chinese government subsequently. As English was widely spoken, there was no problem of communication. I noticed a large number of Indians settled here doing thriving businesses. When I mentioned to them about this territorial change in governance, I found most of them were not quite happy and they earnestly prayed that such a decision would be reversed.

All this, of course, was soon to become a part of history.

1983 MADRID VISIT

Just a year after my visit to Japan, I was invited to the next world economic congress held in Madrid. Here I had to contribute a paper in the energy session, and another paper on India's experience on emigration to foreign lands. Incidentally, this trip was also a parting gift from my university, where, after serving for 18 years, I was retiring in September 1983, since I had reached the age of superannuation. However, as per convention, I was asked to complete the term, which meant my serving the university for a few more months.

This time Victor Urquidi was the president of the International Congress. It has always been a great pleasure to meet him, as well as the large circle of friends, that I had come in contact with meanwhile. Several new ideas were emerging. The conferences were becoming more complicated and the size of the participants was growing fast.

There were quite a few participants from India as well. Since the conference being held in Madrid, it made their participation easier, as several of them were already in this part of the world.

SAD EXPERIENCE AT THE ROME AIRPORT

On my return journey, I was keen to spend a day in Rome, which I had missed earlier, though at the cost of foregoing the Madrid closing session. But as bad luck would have it, I reached Rome rather late and it being a holiday, it was not possible for me to secure the transit visa. Also, the language problem proved far more formidable here than even in Paris. The attitude of the airport police was also somewhat aggressive as they were not prepared to entertain any plea and everything fell flat on their ears.

So, I was put in the worst possible situation and did not know what to do. Soon it was getting quite late and there appeared to be a very slim chance of reaching a hotel for the night. A local gentleman gave me a patient hearing and was quite sympathetic with my plight, but even his pleas to the local police in their language did not help.

While talking to him I realized that in my struggle to get the transit visa, I had completely ignored to check my luggage. This gentleman volunteered to do this on my behalf and took my baggage ticket. Soon when he returned, I was disappointed to learn that my baggage was not traceable. He felt that it might have been transferred to the next airport where this flight was to terminate. He added that it often happened on this route.

This was a totally unexpected development. Having faced a similar situation in Mexico recently, which had upset me so much, I forgot completely about the Rome visit. Thanks to the intervention of the stranger, he got the message flashed to the next airport, requesting that in case my baggage had reached there, it should be reloaded in the morning flight to Rome.

To help me keep a track of this he had got an extra copy of the message for me, to counter the language problem while making further enquiry.

It thus, again turned out to be a sleepless night for me at the airport, wondering about the fate of my baggage and unhappy thoughts again started visiting my mind about the Mexico episode. Although I started enquiring about my baggage from early morning, it was only a little before midday that a message was received that my baggage had been traced and soon it would be reaching this airport. This relieved my anxiety, which this time was fortunately short-lived but I had yet to confirm whether this was my baggage, and that was only possible after it was loaded into the Air-India flight.

While I patiently waited for this, I relaxed and had an easy time and also had a wash and felt fresh. Indeed a major headache was over. I felt that if I had not met the gentleman who came to my rescue at that hour, possibly I would not have checked my luggage and wondered what would have been the consequence.

Didn't I say earlier that strange are the ways of Nature which comes silently to your rescue at odd times?

After having learnt a lesson from my earlier experience, this time before boarding the Delhi flight I insisted that my baggage be shown to me, before it was loaded in the plane.

IN BUDAPEST AND VIENNA

Insofar as my visit to Rome was concerned, it fortunately materialized the very next year when I was invited to yet another Round-Table Conference of the IEA being held in Budapest as well as Vienna. On the way to Budapest I had much of the day and whole of the evening for a visit to Rome. Here I was fortunate to have the company of an Englishman who stayed close to my hotel and had volunteered to show me the important landmarks around.

I could not have asked for more. My problems of language as well as locating different sites in such a short time, were solved so effectively.

The best part of this trip was the time spent in visiting the Pope's headquarters in Vatican Palace. It is a colossal structure that enjoys its own status, administration and governance. A very large number of tourists had thronged this place. We took a complete round of the palace admiring its architecture and other related aspects.

A good part of the evening was spent enjoying the glitter of this city. We had snacks in an open-air cafe watching the traffic and crowds of people moving about in a highly hilarious mood. It indeed turned out to be one of the most pleasurable evenings. Thus, I was more than compensated for having missed a visit to the city during my last stopover. I thanked the gentleman for giving me company and showing me around. It was quite late when I returned to my hotel and enjoyed a sound sleep.

Budapest those days was a part of the vast communist empire, but like Poland it was far more tolerant and open. It enjoyed a picturesque location on the banks of Europe's famous river Danube and incidentally, had derived its name in 1873 from the merging of two towns—Buda and Pest—situated on either side of this river.

It was seeped in rich culture and history and at the same time was shaping into a highly modern city. The delegates of the Round-Table stayed in a hotel located in the wooded part of the city amidst calm surroundings and traditional buildings.

The atmosphere here was so different, unlike the other part of the city across the river, which was the commercial hub, full of modern activity and the main centre of the tourist attraction.

We were around 25 participants, and presentation of papers and discussions were held in the conference room of the hotel. The main theme was how the development of both Eastern and Western parts of Europe could be more effectively synthesized. It was like a trade-off between the two worlds where lots of changes had occurred and both had moved closer to each other, though a lot yet needed to be achieved with due care.

Interestingly, soon after this programme, tremendous changes actually occurred in the socialist world. In 1985 major changes in the outlook of the top leaders of the socialist empire were visible, which later resulted in the disappearance of the old world iron curtain and there was a rapid move towards the western brand of capitalism. While we looked closely at these expected changes, we did not visualize the speed of their occurrence. The likely impact of such changes on the third world countries was also deliberated upon.

When I landed in Budapest, the programme had already begun. I was late by around two hours and found that my paper was slated for presentation that very morning. Thus, suddenly I was caught in a strange situation and had not anticipated speaking before the learned participants so soon on my arrival.

However, I had to rise to the occasion. Taking the help of the main points I had already posed in my paper, I tried to develop these systematically during the presentation, which took about 40 minutes.

In the discussion that followed, I tried to resolve some critical doubts expressed on my observations. Indeed, it had sparked a small lively debate between the socialist and capitalist lobbies.

After Budapest, the closing and final session was held in Vienna. The organizers had arranged a comfortable boat journey through the river Danube, which provided a welcome change to the delegates. However, I had failed to get my visa for this journey in Delhi and the time to arrange it was very short. I was advised to contact my Embassy. I personally visited the officer in charge for this purpose. Luckily, the Indian Embassy was not far from our hotel.

The gentleman agreed to my request and thus, soon this visa was arranged and I was able to join the group and revelry.

UNFORGETTABLE BOAT JOURNEY

The boat journey through the river was indeed an exciting experience. The river was in an unusual calm and serene mood and also this long trip of about 280 km was equally peaceful. We moved around its spacious deck quite freely and enjoyed the lovely scenery of the rich fauna on both sides of the river. Most of us relaxed on the deck chairs, while others got involved in interesting discussions on global happenings.

I preferred the company of a Chinese delegate whom I had also met earlier in Tokyo and we had become quite friendly. Soon, a British scholar joined us and three of us exchanged views on the changes that were occurring in our respective economies.

That day, I had unfortunately run into a small health problem, which I shared with my Chinese friend, who got some medicines for my stomach ailment. This was probably the consequence of carelessness in food and drinks, which are an integral part of such international programmes.

The other evening, we had visited a traditional pub outside the city and spent a few hours over drinks, shared jokes and songs and topped it with a sumptuous dinner. It was here, I realized how even senior faculty members could get fully lost in the drinking spree and even indulge in all sorts of frivolities.

I had also observed this type of thing as a student during the weekends at Passfield Hall in London. The warden and other senior members did not mind getting drunk and joining the young residents of the hall in humour and singing.

Before the evening cast its shadow, we had reached our new destination, Vienna, a city which appeared to be highly glamorous. Had the organizers not arranged the closing session here, we would have certainly missed this exquisitely lovely city full of its own culture, tradition and history and a paradise for tourists, who thronged it the year around in large numbers.

Arrangements for our night's stay had been made among the picturesque surroundings of its suburb in a traditional building, which was centrally heated and cosy. When we woke up the next morning and were greeted by the warm rays of the bright sun, we could have a full glimpse of the area around and were charmed to find a white castle building not far from that place. This was a rich remnant from its past and it had been maintained with great care.

Unfortunately, we were short of time, as we had to move back to Budapest that very afternoon, on the last lap of our journey. Thus, a visit to its landmarks was out to question. However, to compensate us partly for this, the organizers had arranged the closing session right in the heart of the city so that we could find time to look around the shopping plazas.

During the concluding session, reports on the programme were presented and some discussion also followed, where the participants set the records straight about the missing links in the report. All this took around two hours and then followed a lavish lunch, where of course, due to my weak constitution, I was quite careful and especially when I had to take the morning flight.

Our return journey had been arranged in a luxury train, which like the boat journey undertaken the previous day, was exclusively for our travel. The train was luxurious right from one corner to another and it chugged at a comfortable speed through the rich landscape of woods and forests wrapped in greenery, where peace ruled supreme. Most of us took a small nap or relaxed. We also exchanged some last-minute greetings, as all of us would be moving to other destinations by next forenoon. If anyone needed to stay further in the hotel, he would have to foot the hefty bill. Unfortunately, my return ticket was not yet confirmed and I was told that I would have to wait for a couple of more days, because of the heavy rush. This put me in a great dilemma and I could not afford to stay here any longer. As a last resort, I contacted the Indian Embassy gentleman again at his residence and told him of my problem. He quite understood my predicament and promised to resolve it.

He spoke to the airlines authorities and from the diplomatic quota, managed a confirmed seat for me in the morning flight, which was for travel up to Frankfurt, from where I was required to board the Air-India flight to Delhi. He also told me that there should be no difficulty in finding a seat in the Jumbo Jet flight of Air India. But in case some assistance was required, he gave me the reference of a particular gentleman at the Air-India counter who would help. I again got a taste of how helpful our Embassy people were. My experience in other foreign visits had been similar, especially in Warsaw where during my three-month stay I felt at completely at home because of the help extended by the Embassy staff in several ways in times of need. I was even permitted to use the diplomatic bag for getting my mail from India, which otherwise would have taken a number of days to reach.

I often wonder why their counterparts in the government in India fail to learn from them. If they did, our country would also improve a lot.

Post-retirement Problems

As I have pointed out earlier, though my retirement was due in September 1983, I was permitted to stay in the department till the academic session ended in April next year. This extended period was of great help to me to plan my retirement, which indeed comes about so suddenly that one is hardly prepared to face it.

Here the foremost problem was of a house, for, after getting used to the comfort of an official accommodation, I had seldom bothered about it.

I looked forward to settling down in the family house, which now appeared to come to my rescue. But it was not going to be that easy since there was hardly any unoccupied space in the house, as other members had taken possession of every conceivable constructed space. So, there was little possibility of my finding an easy entry, especially with all the paraphernalia accumulated during the long stay on the campus.

Simultaneously, with no pension to fall back upon, which I would have at least earned in a government job, I faced an insecure and bleak future. More so since my two children were yet quite young and would take time to grow and settle. Thus, a real challenge stared at me. A major part of the small income earned through the interest on fixed deposit raised against my provident fund and gratuity had been earmarked for the repair and renovation of the house to make it fit for us.

HOUSE CONSTRUCTION

Thus, this extended period of service was a real boon. When none of the family members was prepared to cooperate, we virtually barged into the house and made our presence felt with a plan of construction prepared by my son, who was then a student of the college of architecture. The house had a lobby, which was being used for dumping extra goods by a family member. We planned to carve out a kitchen and toilet, as well as couple of *mianis* (storages) for baggage and extras in this area. The lobby extended to the spacious *verandah* used mainly for sleeping purpose during summer. We planned to convert it into two small additional bedrooms for our requirement.

And there was the family drawing room, which was rarely used. Gradually, it was to be made a part of our accommodation since we sought an equal share in the house. The old dining room had, meanwhile, been converted into a living room by my younger brother who had died in 1973 in a road accident and his wife, who did not have any issue, had since then shifted to her family house and locked this room.

She happily had a soft corner for our family and when we approached and convinced her about our urgent need of accommodation, she agreed to vacate her room after we had suitably compensated her monetarily. We promised to take care of her goods, in case she was not interested in removing them.

During this construction period often angry remarks were exchanged, as it caused inconvenience to the other family members.

Incidentally, the annexe in the house, where we had stayed before shifting to the campus, continued to remain under our possession. Just sometime before my retirement, the wife of my younger brother, who stayed in a room in the main house along with her family members had visited us on the campus and requested for being allowed to shift to the annexe and they would vacate their room occupied in the main house in our favour.

They were not happy to share the common toilet and bath with the family of other brother who stayed in the adjoining room. In the annexe, on the other hand, they would have independent facilities, including the kitchen. This arrangement suited us as with this our claim to the main house was strengthened. Also, my other younger brother who was the co-sharer of the common toilet-cum-bath facilities would become more cooperative, for he would now have the opportunity to get hold of this room in case we vacated our claim on it and, in fact, he needed it urgently for his growing family.

And thus members of this family, who had initially created much noise on our undertaking construction, were now far less vociferous. So, gradually things had settled down and before the extended period of our stay on the campus house expired, we handed it over to the university.

NORTH-EAST ASSIGNMENT

However, at the time of final shifting from the campus, I was not in Chandigarh. I had meanwhile, left for Calcutta to participate in a couple of programmes there. And after that, I went to Shillong to join the North East Hill University, as I had got an offer of a visiting assignment for a year from them. In fact, as I learnt later, the offer was for their campus at Aizawl in Mizoram, frankly a place of which I had very little knowledge.

I soon got to know that it was a difficult area in the extreme corner of the country, mostly surrounded by a thick jungle belt, cut off from means of communication and, above all, it was a highly disturbed area. All this was disheartening and I was not sure whether I would be able to join that place. I planned to decide after a personal visit there.

Meanwhile, I found Shillong—where I was allowed to join for the initial period of couple of months—to be a pleasant place in summer, as compared to the terribly hot conditions of Chandigarh. Also, arrangements for my food and stay in the guest house were satisfactory, though it suffered from water problem.

While in Shillong, I had taken a week off and visited Aizawl. Fortunately, I did not find its topography as frightening as I had imagined. In fact, I liked its thick green cover and the extensive jungle stretch that surrounded it. The communication system was also not that bad, though there was acute water problem. The climate here too was mild and pleasant.

I visited the department there and also my room, which was satisfactory. Also, my colleagues, including Mizos, were quite friendly and helpful. So, I decided to join this campus after the fortnight break in July.

I visited Chandigarh during the July break. In the North East, travel by air was the most convenient mode. The government had also substantially subsidized it. I had been cut off from my family for the last couple of months. While they had shifted to the new place after the major construction work was through, several internal fittings and other facilities had yet to be attended to.

Meanwhile, our daughter had run into a difficult health problem which, by the grace of God and timely diagnosis, was controlled. But it had caused a heavy strain on my wife in particular.

Our new accommodation presented a praiseworthy look. It was a great improvement over the accommodation occupied by my other brothers. It reflected the good taste of my son who had used the latest designs. Its modern kitchen, toilet, two additional bedrooms, apart from the master bedroom and a large sitting-cum-dining room, along with plenty of storages planned by completely reconstructing the old area, earned good praise from those who visited us.

A formal *Greh Parvesh* (house-warming) ceremony—auspicious house entry ceremony—was performed, after I visited Chandigarh, with *havan* (prayer) and distribution of sweets, followed by a special lunch. Certainly the generous income I had earned in my new assignment proved to be of great help at this critical time.

On my return journey, I had stayed for a few days in Shillong and then finally moved over to Aizawl, where my stay arrangements had also been made in the university guesthouse. While rice was the staple food in that area, our cook, who was a non-tribesman, also prepared *chapattis* and *paronthas*. So, I did not face any problem and got adjusted to it.

Despite the fact that the North East area was highly rich in rainfall, in fact, some of its areas received the maximum rainfall in the country, the tragedy was that it faced the worst water problem, especially during the lean season. Also, potable water was a problem, for one was never sure about the quality of water available even after boiling and filtration.

ROLE OF MISSIONARIES

As I had plenty of spare time in that lonely and sparsely populated place with hardly any social life since the locals retired early, I would often read travel accounts by the British missionaries in particular, who had contributed enormously in reforming the tribal areas during their visits to these difficult places.

I derived inspiration from these writings and appreciated their adventurous spirit for coming all the way from their homeland to these distant jungles, which were not safe to travel, much less to work among the most difficult tribesmen. Their contribution in civilizing the tribesmen is indeed remarkable.

The missionaries also shaped the local language and gave it a written shape. They also brought medical help, education and sanitation to their doorstep and thus succeeded in transforming them in several ways.

Now if the locals had any grudge against India, they were justified, for the new government had failed to meet their aspirations. Rather, for quite a number of years after Independence they were virtually ignored.

It was only after the Chinese incursion through the North-East, when they had a safe passage over a large Indian territory without facing any resistance, that the Indian government woke up from its long slumber and realized that it had neglected these highly vulnerable borders.

Thus, now the attention had begun to be focussed on the development of this area. But, the government's policies lacked a realistic touch and a large amount of money that was filtered into these areas for local development actually failed to reach the beneficiaries as a substantial part of it was wasted on non-productive programmes, or siphoned into the pockets of corrupt administrators and politicians.

The long period of insurgency, especially by the Nagas and later by the Mizos, which spurred so frequently, had caused a great damage to the government's relations with the tribesmen. Also, the Indian forces suffered a heavy loss when several of them perished in these difficult terrains. Much of this could have been averted had the government tackled this sensitive issue of insurgency with care and thought, through the cooperation of the local leaders, the way it was done by the British.

I recall the ignorance of an average Mizo, when several of them gazed with utter amazement at the statue of Mahatma Gandhi that was installed in a park opposite the Raj Bhawan in Aizawl. Many felt amused at the sight of this semi-naked, dull looking figure, even after reading it was Gandhi. But who is Gandhi? They asked this question even after almost four decades of Independence. Whose fault was it? Surely, of the Indian government which treated these areas as if they were foreign pockets and had nothing to do with India.

In fact, our attitude towards these tribal areas had long been of indifference. In such an atmosphere, if they had turned out to be hostile towards India it was understandable. Our leaders have hardly cared to visit these areas and listen patiently to their grievances or educate them about the changes emerging in this country. Their knowledge was derived from the teachings of foreign missionaries. Unfortunately, we have never tried to re-educate them properly after the British left. They were completely ignorant about the Indian history, culture and civilisation and the struggle made by its leaders in securing freedom.

Thus, their hostility towards the Indian government needed to be appreciated against this background. And, unfortunately, the situation was made still worse due to pursuing of wrong policies by the administration that went counter to their aspirations.

Personally, I found them to be quite friendly and even helpful. Of course, much of it depended on how one approached them and took interest in their language, culture and values. They could be very ruthless and callous in case you asserted your views and failed to listen to them. They might initially appear to be unfriendly and hostile, but once you got to know them they would extend their full cooperation and friendship.

During my stay in Aizawl, I also tried to contribute writings on the complex socio-economic problems faced in this region and here I got especially interested in the local agrarian system. Like in the rest of country, agriculture was the stay of the local people here, as modern industry had not taken its roots and was not likely to either, for a long time to come because of the constraints of infrastructure, technology as well as market forces. Even with a high rate of literacy, including among women, technical knowledge was almost missing.

Even in the area of agriculture, though it was the principal means of subsistence, transparency was missing since a large percentage of the population scattered over isolated hamlets not easily accessible, practised a highly wasteful method of *jhum* (shifting) cultivation, which had already destroyed over a quarter of the rich forest cover, thus, converting it almost into a wasteland. The situation was no different in several other areas of the North-East.

Thus, a good part of the rich fauna had turned into not only unproductive wasteland and dusty area, but also posed a major danger to the local environment, especially during the month of March, when high velocity dust-laden hurricanes ruthlessly struck houses and other property, causing huge damage.

All this was the result of destroying the natural balance in this area through reckless human activity of carving agricultural land out of the forest cover. The Mizo government was also quite aware of this problem, and was keen to come out with a concrete plan for putting a permanent end to this mode of cultivation. It was keen to encourage a stable, environment friendly and less forest destroying programme within the reach of farmers, which would also yield them a good return.

In fact, in 1985 or so, the government had launched a vigorous crusade against the *jhum* cultivation, creating awareness among the people about the tremendous damage caused by it to the local environment. It appealed to them to desist from this system and take to settled land cultivation, or even undertake other allied activities which would help save the forests. People were made aware of it, through frequent programmes on the radio, appeals from politicians and other leaders, public meetings and in several other ways. The government announced that the *jhum* system (shifting) of cultivation would be closed down totally by 2001 and anyone found practising this system subsequently would be severely dealt with.

It simultaneously realized that this crucial system of agrarian reforms could only succeed if the farmers were provided with an alternative mode of production through the creation of settled land area. And those who could not be adjusted under this system should be provided with alternative good income yielding vocations.

I happened to be in Aizawl in 1985, and had already shown an interest in the development of this area. I was approached by the government to help them prepare a 15-year-plan for the execution of this project so that by 2001 there was a complete closure of *jhumming* and farmers were suitably accommodated both in agricultural and alternative activities.

I agreed to help them and prepared a prospective 15-year plan, which was split into three mini five-year plans. The initial mini plan pertained to creating settled land itself through land surveys and other technical inputs and investments. It, by and large, laid emphasis on the existing disturbed land, which needed to be systematically developed for settled cultivation. In addition to it, lands close to the villages, which could also be brought under permanent cultivation with the least environment disturbance, should be identified and systematically developed. Thus, both the already disturbed land as well as the new land carved out from the village surroundings, constituted the initial corpus of settled land on which the farmers should be settled on a permanent basis, after these areas had been suitably developed.

Since during this crucial phase of land development, farmers would be disturbed and would not have any source of livelihood, they should be suitably compensated for it by the state. During the second phase of the 15-year plan, it should be possible to settle down the maximum number of them on the land so developed.

Even so, as there was a likelihood that a large number of farmers would still not be settled, attention should be focussed on them during the second and third mini plans, where the maximum opportunities should be identified in areas close to the villages in horticulture, plantation of coffee, tea and rubber, piggery, dairy, poultry and other allied activities, as well as processing activities which should be encouraged.

Ultimately, I had suggested that more people should be shifted from farming to alternative activities, which should provide them with a comparatively higher income. Further, such a mode of transformation would also reduce pressure on agricultural land, as well as enable the fewer people practising it to make the best of the land use.

I was also of the opinion that in the last phase of the 15-year cycle, the whole programme should be integrated effectively for encouraging self-sustained programme in rural development.

I had also worked out the total investment that would be involved during this 15-year period at the 1985 prices.

This exercise had provoked a good interest, as I learnt. The whole scheme was also taken to the Planning Commission for their knowledge, as well as for the release of necessary funds. The Planning Commission, it appears, had suggested that they would get it examined first by sending a team of their experts to Mizoram before sanctioning this programme.

It was of course, an exploratory exercise in agrarian reform in this tribal area based on the scanty information available. Before it could be considered, it needed to be worked out further with great care and imagination, keeping in view the peculiar land related problem in the North-East. I had also added that unless such an exercise was given a trial, we would not be able to enter meaningfully into the complex area of tribal land reforms.

Above all, such a drastic change in this sensitive area of agriculture needed a strong political will, as well as cooperation and understanding from the farmers. Experience the world over has shown that farmers are the most difficult people to change, as agriculture itself is a highly risky business, where Nature plays the supreme role.

I do not know what exactly happened to this exercise subsequently. Possibly, it was forgotten under the subsequent developments, when a new government headed by the strong man of Mizoram—Laldenga—who had spearheaded one of the longest as well as the bloodiest insurgency battles in the North-East, was voted into power.

Despite several constraints faced in creating settled land in the difficult terrain of the North-East, I felt that unless determined efforts were made in this direction, it would be difficult to change the current mode of agriculture and thus this area would continue to face difficult environment problem.

SURVEY OF LUNGDAI VILLAGE

During the last few months of my stay in Aizawl—I left it in mid-1986 after the completion of my term—I was associated with the socio-economic survey of the rural areas on behalf of the university. Here we had made a beginning with Lungdai village, which was not far from Aizawl. We initially carried out a house-to-house survey with the help of a comprehensive schedule, where the Mizo colleagues in the department were a great help, especially in overcoming the barrier of the language problem in contacting the local households. Before I left, a substantial part of the report too had been prepared. It was finalized and published later. The Lungdai survey, which was the first comprehensive work on rural development in that area, became a landmark for the future rural surveys among the tribal areas in the North-East and revealed quite a number of interesting socio-economic features in rural development.

Seeing the success of the Lungdai survey, I was keen that more similar surveys be conducted in other rural areas of Mizoram, which would provide a useful training ground to the young Mizos in socio-economic surveys, as well as help them in formulating important policy issues for rural development.

I also found that my experiments of conducting weekly seminars on current economic issues, were also well participated by teachers from different local colleges, which in turn helped them to learn more about the current developments occurring in the Indian as well as world economy. I also found that this was a good way of keeping them well informed about current affairs.

SEMINAR IN AIZAWL

I had also been approached by the North East Council, an official body which coordinated development programmes in all seven states of that area, for holding a regional seminar on the 'Emerging pattern of North Eastern economy' for which they had sanctioned some funds. This seminar was duly organized with good participation by teachers in the North East, as well as the neighbouring universities and also by bureaucrats.

After I returned to Chandigarh, I got two volumes, based on my stay in the North-East, published. Of these, one volume was exclusively based on the seminar.

Thus, though initially I was hesitant to visit the difficult terrain of the North-East, I had subsequently a very busy time there during my stay, which had been extended by one more year. I involved myself in different socio-economic activities, as well as found time to read extensively about these people.

Of course, the most prized contribution of my stay in Mizoram was the drafting of a 15-year-plan for converting *jhum* cultivation into settled agriculture and also modernization of the local economy through other thoughtful programmes. This 15-year-plan was also incorporated in a published volume on the North-East.

Later, despite distance and other constraints, I did not cut off myself completely from the North-East. I maintained occasional contact through programmes held mainly in Shillong, though could not visit Aizawl again.

Back to Chandigarh

In 1986, when I had settled down in Chandigarh, I had another opportunity to participate in the IEA Congress of world economists, this time being held in New Delhi, in the capacity of a rapporteur. This was my third consecutive participation in this congress, which had begun in 1980 from Mexico. Thus, I served in this body as a discussant, paper contributor and finally rapporteur.

The Delhi congress had a very large participation, where several Indian economists also joined, besides several others from the neighbouring countries.

Incidentally, from 1978 to 1986 I had found quite a few opportunities to visit foreign countries, as an invitee of the IEA which, except for the Warsaw Round-Table, also financed my travel expenses as well as provided me with five-star hospitality. I could not have asked for more. I had participated in four Round Tables and three global conferences of the IEA which also helped me come in contact with several renowned economists and I was also able to interact with them on several vital issues. These programmes also provided me with ample opportunities to make my presentations, as well as interact with the participants from the world institutes during discussions. This has provided me with a rich experience that I cherish.

But the Warsaw visit and subsequent travel to several

countries stands out amongst all the trips. I got an opportunity to visit a good part of the communist world. Besides Poland, where I spent three months, I visited DDR (East Germany, which was then a part of the communist empire) and in the last lap of this journey I had visited the mightiest communist country, Russia. At that time the world was virtually controlled by two superpowers, the USA (leader of the capitalist world) and Russia (leader of the communist world). It was thus my best foreign trip when I essayed several western as well as socialist countries in a single go and also travelled extensively within these countries.

My subsequent visits unfortunately were not well timed, as they occurred when the teaching sessions were on. Had these too fallen during the vacation period, I could have visited more countries also.

STINT WITH PLANNING COMMISSION

After the Mizoram stint, I had one with the Planning Commission. It was a short-period contract job as a consultant, under their project "National transport perspective for 2000 year." It was a part of similar studies being undertaken at the behest of Rajiv Gandhi who was then the Prime Minister and keen that India, while entering the next (21st) century, should play a crucial role in the global scenario. For that it was essential to kickstart suitable programmes in different areas of the Indian economy and for identifying these programmes these national studies were essential.

In my new position, I was attached to a core group in the area of India's waterways, where even after several years of planned development, nothing concrete had emerged for the transport of bulky traffic, which was fast rising and imposing a heavy pressure on both roads and railways. Thus, if we could divert even a part of the bulky goods traffic from the choked roads and railways to waterways it would mean a tremendous relief to the surface transport.

It was a perfectly justified argument, particularly when we were blessed with rich waterways, covering the entire length and breadth of this country. However, there were several constraints in taming them for bulk transport. Foremost, these waterways did not follow any disciplined route or behaviour. They received the maximum water during a couple of months of the rainy season, when several of them would even flood the surrounding areas, causing heavy damage to a vast area.

And for the rest of the time, most of these rivers received scanty supply and some even ran completely dry, thus becoming unfit for navigation. So the first job was to select those waterways, which enjoyed perennial water supply the year around and also touched a large number of important destinations. These rivers could constitute potential traffic routes and be utilized for the transportation of bulky traffic. Of course, a lot of homework would have to be done before they were made traffic-worthy.

Gradually, as more experience was gained about the functioning of these routes, further improvements should be effected and more potential waterways explored, and steps undertaken to make them traffic-worthy. In this way, a perspective waterways plan would itself take shape, focussing ultimately, at the linking of major waterways and their tributaries in a nationwide system for making the optimal use of our water resources, which currently flow unutilized, into the sea.

In other words, a carefully thought out and implemented plan for wedging the gaps in our waterways system within a reasonable time alone would assure a long-term development of this crucial source of carriage of bulky cargo over a long distance. Such a system would also provide a great relief to the highly choked land routes, especially considering the expanding human and light goods traffic.

We started with the study of the Ganges and Brahmaputra river systems, which spanned much of the northern and eastern areas of this country. They possessed vast potential for the carriage of bulky traffic the year around and fortunately also various important cities fell on their routes. Currently, the studies revealed, they carried insignificant traffic as well as the distance these covered was usually short.

First we had to identify the deficiencies which were a hurdle in the smooth flow of traffic, so that these were suitably tackled for carving out long traffic stretches. Therefore, with necessary changes in the river behaviour, its topography, flow of water and allied areas, these rivers would get ready for the carriage of bigger loads as well as the traffic would be able to cover longer distances.

Thus, within the time at the disposal of the group, an effective beginning had been made in tackling the numerous segments of the country's complex transport system for the carriage of goods traffic in particular, on which also depended the future development of this country.

While these studies were in progress, I unfortunately met with an accident when a fast moving scooter hit my left leg hard while I was crossing a road in the Connaught Place area of New Delhi. This caused multiple fractures and my left leg was ultimately put under plaster, which spelt a couple of months' complete confinement to bed. This unfortunate occurrence also deprived my participation in this interesting project. Soon, however, the final report on all modes of transport for the transport plan was finalized by the group and presented to the Planning Commission.

In this way, a number of useful studies for the planned growth of different sectors of the Indian economy were prepared during this period. Had these been properly pursued and further worked out they would have been of great help for a more transparent growth of the economy, especially during the era of globalization. But soon when the new government at the Centre was voted to power, most of these studies were forgotten and possibly dumped into the government archives.

Working with the Planning Commission also provided me with useful insight into the functioning of this august body. It was like a mini parallel government presided over by the Deputy Chairman of the rank of cabinet minister, helped by a coterie of members enjoying the central ministers' rank, while advisers who followed next ranked like secretaries and so on.

It had its own generous budget for meeting salaries, travelling allowances and other expenses of its multiple activities and generally the way it was spent was not questioned.

It thus, enjoyed a special status, normally not found in by any other government organization. Since the Prime Minister was its chairman, it added further to its glitter and authority. It had its own secretariat where a large number of officers and other rank employees worked. A large number of full-time as well as part-time consultants and other specialists also helped in the commission's several odd activities.

The activity of seeking the final approval to their annual plans by the states, often turned out to be a big show as several senior officers would crowd the corridors of the Commission, anxiously waiting for their turn to discuss their individual state's problems with the member concerned. Well aware of the fact that large cuts would be applied to their demands, the states would initially present inflated expenditure figures, well beyond their own capacity to spend.

ACCIDENT AND RECOVERY

As mentioned, while working with the Planning Commission I had met with an accident, leading to a long detention in bed. In view of the multiple fractures suffered on the left leg and considering my age, the attending doctor had declared that the confinement period could be a minimum of three months. That was indeed terrible, for I was not used to such a long period of inactivity as I had always been occupied with several programmes. But with this accident, I seemed to have no choice.

Meanwhile, I had shifted to my home in Chandigarh, where I could get better care. In that condition, I could still attend to my urgent mail as well as follow the reading and writing routine. But I was unable to handle my typewriter for which I would have to wait.

Thus, most of my written work was passed on to a typist. Happily, I carried all along a strong urge for early recovery, and took measures to achieve it, like frequent exercising of the toes of my injured left leg. I also followed other precautions as advised. Soon the situation appeared to be in my favour, which was reflected in the x-ray reports. And, fortunately I was able to move about after two and a half months of confinement against the three months predicted by the doctor. I remember when I made my first attempt to stand. It appeared to be an almost impossible job. I failed every time I tried this, and felt that my energy had dissipated. Next, I attempted walking, which again seemed an insurmountable job. Even after practice, I found I could only walk with a support. Worse, I limped which I did not like at all. I wanted to walk straight and erect like before the accident.

That, however, appeared to be a far-off thing. I feared I might have to end up ultimately with a lifelong limp, which sent a cold shiver through my body. I resolved to walk straight and erect. From then onwards I walked little but tried to walk straight even though it meant putting up with an excruciating pain.

Once, while I was practicing learning to walk, a homeopathic doctor friend walked in. He strongly advised me against cultivating the limping habit for soon it would become a permanent feature in my life, he feared. But when I narrated to him the unbearable pain I experienced while walking straight, he made me lie down and examined my injured leg closely. He found some bends beyond the injured spot and tried to straighten these. He had, however, warned me of the terrible pain I would suffer, but told me to bear it for this was the only way it could be corrected.

I tried to cooperate with him. However, when I could no longer stand the pain, it had to be given up, but soon the situation improved a lot. He gave me an ointment which he had prepared and asked me to apply it frequently on the injured portion as well as surrounding areas, which would provide a healing touch and also help in my walking straight.

I followed his instructions and it was not long before I was walking straight and erect almost the way I always did and also took a small walk in the house and the close by area. Thus, I acquired confidence in walking and soon had also discarded the walking stick. Just a little later, I was also able to visit Delhi independently and the Planning Commission. Here I faced difficulty while climbing up the steps to the first floor and even more while descending to the ground floor.

This difficulty too was soon conquered through practice. And after some time I even managed to attend a programme in the Simla hills and faced little difficulty in reaching the guesthouse and climbing up its stairs. Here I could also negotiate a small climb but rarely tried the difficult climbs for which I had to wait.

Thus, on the whole I found that within a month and a half of my recovery I was on the way to my earlier activities. This experience taught me that if one was really determined and did not give up easily, there was no reason why success could not be achieved. This lesson on determination stood firm with me even later, and whenever I faced any difficulty, I was reminded of this experience.

Settling to a New Life

After the Planning Commission stint I settled down in Chandigarh in my family house where, as mentioned earlier, we had made the necessary alterations. I had also reached the age of 65 and did not look forward to any more assignments. However, to lead an active and purposeful life even after retirement, I established a small non-governmental organization (NGO) to undertake research projects, organize seminars, publish a journal and engage in allied activities. The institution—Centre for Indian Development Studies—was duly got registered under the Indian Societies Act.

NGO CENTRE

The Centre soon became my field of interest and activity, for which I was also able to have the support and cooperation of my former students, colleagues and other well-wishers. Gradually, we were able to chalk out the programme of our activities, where we planned to move slowly but effectively.

But the greatest challenge we faced was of finance, which I think applies to all new NGOs. Since I was running the Centre from my residence, I had to be careful so as not to bedevil the house with the clutter of a growing number of files, papers, journals, stationery material and other items needed for its day-to-day operation.

Initially, we did not have any funds for starting the functioning of our Centre and neither was there any provision for paid membership in our constitution. Funds could be raised only through the Centre's programmes, fees and donations, which were likely to be generated only in due course of time. But how we were to get funds initially? That was the challenge we faced.

But not to be let down so early or think of closing the institute, I had injected some funds of my own which I thought could be recovered later as we moved along. It was thus a sort of loan to the institute. Insofar as the space problem was concerned, I used my bedroom for the purpose. Already I had an office table in this room which now served the dual purpose—of my own writings and the activities of the Centre. I also had a portable typewriter, which too helped in the institute's correspondence and other activities.

An empty shelf in the room was commissioned for storing the Centre's files, stationery, meeting registers and other papers. As I knew typing well, I drafted and typed out its correspondence as well as noted the minutes of its meetings. Even the notices for the meetings were typed on this typewriter. This indeed was a great asset, which besides sharing a good load of correspondence also helped in typing out urgent messages and articles at odd hours, when no office staff was available.

This arrangement also helped us save expenses on employing a typist/office assistant, which frankly we could not afford. We made it going with thoughtful planning and vision.

Soon, we had arranged our first one-day programme. It was a regional seminar on energy, an area which was also on the top priority of the country's agenda and called for a close examination by experts from different organizations and suggestions of viable solutions. We had an encouraging participation by quite a few experts who presented papers as well as deliberated on the issue, the whole day long.

It was an encouraging beginning, which also helped us to raise some funds through the publication of advertisements in the souvenir released on the occasion. And after meeting the expenses of this seminar, we were also able to earn a small surplus amount, which constituted the initial corpus of this Centre.

Next, we moved on from a regional to national-level seminar. It was again on energy, an area in which we had by now developed contacts and were assured of good papers from different parts of the country. This time the seminar was for two days and like last time, held in Panjab University in a spacious seminar room, fitted with modern facilities.

A few outstation participants also joined and we provided them with a small financial help as well as warm hospitality. This time we were also able to collect more funds through advertisements and add a larger amount to the Centre's account.

In this way, we had kickstarted our activities and created more interest in the functioning of this Centre. On the basis of papers collected on both the energy seminars, we brought out one full volume on energy, which also brought popularity to the name of our Centre.

PUBLICATION OF JOURNAL

In 1992, we planned to extend the activities of this Centre by publishing its own journal. While I wanted it to be a quarterly publication, but with the resource crunch and several other problems, we had to be content with a biannual journal. But the publication of an academic journal itself was fraught with several complications like, getting good papers for publication, their careful editing, finding a good publisher on reasonable budget, ensuring accurate statistical data and references, careful proof-reading to weed out possible howlers, printing an attractive cover page, which should reflect the inside material etc. Then there was the major problem of finance, as well as finding a good market for its sale.

Further, 1991-92 was the time when universities and other educational institutes were told by the UGC to stop subscribing to new journals and were even asked to stop renewing costly journals. Thus, it was an inappropriate time for the start of a fresh journal and I had been warned of this by several well-wishers.

But I had made up my mind on starting the journal and in 1992 its maiden issue was published. It was devoted exclusively to the regional problems of Indian agriculture, an approach also in line with our policy to encourage regional bias so as to distinguish our journal from others.

This issue was well received, though we did not have a single paid subscriber.

Luckily, we were able to finance it through advertisements which also left us with a small surplus amount.

We naturally did not anticipate any market sale of our first issue, nor could the libraries subscribe to it in view of the blanket ban imposed by the UGC on the new journals. So practically all the copies were used for the sale promotion drive, which did pay us in due course of time. Apart from subscribers, we also planned its market sale.

The next issue was devoted to rural development, for which we managed to get some good papers from reputed contributors. We were loaded with papers which needed a good deal of homework before they could be brought to the level of publication. But where was the time for all this? Thus, often we had to depend upon reprinting some good papers relating to the main theme of a particular issue that had already appeared. This also saved us the bother of editing, an area in which we were woefully short.

We were, in particular, disappointed by the poor response from young contributors whom we wanted to encourage. Even those who contributed often did it without doing proper homework. I have often wondered why efforts are not made by the university departments to train senior researchers, in the art of good and meaningful writing supported by necessary tables, notes and references. In fact, though they are guided by senior teachers, the outcome is poor.

But, despite the several constraints our journal has survived. Though I have often wondered that while we talk with pride of both liberalization and globalization of the Indian economy, why can't the UGC and other higher authorities apply the same yardstick in the case of journals subscribed by the university and college libraries which happen to be the major patrons of academic journals?

PROJECT WORK

Soon after we had entered the area of journal publication, we were blessed with a small project by the ministry of agriculture in New Delhi. This was our first such venture and helped the institute to push itself further, especially in the field of data collection.

This project for the data collection from the border villagers in Punjab was around 1991-92, when militancy was at its height and no one was prepared to visit the border areas. It was quite a risky and problematic venture and it seemed almost impossible to undertake this job. But, with a determined effort we tackled this knotty issue by managing to get the support of field investigators from the Punjab Agricultural University in Ludhiana who possessed similar experience. Thus, with their support and cooperation, this job was completed satisfactorily.

Now taking stock, a little after a decade and half existence of this Centre, I find it has definitely covered a reasonable stretch, completed five projects in different areas mainly involving evaluation of ongoing programmes. Barring the first project, in all other projects, besides the collection of field data we were also asked to complete the final project reports. Working with a group of people, as well as funding them and learning from them, has indeed been a fascinating experience.

I am glad to add that after settling down in Chandigarh, following my last assignment with the Planning Commission, it has been possible to lead an active and purposeful life.

My Mother-in-law and our Children

This autobiography would remain incomplete without mentioning the services rendered by my mother-in-law Santi Devi to the family. She joined us in the early 1970s and stayed with us till her death in 2004. As I have already mentioned, my mother Maya Devi had died in 1952 in Simla. It was my mother-in-law who filled the void created by the death of Bebe.

She took full care of me, as well as our son Rajeev and daughter Jyotsana, who were barely eight and six years old, respectively, when she came to us. She was also a great help to her own daughter and other family members, who visited us quite frequently.

It was only because of her presence that my wife Santosh could complete her degrees of M.A., B.Lib. and Ph.D. and become the most academically qualified member in her family.

The children were so attached to their *nani* (maternal grandmother) that they would feel uneasy when she was not at home. At the same time, they also dared not disobey her, and she had a strong hold on them. In fact, we were happy when she was in full control of household affairs. We rarely interfered in her functioning, and that was what made her all the more attached to us.

Possibly, this was also one of the reasons that a lady of her dominating nature could stay with us for a long time. This was obviously missing in her own son's house where it was his wife who zealously took over this job, thus pushing her mother-in-law into the background. And neither her son Raj, who was of a difficult nature—though blessed with a scientific and argumentative mind, which unfortunately often yielded unproductive results—bothered about this issue (or possibly he felt helpless)? The net result was that his mother felt slighted and ignored under these circumstances.

She had led a distressed life right from early days when she lost her husband. She had two sons and four daughters to take care of with hardly any regular source of income. The elders in the family took care of her and the family, as the majority of the members were still minors.

Under the circumstances, it was tough going. She also lost her elder son when he was yet in his teens. Now the burden of maintaining the family fell on the younger son Raj. They started staying independently in a rented accommodation when he got a job.

It appears that the heavy burden of the family falling on the shoulders of her son at a tender age, also contributed to his harsh nature. However, their mother who was used to facing hardships, was able to get her two elder daughters married in good families, which indeed was a remarkable achievement.

How all this happened remains a puzzle, at least for me, particularly for a family with grossly limited resources. Soon her two younger daughters had also begun to contribute their share to the family kitty when they found employment, and they also completed their B.A. degrees.

As I mentioned, her stay with us helped Santosh complete her M.A., B.Lib. and Ph.D. degrees. Thought it was a great achievement, she never picked up any assignment.

My mother-in-law was a highly religious lady who spent a good part of time daily in the *puja* room (prayer room) that was set up for her in the house. All festivals were celebrated with much zeal, where she took the leading role and made all of us join in the festivities.

Here, it was particularly Rajeev who helped his *nani* and thus every *puja* was a great success. His *nani* also took a lot of interest in his welfare and made sure that he ate good food and drank plenty of milk.

It was because of such an atmosphere in the family that our son did not fall into any bad company, which he could have easily done, when I was often away from the house and even when at home hardly took any interest in the children.

I hardly bothered about the education of my children. It was Santosh who took up this onerous job. In fact, I never visited Rajeev's college—College of Architecture. At one time, he ran into health problems while undergoing training with a firm of architects in Ahmedabad and it was Santosh who had to rush to this place. At that time I was in Aizawl.

Another time, Jyotsana faced a rather serious health problem. This time also I was away and again Santosh, Rajeev and others had to take full care of her. Luckily, she was restored to normal health after some time.

On these and similar occasions, it was my mother-in-law who took full care of the house, thus making the others free to pursue their activities.

In fact, my assignment in the North-East was for more than two years, and this area happened to be a very distant one with poor communication systems. Again it was the presence of my mother-in-law throughout that made things easier for the family back home in my absence.

I was not quite sure how successful Rajeev would be in his career as an architect. I thought he would be better off on a job instead of venturing into an independent career. How wrong I was in my calculations, I realized later. Today he is one of the known architects in the city with his independent, modern office and a team of assistants.

His wife Asha is also an architect. She is in a job with the government and doing quite well. So it is the story of a successful couple. Asha has been his classmate and they decided on marriage after a short courtship. And their marriage has worked well. Apart from small family tensions, which are an integral part of any family, their lives are smooth. They are blessed with a son and a daughter.

Jyotsana, who has specialized in finance, is married to Kulwant, again after courtship. They too are blessed with a daughter and a son. Kulwant is an officer in the Haryana government.

Thus, unlike me who was unsuccessful in his love affair, our children have been more adventurous and daring and their love marriages have worked well. Like this, all four daughters of my younger brother Shanti Sagar are leading successful love marriages.

Coming back to my mother-in-law, though she had a long life, outliving all other senior members in her family, she, however, had a tough end in her life, like the tough time she had to face in her lifetime. For almost five years at the fag end of her life, she was bedridden. This was a great punishment for this noble lady, who became dependent on others for a long period.

She was helpless. But even during this period, when faced with agony, I hardly saw her grumbling. She bore all the pains courageously. That showed her will power to face boldly even the worst possible adverse situation.

Thus even in pain she has left a lesson for us. Rajeev, who was most attached to her was highly affected by her death. He arranged the most befitting funeral for his *nani* and took an active part in the ceremonies connected with her death.

Epilogue

PARENTS AND SOCIETY

In the end it may be asked what sort of influence my parents and family on the one hand and society on the other has had on me?

Though it is an important question, at the same time it is difficult to answer, for there are so many aspects of one's life that it becomes difficult to attribute them to anyone in particular. It is certainly true that as a child, one is more in contact with parents than anyone else. And as one grows up, he is likely to be more close to the society, say as a student and further on as one settles down in life.

My father Hem Raj Mahajan was well educated. He had joined the Law College and obtained his degree in law from Panjab University, which even in those day was considered to be a reputed university recognized in the English-speaking countries. But it was so different in the case of my mother. She had never gone to any school, nor was she educated at home. She was completely illiterate.

It was remarkable that even so, both of them were able to pull on so well and there hardly arose any occasion when Baujee raised any issue about Bebe's illiteracy. It never was in his mind. He accepted her as an equal partner, who was well-versed in managing the household affairs and raising the family of five children, despite her poor health for she was a victim of diabetes.

It is also remarkable that Baujee never ignored her health problem, but attended to it personally and tried to make her comfortable. He employed a full-time domestic help to take care of the kitchen, children and guests. Our family consisted of not just us parents and five brothers. It was an extended family when several other members, from students to grown-ups, stayed as long as it suited them and there was a joint kitchen for all. In addition, several other relatives dropped in for short periods. Thus, the house was always humming with a large number of family members and Baujee patiently put up with it. I don't think he ever lost his patience or let it weigh on his profession, which often requiring his sitting late in office, preparing briefs. He generally slept around midnight and woke up early in the morning for a walk, and even occasionally spent some more time on his work before leaving for the court.

This aspect of his life—patience, care of his guests and hard work for his own profession —had an impact on my line of thinking, and later on in my life, I too tried to follow in his footsteps. It was particularly his honesty and hard work that had impressed me.

Baujee was also extremely God-fearing and a strict Arya Samajist. He had cultivated a rational attitude towards life (the effect of Arya Samaj). At the same time, he didn't interfere with the traditional religious beliefs of Bebe, several of which were quite opposed to the Arya Samaj philosophy.

So we were brought up in an environment where we were exposed to both aspects of Hinduism. In other words, we were liberal, though personally I too had more belief in Arya Samaj. In fact, we were sent to study in schools run by Arya Samaj, where we were taught about various aspects of this religion. In my early days, like Baujee, I also said my prayers regularly twice a day, both morning and evening, though later this practice somehow eased out of my daily schedule. I realized at times that this was not a good change, for regular prayers brought about mental peace.

While externally Baujee was grim-faced and harsh, and we were afraid of approaching him unless we were called or had some urgent work that could not be executed without his permission or consultation, internally he was so different—soft, sympathetic and helpful, and he possessed an understanding nature. Even when he rebuked any one of us or uttered harsh words, he would feel bad about it and tried to make amends later.

Late in his life, I developed closeness with him when he would consult me in family matters, including the slow progress being made by two of my immediate younger brothers who were twins. They were not able to make any headway in their education—one ended with a matriculation and other with F.A. degree, as he was not able to clear B.A., despite a couple of efforts. Baujee got them employed according to their qualifications.

The most remarkable thing about him was that he never showed any distinction among us. He treated all of us alike, though we were at different levels in education and professions.

Not only did he help his own children, he was equally helpful towards other family members.

This aspect of his life too rubbed on me when I too learnt to help family members and even my students. While I helped others, I myself would normally refrain from seeking their help when faced with similar situations. I never believed that help should be rendered on a reciprocal basis.

Here, I was certainly greatly affected by the selfless nature of Baujee.

The death of Bebe in January 1952 created a big void in Baujee's life for he was greatly attached to her, though he rarely demonstrated it as was his nature. He realized that she was a great support to him, even though she was bedridden. Her presence itself was soothing for him. And this aspect, I think, also contributed to his early death, when he was barely 71. He felt lonely from 1952 till his death in 1965.

At the time of Bebe's death, none of us was married. The last to marry, in 1963, were myself and my younger brother. Thus, barely two and a half years after the last marriage in the family, when all of us were settled in the large family house that he had purchased, he breathed his last.

But he was not quite happy with the new environment, with all of us with small kids crowding in the same house. In fact, a stage had come when he had to share his bedroom with a member of the family, which weighed heavily on his mind, especially when he was recovering from the stroke that had partially paralysed the left portion of his body. Thus when he needed more rest and care, he could hardly get either.

During the last days of his life, he had shifted to the family drawing room where he could have some peace and also sit in his office which was next door, and prepare his briefs. He was attached to his office till the last day, where he found mental peace.

In fact, at the time of his sudden death, he was preparing a brief. So, he virtually died in harness.

What did I pick up from the society, from my educational career and afterwards?

As also mentioned earlier, my early school life was a disaster, where instead of learning some good things I was persecuted by the class teacher, which made my life hell until I was saved by a relative. On the whole, the school career wasn't productive. It only helped to memorize lessons like a parrot without understanding them or arousing any interest.

We rarely used the library facility. The books there were mere ornamental pieces. Except for some books on fiction and short stories, I don't recollect having ever picked up another book, since that interest was totally lacking. Often the library card remained unused and we depended solely on class notes or cheap texts.

No teacher ever took the trouble of explaining what was said in the texts. They goaded us to memorize the important passages. If in the classroom any questions were asked, they were from these passages and those who had memorized them well would escape the teacher's wrath while others faced punishment. Punishment, thus made them all the more aware of the fact that unless they memorized their lessons, they would continue to be victims of the teacher's wrath.

And unfortunately, things hardly changed even in higher education. Almost all lecturers appeared to be specialists in memory test and hardly anything beyond that. Very few took the trouble of explaining the text in a way that would arouse the interest of students and encourage them to use their own faculties to ensure a scientific approach to their studies.

Unfortunately, even the minimum approach to the process of self-thinking and finding a rational answer to a particular situation, was lacking. It was all the way just a memory test. And we were almost indoctrinated to specialize in this respect, if we wanted to obtain a good result in the exam. The more we used our memory in the exam, higher the marks we would secure.

Both teachers and students passed on this trait from one generation to the next.

Little surprise that, groomed in this atmosphere, most of us who sought admission to the institutes of higher studies in the Western countries often faced difficulty in adjusting to their method of education and research, as we found it difficult to give up this memory approach even under the new environment. We had to prod a lot to shift to their level of approach, which called for sustained effort.

While this task was easier for those who were already in the teaching profession, it was tough for those coming from the non-teaching or non-academic streams, having lost their active contact with such an environment for years.

This was very much the case with me. I had taken a long time in realizing why despite my hard work and constant sitting in the library for late hours, I wasn't making any progress in my writing or meeting the standard expected of my supervisor. I made the basic mistake of continuing to write one draft after another by following meticulously the long-winded, historical approach of what was already said without any contribution of my own, which was not acceptable to my supervisor.

While I blamed my supervisor for being biased and unusually harsh towards me, little did I realize that unless I changed my strategy towards research, which called for scientific investigation and not to nearly reproduce quotes from writings in books and reports, I hardly stood any chance of being accepted for a Ph.D. degree or a masters degree, to which I had been shifted subsequently with the hope that through attending regular lectures and seminars to which I was directed, I would change my strategy. But even that failed to happen. While I had shown a considerable improvement later, it wasn't sufficient enough to earn even this degree.

At the same time, it is also true that quite a few research students, who didn't change themselves sufficiently in their system of approach, did earn their degrees, unlike me. But then that depended on the perceptions and sympathies of the supervisors. That way perhaps I was not so fortunate, for my supervisor was an unusual stickler for high quality research.

Also, very slow change in my perception towards research had followed from the fact that for long I had worked on a civil service job where the nature of work was quite different.

It was only towards the end of my stay at the LSE, after I had faced a chain of failures and frustrations that I got near the realization of the basic error in my approach towards the work. In fact, it emerged after writing a series of essays. It was too late, however, to repeat the whole process again. But I learnt and resolved that in future I would use the technique of thorough investigation before venturing into writing any piece of economic research. And that is exactly what I did subsequently, with success and still higher success. All this has been mentioned in detail in my autobiography.

I have often wondered why we continue to stick to the memory method in our teaching, hardly exposing our students to scientific enquiry of what is said or what we teach. There has hardly been any change from pre-Independence era to the post-Independence time.

Also there is the question of why the British, who brought the Western (or English) system of education in this country, used one approach in their own country and another in India. Was it that they didn't want India to raise to a higher level of education? Did they want us to be mere clerks to serve their interest, as is often claimed?

I have not been able to find the answer to this question. But the fact remains that the average level of our students as well as of teachers has unfortunately been close to such thinking. It is simultaneously true that with fast changes in education and levels of skills of our teachers, there have been encouraging changes here and there. But these are restricted to only a few institutes, while a majority of our institutes and universities still follow the traditional approach of teaching. Even today a very large section of our students continues to be a victim of the memory method, rarely moving beyond this.

Most of us would agree that this archaic method of learning needs to be drastically changed, so that we can get better products from our educational system.

MY PHILOSOPHY

It would be appropriate to end it with my philosophy in life, which has been:

1. Strength lies in determination and not giving up.
2. There is always some Invisible Power ready to help you, provided you are prepared to accept it.

3. With deep faith and courage, even the most difficult situation is possible to tackle.
4. While dark clouds have often chased me in life, but then simultaneously, there has been enough inner Shakti (strength) to drive them away.

Index